D0290485

Child Abuse

OTHER BOOKS OF RELATED INTEREST

Child Abuse

Bryan J. Grapes, *Book Editor*

David L. Bender, *Publisher*
Bruno Leone, *Executive Editor*
Bonnie Szumski, *Editorial Director*
Stuart B. Miller, *Managing Editor*
Brenda Stalcup, *Series Editor*

Contemporary Issues
Companion

Greenhaven Press, Inc., San Diego, CA

Library of Congress Cataloging-in-Publication Data

Child abuse / Bryan J. Grapes, book editor.
        p. cm. — (Contemporary issues companion)
    Includes bibliographical references and index.
    ISBN 1-56510-892-2 (pbk. : alk. paper) —
ISBN 1-56510-893-0 (lib. bdg : alk. paper)
    1. Child abuse. 2. Child abuse—Prevention. 3. Abused children.
4. Adult child abuse victims. I. Grapes, Bryan J. II. Series.

HV6626.5 .C486 2001
362.76—dc21   00-056121

CONTENTS

FOREWORD

In the news, on the streets, and in neighborhoods, individuals are confronted with a variety of social problems. Such problems may affect people directly: A young woman may struggle with depression, suspect a friend of having bulimia, or watch a loved one battle cancer. And even the issues that do not directly affect her private life—such as religious cults, domestic violence, or legalized gambling—still impact the larger society in which she lives. Discovering and analyzing the complexities of issues that encompass communal and societal realms as well as the world of personal experience is a valuable educational goal in the modern world.

Effectively addressing social problems requires familiarity with a constantly changing stream of data. Becoming well informed about today's controversies is an intricate process that often involves reading myriad primary and secondary sources, analyzing political debates, weighing various experts' opinions—even listening to firsthand accounts of those directly affected by the issue. For students and general observers, this can be a daunting task because of the sheer volume of information available in books, periodicals, on the evening news, and on the Internet. Researching the consequences of legalized gambling, for example, might entail sifting through congressional testimony on gambling's societal effects, examining private studies on Indian gaming, perusing numerous websites devoted to Internet betting, and reading essays written by lottery winners as well as interviews with recovering compulsive gamblers. Obtaining valuable information can be time-consuming—since it often requires researchers to pore over numerous documents and commentaries before discovering a source relevant to their particular investigation.

Greenhaven's Contemporary Issues Companion series seeks to assist this process of research by providing readers with useful and pertinent information about today's complex issues. Each volume in this anthology series focuses on a topic of current interest, presenting informative and thought-provoking selections written from a wide variety of viewpoints. The readings selected by the editors include such diverse sources as personal accounts and case studies, pertinent factual and statistical articles, and relevant commentaries and overviews. This diversity of sources and views, found in every Contemporary Issues Companion, offers readers a broad perspective in one convenient volume.

In addition, each title in the Contemporary Issues Companion series is designed especially for young adults. The selections included in every volume are chosen for their accessibility and are expertly edited in consideration of both the reading and comprehension levels of the audience. The structure of the anthologies also enhances accessibility. An introductory essay places each issue in context and provides helpful facts such as historical background or current statistics and legislation that pertain to the topic. The chapters that follow organize the material and focus on specific aspects of the book's topic. Every essay is introduced by a brief summary of its main points and biographical information about the author. These summaries aid in comprehension and can also serve to direct readers to material of immediate interest and need. Finally, a comprehensive index allows readers to efficiently scan and locate content.

The Contemporary Issues Companion series is an ideal launching point for research on a particular topic. Each anthology in the series is composed of readings taken from an extensive gamut of resources, including periodicals, newspapers, books, government documents, the publications of private and public organizations, and Internet websites. In these volumes, readers will find factual support suitable for use in reports, debates, speeches, and research papers. The anthologies also facilitate further research, featuring a book and periodical bibliography and a list of organizations to contact for additional information.

A perfect resource for both students and the general reader, Greenhaven's Contemporary Issues Companion series is sure to be a valued source of current, readable information on social problems that interest young adults. It is the editors' hope that readers will find the Contemporary Issues Companion series useful as a starting point to formulate their own opinions about and answers to the complex issues of the present day.

INTRODUCTION

On September 28, 1999, Sheriff Elry Faulkner drove to the home of Donna Duncan in Lake of Egypt, Illinois, to investigate some disturbing comments that Duncan had made to her coworkers concerning her eight-year-old son, Joseph. In searching the home, Faulkner discovered Joseph's battered body in a suitcase in the bathroom. An autopsy later determined that Joseph had been beaten two or three times a day during the three weeks leading up to his death. Tragically, surveys indicate that Joseph Duncan's experience is repeated with frightening frequency: Each year almost 1 million children are abused in the United States, nearly fifteen hundred of whom eventually die from their injuries.

According to statistics gathered by the U.S. Department of Health and Human Services (HHS), 963,870 children were identified as victims of abuse in 1997 (the latest year for which statistics are available). This number marked the eighth straight year that the total number of substantiated cases of child abuse approached or surpassed 1 million. Some experts believe that this number represents the tip of the iceberg, arguing that many other cases have gone unreported or unconfirmed. Despite this contention over the accuracy of the HHS figures, the statistics from the 1990s do reveal a striking increase in confirmed cases of child abuse from levels of previous decades.

The charge of child abuse includes three main kinds of mistreatment: physical abuse, sexual abuse, and neglect. Physical abuse is defined as harming a child through punching, beating, kicking, biting, burning, or shaking. Sexual abuse involves fondling a child's genitals and persuading or forcing a child to engage in sexual activity. Neglect is defined as the failure to provide for a child's basic physical requirements (for example, food, clothing, shelter) or emotional needs. Though horrifying cases such as Joseph Duncan's receive the most media attention, physical and sexual child abuse combined account for less than half of all child abuse cases. The majority of substantiated reports of child abuse—52 percent—involve neglect.

Although child abuse occurs in all racial, ethnic, and socioeconomic groups, research has indicated that abuse and neglect are more likely to occur in families that are economically deprived. "Poverty is the most frequently and persistently noted risk factor for child abuse," states Dr. Lesa Bethea, a professor of family medicine at the University of South Carolina School of Medicine. Many researchers believe that the stress associated with poverty aggravates some parents' depression and anger, leading to violent outbursts directed toward their children. Poverty-stricken parents also have a higher incidence of neglect: Children of poor parents are more likely to go without adequate food and clothing. However, as many experts point out, in such cases poor parents may not be intentionally neglecting their children but are simply unable to afford proper clothing and food.

Other experts believe that the primary contributing factor in child abuse is parental substance abuse. The National Center on Addiction and Substance Abuse (NCASA) at Columbia University in New York City has determined that children of substance-abusing parents are three times more likely to suffer physical or sexual abuse and four times more likely to be neglected than the children of nonabusers. "At least seven—some professionals say nine—of 10 cases of child abuse and neglect are caused or exacerbated by alcohol and drug abuse and addiction," charges NCASA president Joseph A. Califano Jr.

Some commentators blame the breakdown of the traditional nuclear family for higher levels of child abuse. Patrick Fagan, William H.G. Fitzgerald Senior Fellow of the Heritage Foundation, a conservative public policy research institute, contends that cohabitation is the primary risk factor for child abuse. Citing studies from England, Fagan points out that the rate of child abuse is thirty-three times greater if a child's mother is cohabiting with a man who is not the father of her child. In addition, Fagan maintains, parents who raise children outside a stable marriage are subject to more stress, thereby making them more likely to abuse their children.

Yet another risk factor frequently cited by child experts is a parental history of abuse. According to Susan Mufson and Rachel Kranz, authors of *Straight Talk About Child Abuse,* many parents who themselves were abused as children repeat the abusive behavior with their own children. Researchers theorize that many parents who were abused when young never learned other ways of relating to children. As Mufson and Kranz explain, these parents "may believe that it's normal to beat a child or to vent one's anger with harsh insults."

Experts disagree on the relative importance of particular risk factors, but most concede that child abuse usually results from the complex interaction of a number of factors. In recent years, a rash of high-profile child abuse fatalities like Joseph Duncan's has shifted the focus of the debate away from the causes of child abuse and toward the problem of America's collapsing child welfare agencies, which seem to increasingly unable to adequately protect vulnerable children from abuse.

In the case of Joseph Duncan, for example, Illinois child welfare authorities had repeatedly been notified of the abusive conditions in which Joseph lived and yet failed to remove him from his life-threatening situation. In a 1995 case that received a great deal of media attention, six-year-old Elisa Izquierdo was killed in New York City by her drug-addicted mother, who had physically and sexually tormented the child for years. Records revealed that despite numerous warnings from teachers and neighbors, child welfare officials had decided to leave Elisa in her mother's custody. In 1997, five-year-old Daytwon Bennet was beaten to death by his mentally unstable mother in the

Bronx, New York. Daytwon weighed just thirty pounds at the time of his death, and an autopsy determined that he had sustained multiple blunt-impact injuries over a long period of time. Such cases understandably outrage most citizens, who cannot understand how the child welfare system so tragically failed these children.

Writing of America's troubled child welfare agencies, authors David Stoesz and Howard Jacob Karger state: "No government function is more crucial than protecting those who cannot protect themselves. . . . Yet few government services are in as much disarray." Most social workers concede that child protection agencies across the United States have been unable to cope with the rising tide of child abuse. By 1996, conditions at child welfare agencies in twenty-one states and the District of Columbia had deteriorated so badly that they had to be placed under court supervision. An investigation of New York City's Child Welfare Administration (CWA) determined that the agency's own neglect directly contributed to one-third of the child abuse fatalities in New York in 1996. Child welfare workers in Washington, D.C., were unable to locate one in four children placed in that city's foster care system. A 1995 report by the *Chicago Tribune* indicated that the Illinois Department of Children and Family Services did not know the whereabouts of more than twenty thousand of its wards. Clearly the child protection system in the United States is faltering, but experts and commentators disagree over the root cause of this problem.

Some experts blame the failure of the nation's child welfare agencies to protect children from abuse on a chronic shortage of funding. Federal and state funding for child welfare agencies has not kept pace with the substantial increase in caseloads, which has led to a chronic shortage of qualified social workers. Most social workers do not stay in the field long: Low pay and the stress of daily exposure to shocking cruelty have led to staff turnover rates as high as 50 percent per year in some states. Those social workers who do remain are quickly overwhelmed by the sheer number of cases involved. The Child Welfare League of America recommends that a caseworker handle just twelve cases at any one time, yet the shortage of qualified personnel has forced some social workers to juggle as many as forty cases simultaneously. According to journalist Skip Hollandsworth, social workers in Texas are so overwhelmed that they have taken a "triage" approach to their jobs: "Less serious wounds that would have been investigated five years ago (such as bruises on an older child as a result of a spanking) are now ignored so that more attention can be paid to the worst cases." Because social workers are inundated with cases, Hollandsworth argues, vulnerable children are slipping through the cracks in the system: "Some of the kids who are dying or showing up in emergency rooms with their bones broken have been the subject of previous . . . investigations that were closed too early. Others are not saved because overly stressed caseworkers are starting to make mistakes."

Some commentators, however, do not believe that the failures of America's child welfare agencies stem from lack of funding or trained personnel. According to journalist Dennis Saffron, child abuse victims are often misrepresented in the media as "casualties of an overworked, understaffed, and underfunded bureaucracy that 'let them slip through the cracks.' The subtext: more money will solve the problem, allowing authorities to investigate more reports of abuse." However, Saffron and other critics point out, the cases of half of the fifteen hundred children who die each year as a result of child abuse have already been investigated by the child welfare agencies. These children, critics charge, are victims of a faulty policy, known as family reunification, which has been widely promoted by most child welfare agencies during the last two decades.

Family reunification laws originated with the Adoption Assistance and Child Welfare Act of 1980, which requires states to make reasonable efforts to keep a family together before removing a child from an abusive household. If a child is removed, states are required to attempt to reunify the child with his or her parents, even if the parents have a long history of neglect or abuse. This policy is based on the belief that removing children from their natural parents is extremely disruptive and compounds the trauma already experienced by the children. "The damage caused to a child by the removal [from his or her parents] is far greater than the protection he or she receives," argues CPS Watch, a national watchdog group that monitors child protection agencies. Supporters of family reunification policies contend that intensive therapy can help most abusive parents correct their behavior and provide a more functional environment for their children.

However, an increasing number of observers believe that the family reunification policy lies at the heart of the dramatic rise in child abuse and that family reunification laws are the primary contributing factor to the inability of the child welfare system to protect at-risk children. These critics point to cases in which parents who were convicted of abusing or murdering one of their children were awarded custody of their remaining children, thereby exposing them to repeated abuse. "I believe in keeping families together, but not when it means sacrificing children," writes Kellye R. Wood, a teacher in Six Lakes, Michigan. "The sad truth is that some parents will never or can never care for their children in even a minimal way." As long as child welfare agencies insist on adhering to the policy of family reunification, critics maintain, severely abused children will continue to fall through the cracks of the system.

The controversy surrounding family reunification policies and the risk they pose to vulnerable children is one of the issues examined in *Child Abuse: Contemporary Issues Companion.* In the chapters that follow, discussions focus on the causes of child abuse, the prevention of child victimization, and personal narratives of survivors as well as perpetrators of child abuse. These essays provide a comprehensive overview of one of the most disturbing issues facing American society today.

CHAPTER 1

THE SCOPE
AND NATURE
OF CHILD ABUSE

Contemporary Issues
Companion

THE RISING INCIDENCE OF CHILD ABUSE

Alex Morales

In the following selection, Alex Morales, executive director of the Children's Bureau of Southern California in Los Angeles, reports that the prevalence of child abuse is increasing dramatically. According to Morales, each year 1.5 million children are abused in the United States physically, emotionally, or sexually; more than half of these children are victims of neglect. Birth parents commit nearly 80 percent of all abusive acts toward children, he writes. Though substance abuse and stress are major contributing factors, poverty is the social condition most associated with child abuse, Morales explains. He also contends that the child welfare system, while a necessary component in the fight against child abuse, is not enough to eliminate it. If child abuse is to be prevented, Morales argues, society must place a greater emphasis on responsible parenting and increase the resources available to at-risk families.

Mary Ellen, a frail eight-year-old, stood before the Supreme Court of New York in 1874 and told the painful story of how she did not recall ever being kissed or hugged, and testified that she was beaten and whipped daily by her mother. A neighbor had become concerned about the girl's suffering and shared her fears with a social worker. Together, they attempted to get society's attention, but no one would respond.

Finally, the social worker and neighbor turned for help to a community activist who had founded the Society for the Prevention of Cruelty to Animals. He had compassion for Mary Ellen and used his resources to bring her plight before the court. The girl's mother was placed in prison, and Mary Ellen later was adopted. Shortly thereafter, the Society for the Prevention of Cruelty to Children in New York was formed, thus formalizing the regrettable need to protect youngsters from their parents.

Reprinted from "Seeking a Cure for Child Abuse," by Alex Morales, *USA Today* magazine, September 1, 1998. Copyright © 1998 by the Society for the Advancement of Education. Reprinted by permission of *USA Today* magazine.

Today, Mary Ellen's story still raises two challenging questions: What are we—neighbors, the business community, concerned citizens, and professionals—going to do about the escalation of child abuse? Most important, can we truly act to prevent it?

The Rate of Abuse

It is estimated that each year in the U.S., 1,500,000 children (up from 900,000 in 1986) are moderately to seriously abused. Three thousand of the youngest victims will die because their bodies are too weak to stand up to the abuse, with half of victims being under the age of one and 90% under the age of four. In 1998, out of every 100 American kids, 2.3 (up from 1.5 in 1986) will be abused. If nothing in American society changes, one out of 10 babies will be abused before they reach adulthood. As of 1998, there are 72,000 abused youngsters receiving protective services from the Los Angeles County Department of Children and Families Services. Approximately 42,000 of them have been removed from their parents, with half living with foster parents or in institutions and the other half with relatives. The financial cost of a child in institutional care is more than $50,000 per year.

There are four major forms of child abuse. Approximately 55% of the kids who are seriously mistreated suffer from severe neglect. These include very young children who are abandoned or left alone for more than 48 hours, aren't fed, do not receive needed medical treatment, or are not sent to school for days at a time. Approximately 25% are physically abused to the extent that the injuries will take at least 48 hours to heal and, in some cases, they never will do so. Twenty percent are sexually abused—and the risk of this happening is the same for a three-year-old as it is for a teenager. Emotional abuse underlies all the other forms of abuse and, while not outwardly visible, is insidiously present nonetheless. The latter often causes the most disabling and lasting injury, as the emotional foundation of the child is eroded and he or she feels unloved, unworthy, exploited, and enraged.

Seventy-eight percent of all child abuse in this country is committed by birth parents. In American society, despite women's increasing role of participating in the workforce, the mother—whether working full or part time or staying home—remains the primary parent who faces the daily challenges of raising the youngsters. Therefore, one erroneously might think that the problem invariably lies with mothers. This is not so. Physical abuse is carried out relatively equally by mothers and fathers. Sexual abuse, in 90% of the cases, is perpetrated by a man. Sexual abuse is the one form of abuse in which the majority of perpetrators are neither the mother nor the father, but, most often, a male adult who has an ongoing relationship with and access to a child. In 87% of the neglect cases, it is the mother who is the neglectful parent.

The Factors Behind Child Abuse

Research clearly has revealed that child abuse is not associated with race or ethnicity in this country. The strongest correlating factor is poverty. However, abuse is found at all socioeconomic levels. Parents are 22 times more likely to abuse their offspring if they live on less than $15,000 annually than are those who earn more than $30,000 per year. This explains why many professionals dedicated to the well-being of children are deeply concerned that the new welfare reform strategy must assure the economic survival of families, or else the youngsters will pay the price.

Drug and alcohol abuse devastates parents and is highly associated with abuse of children. Substance abuse undermines adults' ability to function in many areas, including parenting, work, and personal life. There are many who have great emotional problems because of unhealed traumatic childhoods or adult experiences, such as growing up in a home with child abuse, spousal abuse, or alcoholism. These parents can be unstable; sometimes, substance abuse is a destructive anesthetic for them.

There is a strong relationship between stress and violent physical outbursts directed at a youngster who is in the wrong place at the wrong time. To understand stress, it is necessary to examine the causes and seek coping resources to manage the condition. One very important resource to help manage personal stress is the support of others—i.e., a spouse, relative, friend, or even a compassionate stranger. However, some people do not have a network of supportive relationships due to the high mobility of society, poor decision-making in forming relationships, or insecurity about forging new ones. Stress can come from many sources, but often its strongest forms are associated with poverty. It can arise when a parent does not know how to deal with a child, especially a difficult one. Mothers and/or fathers who have had a poor upbringing particularly lack good examples for parenting.

Sexual abuse is driven by several destructive factors. Often, the perpetrator was sexually victimized as a child or youth and, unlike others, did not heal from the experience. The result frequently is distorted sexual drives and emotional needs. Divorce and single parenting expose kids to other men who do not have a biological or long-term commitment to the youngsters' well-being. Furthermore, the eroticized sexual society in which we live adds to the difficulty of some men who have not learned or found appropriate ways to manage their sexual feelings.

An Ineffective System

Currently, society has a limited—and often ineffective—arsenal to fight child abuse. These include the child abuse reporting law; the stern, watchful eye of society over families who are abusing their offspring; and the temporary or permanent removal of kids from abusive households.

The child abuse reporting and subsequent investigation system, while necessary in a civilized society, clearly are not the answer to the prevention of the syndrome. The majority of the public detection of child abuse—more than 60%—comes from the public schools, which typically do not even begin to observe youngsters until the age of five. Unfortunately for the victims, much abuse starts long before that time. Nearly 60% of all child abuse investigations in California results in dismissal because the evidence is insufficient to prove that abuse occurred or it is proven that the offense did not, in fact, occur. The process of investigating a family is psychologically devastating to kids and parents, even though it must be done to protect some children from further harm. Moreover, a mere 28% (down from 44% in 1988) of moderate to severely abused children are investigated. Thus, the system is ineffective because it does not even see many of the abused children and therefore is unable to help.

The stern watchful eye of society in which the Juvenile Court—with the help of the government's social workers—periodically checks up on abusive parents and offers limited tangible help is only modestly effective in stabilizing a family on a long-term basis. Many families—20–30%—will be back in the system within a few years.

The process through which children are removed from their parents by placing them with their often economically poor relatives (mostly grandparents), as occurs in 50% of the cases, or with foster parents and institutions in the other 50%, is a weak solution. It not only is costly, but frequently leaves youngsters in a state of emotional instability; adds economic and emotional stress to financially poor grandparents who are trying to raise kin; and often intervenes too late to prevent permanent damage to the child from years of abuse.

The Importance of Good Parenting

Is there hope to prevent much of this? The answer is yes, but success requires a strong commitment on society's part. To lay a foundation of prevention, it is necessary to build in three areas. First and foremost, a new societal norm must be created and sustained which sets an expectation for prospective and new parents to prepare themselves for the role. Parenting is the most important job an individual ever will hold, and it must be taken on with the utmost responsibility.

If this value deepened in our society, many good changes might be expected. No longer would 60% of births in the U.S. be unplanned. (For teenagers, it is 80%, though teens account for just 10% of all births). All parents would aggressively seek out the most advanced information that would allow them to learn from experienced parents and professionals about the unique needs and problems of their offspring. They would learn how to meet these needs, so that their children could blossom intellectually, emotionally, and with character ready to face the future. Mothers and fathers would take it upon themselves to redouble their efforts to build a network of supportive relationships, realizing that they must do this not just for themselves, but to help them be strong parents. They would spend more time with their kids, realizing it takes a great quantity of hours to get one quality hour with their offspring.

Second, private and public organizations must create family resource centers for all parents with children from birth through age three. These centers would be a resource to help them find practical information on parenting, opportunity for new supportive relationships, and a place to facilitate the cooperative voluntary efforts of groups of parents. The latter might provide periodic baby-sitting for each other or even emergency baby-sitting when members of their group find themselves in that unplanned desperate moment. There could be childbirth and "Mommy and Me" type classes for parents and their kids. Organizations such as religious institutions, YMCAs, community colleges, and city-funded community centers could take the lead in creating these family centers. The key is to have a center that has a clear vision that its ultimate goal is not just to host a lot of activities, but to support those who are investing in preparing themselves for their job as a parent.

Such family centers might be made available to parents of children who are older than age three. However, if these centers really are going to lay a foundation for prevention of child abuse, they first must help parents with their offspring from the womb through the critical formative years. These centers, in order to be effective, would require the volunteer efforts of parents and other community residents to help administer them and work with the families. Family resource centers should be established in all neighborhoods. Where such centers require the support of tax dollars, though, they first should be developed in low-income communities, where they can do the most good.

Third, a home visitation program with referral services targeted to high-risk new parents at the time of the birth of a child must be developed. Trained parents or professionals would go out into the home of these high-risk families and provide valuable information, teach and model parenting, and offer counseling and support. They would help connect these high-risk families to other needed community services, including parent education, support groups, and drug treatment. Such a program must follow these parents and their child through the first three years of their child's development to prevent the occurrence of abuse and to create a strong foundation for the youngster.

Mary Ellen's appearance before society long since has passed. While enormous and meaningful steps have been made to respond to the problem of child abuse, society has yet to build a foundation for prevention aggressively. Now is a good time to do so.

THE SOCIETAL CONSEQUENCES OF CHILD ABUSE

Blair Sadler

The abuse that maltreated children suffer often leaves behind more than physical scars, argues Blair Sadler, president and chief executive officer of Children's Hospital and Health Center in San Diego. According to Sadler, children who are abused sustain psychological damage that is difficult to overcome. This emotional trauma has negative consequences not only for the child, he contends, but for society as well: Abused children are at higher risk for substance abuse and teenage pregnancy and are more likely to commit violent crimes, both as juveniles and adults. The taxpayer expense associated in dealing with these problems is enormous, he explains. If there is to be any hope of curbing the devastating effects of child abuse, Sadler concludes, America must commit as much to the prevention of child maltreatment as it has to other public health problems such as AIDS and heart disease.

The fact that a 6-year-old could shoot and kill a classmate is deeply disturbing, emotionally paralyzing. [On February 29, 2000, a 6-year-old boy shot 6-year-old Kayla Rolland in their classroom in Flint, Michigan.] Equally disturbing, however, is the environment this little boy evidently lived in every day—cocaine, guns, absent parents. It puts a harsh spotlight on an issue American society can no longer tolerate—child abuse and neglect.

As gut-wrenching and painful as this story is to read about, it's far from being an isolated, faraway incident. In San Diego the parents of a 3-year-old boy were convicted for starving their son to death in 1999.

These tragedies occur every day behind the closed doors of thousands of homes in America. They happen in every community, large and small. They often happen before we, as a society, have a chance to intercede . . . or do they?

Some say you can measure a society's greatness by its scientific and medical breakthroughs, by its educational institutions, by the freedoms given its citizens. How about adding a new one to the mix: mea-

Reprinted from "Child Abuse: The Problems of an Abused Child Stay with Us the Rest of His or Her Life," by Blair Sadler, *The San Diego Union-Tribune,* March 8, 2000. Reprinted with permission from the author.

suring a society by how it treats its children and its willingness to confront the darkest clouds that form a shroud over their potential?

Lifelong Problems

While death is what makes headlines, it's the insidious repetition of child abuse and neglect that should equally turn our collective stomachs. Not only because it maims our children physically, but because it causes deep, profound, emotional scarring that's difficult for children to overcome.

Children who are maltreated are far more likely to run away from home, fall into drug problems, have difficulty in school, get pregnant as adolescents and commit crimes. They are 50 percent more likely to be arrested for juvenile crimes and 40 percent more likely to be arrested for violent crimes when they become adults. In addition, 84 percent of children who have babies before they turn 14 years old were abused by someone in their own homes.

The problems of an abused child stay with all of us the rest of his or her life. They linger, in part, in the form of child welfare, long-term health care for the severely injured, mental health programs, the juvenile court system and remedial education. As taxpayers, we all pay for these programs and services. Unfortunately, they comprise a mere Band-Aid on a gaping wound.

While we continue to see incremental gains with individual child abuse prevention and intervention programs, the overall level of abuse and neglect remains largely unchanged since the 1970s. An average of three children still die every day in the United States at the hands of their own parents, according to the Children's Bureau, U.S. Department of Health and Human Services.

A Need for Serious Commitment

It's crystal clear now that doing business as usual will not reverse this national tragedy. We need to declare war on child abuse and neglect, the same way we did to turn the tide against other public scourges such as cancer, heart disease and AIDS.

Fortunately, the spark for such a commitment has emerged. Members of more than 25 health and child-abuse prevention groups meeting in March 2000 in San Diego for a national child maltreatment conference formed a national collaboration to dramatically reduce the incidence of child abuse and neglect in the United States by 2010. Members of this unprecedented coalition include representatives of the American Academy of Pediatrics, American Medical Association, National Child Abuse Coalition, National Children's Alliance, Prevent Child Abuse America and National Association of Social Workers.

Collectively, these groups and others are pulling behind a national action plan that will:

- Focus first and foremost on reducing child abuse and neglect that comes at the hands of parents and caregivers.
- Put new energy behind prevention, intervention (stopping current abuse; interrupting repeated abuse), research, training and advocacy.
- Stimulate the commitment of more resources to differentiate and promote proven programs so they can be replicated.

This action plan, when fully developed, will focus anew on the mammoth discrepancy between our country's commitment to child abuse and other public health ills. For every death attributed to violence, America invests $31 in prevention, intervention and research, which pales in comparison with other major diseases, including heart disease ($440 per death), cancer ($794 per death), and AIDS ($697 per death).

Enough!

As a country, we must stare child abuse coldly in the eye and say "enough!" We must find the political will to invest enough resources in the problem to make a substantial difference. We need to ensure that every child is given the best chance to grow up and reach his or her full potential without being harmed or having to live under the threat of being harmed. We need to commit anew to be accountable to children in every city and town who are beaten, burned by cigarette butts, violently shaken, thrown against walls, whipped, sexually abused, neglected and undernourished. Children have a right to be protected.

Ultimately, wouldn't it be a tremendous achievement if historians in 2020 are able to characterize the first two decades of the new millennium as a period when the United States undeniably proved it was a nation that truly cared for all its kids?

PHYSICAL CHILD ABUSE: THE MOST VISIBLE FORM OF MALTREATMENT

Deborah Daro

Physical child abuse is the most recognizable form of maltreatment as well as the most lethal, writes Deborah Daro in the following selection. According to Daro, although physical abuse accounts for only 25 percent of all child abuse cases, it causes over 56 percent of all fatalities attributed to abuse. However, she reports, the obvious nature of physical abuse usually enables quick detection and intervention. Common warning signs for physical abuse include broken bones, unusual scars, burns, bruises, and repeated accidental injuries, she explains. A number of intervention options are available for a physical abuse case, Daro points out, and permanent removal of the child from the home is not always necessary. Daro is the director of the Center on Child Abuse Prevention Research and the research director for the National Committee for the Prevention of Child Abuse.

In many respects, physical abuse can be termed the "classic" form of maltreatment. Beginning with Dr. Henry Kempe's 1962 article [an influential study entitled "The Battered Child Sydrome," which appeared in the *Journal of the American Medical Association*] and continuing through today, the popular image of the abused child is one who has suffered physical battering at the hands of his or her parents. Physical abuse is generally accepted as a clear form of child maltreatment and, in extreme forms, to justify quick and extensive public intervention into the private family. Given this universal image of physical abuse, it is not surprising to find that few researchers delineate additional subcategories under the physical abuse heading. Those studies which do suggest a more complex scheme, however, differentiate the population along a number of interesting dimensions. First, the American Association for Protecting Children includes three forms of physical abuse in its summary of statewide reporting data, differentiating cases in terms of their severity. This type of distinction is most commonly made not only by professionals but also by the general public. Very different levels of concern emerge in cases involving broken bones or permanent brain damage versus cases involving minor bruises. In addition, bruises that result from what some may term "normal" corporal punishment are less likely to draw public scrutiny than bruises resulting from an intentional unprovoked attack on a child.

Different Types of Physical Abuses

In contrast to this simple division, others have developed more complex models. Maurice Boisvert constructed a physical abuse typology differentiating families along three dimensions—the characteristics of the perpetrators, the age of the child and the nature of the injury, and the casework strategy as determined by the legal action and the services advocated. In general, Boisvert identified two major types of physical abusers. The first type, "uncontrollable battering," includes such variations as the psychotic personality, the inadequate personality, the passive-aggressive personality, and the sadistic personality. For all of these cases, placement, at least temporarily, is warranted to avoid continued, and progressively more severe, maltreatment. In contrast, "controlled abuse" families are viewed as being far more amenable to therapeutic intervention and can even be treated, in certain cases, without the use of any out-of-home placement options.

Boisvert's concern that physical abuse might be too broad a term has been supported by the work of Dr. James Kent. Kent and his colleagues found that the physical abuse cases they examined clustered into four specific groups which he termed "flashpoint," "spare the rod," "you asked for it," and "who needs it". Basing these categories upon the characteristics of the child, the characteristics of the parents, and the circumstances immediately preceding the maltreatment, he argues that a physical abuse case may be treated in a number of ways and is far from the unidimensional concept depicted in Kempe's "battered child" syndrome. Like Boisvert, Kent outlines specific interventions for each of his four types:

• *flashpoint*—implies the need for psychotherapy to address the individual's psychopathology and/or interpersonal conflict

• *spare the rod*—implies the need for help in learning to use and to trust alternative modes of discipline and socialization to address the parents' overemphasis on teaching "right from wrong" and on ensuring their children grow into "good citizens"

• *you asked for it*—implies a similar need for help in managing the behavior of more assertive and active children without physically abusive methods to address the parents' lack of economic security and self-confidence; and

• *who needs it*—implies a need for therapeutic intervention coupled with the use of a "lay therapist" or "parent aide" to help bridge the gap between the parents' expectations and the kind of help formal therapy can actually provide.

Some 25% of all cases reported to protective services in 1984 involved physical abuse, either as the sole type of maltreatment or in combination with other forms of abuse or neglect. On balance the victims of severe physical abuse are younger than those children experiencing minor or unspecified physical abuse or other forms of maltreatment. A larger percentage of physical abuse victims are hospitalize and physical abuse accounts for over 56% of all fatalities due to child abuse; physical abuse is the major cause of abuse-related deaths among young children. A study comparing victims of physical abuse and sexual abuse noted that the physical abuse victims were five times more likely to die as a result of injuries. Compared to nonmaltreated children and children who have experienced neglect or emotional maltreatment, the victims of physical abuse were noted in one 42-month follow-up study to be the most distractible and least persistent or enthusiastic in preschool settings. When compared to parents involved in other forms of maltreatment, most notably neglectful parents, the physically abusive parent appears more volatile and presents more intraphychic and interpersonal difficulties.

Detecting Physical Abuse

Identification of physical abuse generally results from observations of the potential victims by medical personnel, day care providers, schoolteachers, or concerned neighbors or family friends. Occasionally, older children will report themselves victims of physical abuse, although it is more common for these victims to leave the abusive situation (i.e., running away, moving in with relatives, etc.).

While a variety of factors may trigger reports of physical abuse, the most common "warning signs" include broken bones, bruises, unusual scars or burns, or repeated accidental injuries. Injuries to infants generally receive greater scrutiny than do bruises found on older children. Children who have shown repeated signs of physical injury are more suspect than children who demonstrate an occasional cut or bruise. Finally, the ability of parents or caretakers to explain the source of the injury is often the most critical factor in the substantiation of the report, although it will often not be a factor in whether or not an initial report is made.

Though tempered somewhat by societal approval of corporal punishment, public intervention in cases of physical abuse enjoys widespread support. Identification is primarily made through observation of the victim and reports can be, and often are, made on the sole basis of the child's condition. The nature of the injuries is often such that only one plausible explanation can exist for them. While removal of the child from the home in the most serious of these cases is the most frequent intervention, a wide range of family-based interventions are also employed. The most common service options offered families involved in physical abuse are parenting education regarding alternative forms of discipline, parent aid services to provide a support for parents unable to cope with daily stress, and therapeutic services for the victims to remediate the consequences of the abuse and, in some instances, to improve the child's behavior so that the parent can better manage him or her.

THE COMPLEX NATURE OF CHILD SEXUAL ABUSE

Cheryl Wetzstein

The identification and prosecution of child molesters present a serious dilemma to law enforcement agencies and psychiatrists, writes Cheryl Wetzstein in the following article. Child molesters suffer from a diversity of sexual disorders that are difficult to diagnose, making it nearly impossible for psychiatrists and law enforcement officials to develop uniform legal and therapeutic responses, she writes. Although a number of experts believe that some child sex offenders can be successfully treated and returned to society, Wetzstein explains, others maintain that the majority of child molesters are repeat offenders who cannot be rehabilitated. Also, the author notes, the difficulty in preventing child sexual abuse is compounded by the absence of reliable statistics, as the data suffer from both underreporting and exaggeration. Wetzstein is a journalist who writes on family and social issues for the *Washington Times*.

"I got away with molesting over 240 children before getting caught for molesting just one little boy," convicted child molester Larry Don McQuay has confessed.

"With all that I have coldheartedly learned while in prison, there is no way that I will ever be caught again," he has said. "I am doomed to eventually rape, then murder my poor little victims to keep them from telling on me. . . . Will your children be my next victims?"

These words led to headlines in April 1996 when McQuay was ordered released from a Texas jail after serving six years of an eight-year prison sentence for the 1989 rape of a six-year-old boy. He had served his time, according to Texas's mandatory-release rules.

Before McQuay was taken to a halfway house to prepare for his reentry into society, he pleaded to be castrated to lessen his sexual drive. A victims' rights group in Houston, called Justice for All, began a fund-raising campaign to meet McQuay's request but could not find a doctor who would perform the unusual surgery to remove

This article, "The Child Molestation Dilemma," by Cheryl Wetzstein, appeared in the November 1996 issue and is reprinted with permission from *The World & I*, a publication of the Washington Times Corporation, copyright © 1996.

the testicles. McQuay has since been returned to jail on charges stemming from a previous molestation case.

The case of Larry Don McQuay seems to epitomize society's continuing inability to deal with those who have incorrigible and unspeakable appetites for children.

One obvious permanent solution—capital punishment—is strictly reserved for murder and is likely to remain so. The public remains divided over the merits of the death penalty, child sexual abuse cases are difficult to prove beyond all question of doubt, and most sex offenders are members of or known to the victim's family, making the latter unlikely to call for a death sentence.

As a result, there is a push to sentence child molesters to life in prison without parole or place them in secure mental institutions until they are judged not to be a danger to society.

In the meantime, however, many offenders receive probation or short prison sentences, and thousands are released from jail and back into society each year.

Recidivism Rates

The chances a sex offender will commit another crime seem to depend on the nature of his sexual appetite.

In January 1996, *Congressional Quarterly* reported that, according to international research findings, including a 1994 paper issued by the Washington State Institute for Public Policy, recidivism rates for untreated sex offenders ranged as follows:

- 41 to 71 percent for exhibitionists;
- 13 to 40 percent for child molesters preferring boy victims;
- 10 to 29 percent for child molesters preferring girl victims;
- 7 to 35 percent for rapists;
- 4 to 10 percent for incest offenders.

Some medical experts hold that sex offenders can be successfully treated.

"I don't think the majority [of sex offenders] have a condition that's curable, but I do think that many of them have a psychiatric disorder and can, like alcoholics, learn to control themselves and live safely in the community," Fred Berlin, director of the National Institute for the Study, Prevention and Treatment of Sexual Trauma in Baltimore, Maryland, told *Congressional Quarterly*.

But others are not at all sure that pedophiles—people whose sexual preference is for children—can ever live "safely" in society.

"Pedophiles are always model prisoners and want parole," said John Walsh, whose young son was abducted and found murdered many years ago. The show he hosted for years—Fox-TV's *America's Most Wanted*—once helped catch 37 pedophiles accused of crimes in one six-month period, he said. Ninety percent of them were repeat offenders.

"When you find out how they've conducted their lives, you realize it's their whole life to molest," said Patrick Trueman, former chief of the Department of Justice's Child Exploitation and Obscenity Section and now director of governmental affairs for the American Family Association.

Trueman and others, noting that even notorious offenders seem to get only eight-year prison sentences, strongly believe in very long prison terms, if not life in prison.

Diversity of Disorders

The diversity of sexual disorders has made both clinical diagnosis and uniform legal responses difficult.

For example, virtually all pedophiles collect child pornography, fantasize about children, and engage in infantile or abnormal behavior around them. But not all pedophiles actually assault children. They may instead employ means of self-gratification that are not illegal.

Adults who assault children are child molesters, but not all child molesters are pedophiles. Some child molesters are sexual predators who prefer adult victims but attack a child because an opportunity appears. Such "situational child molesters" are believed to be the most common kind of offender but the least likely to abuse large numbers of children.

Instead, the most worrisome sort of offender is the pedophile who molests, known to law enforcement officials as a "preferential child molester." Such a man is likely to be involved in child pornography, sex rings, and child prostitution. He may molest hundreds or even a thousand children in a lifetime, wrote FBI Supervisory Special Agent Kenneth Lanning in a 1992 booklet issued by the National Center for Missing and Exploited Children (NCMEC).

Referring to a landmark, long-term study of 561 sex offenders by Dr. Gene Abel, an Atlanta sexual disorder expert, Lanning said that pedophiles who targeted boys outside the home committed the greatest number of crimes, with an average of 281.7 acts with an average of 150.2 partners.

Molesters who targeted girls within the family committed an average of 81.3 acts with an average of 1.8 partners. The Abel study also found that nearly a quarter of the 561 subjects committed crimes against both family and nonfamily members, Lanning wrote in *Child Molesters: A Behavioral Analysis*.

A number of punishments have been suggested for child sex offenders, but all have drawbacks.

Meanwhile, nearly every state has enacted laws requiring sex offenders to register in their new homes. Such laws have faced court challenges by civil liberties advocates who argue that sex offenders who have paid their debt to society deserve to rejoin it without undue constraints.

Registration laws have withstood many of these challenges, however, and in May 1996 President Bill Clinton signed the so-called Megan's Law, which requires states to tell local law enforcement officials and communities when a convicted sex offender has moved in.

The law was named for Megan Kanka, a New Jersey seven-year-old who in 1994 was raped and murdered, allegedly by a twice-convicted sex offender who lived across the street and whose background was unknown to the Kankas or their neighbors.

The Quest for Data

"Society's attitude about child sexual abuse and exploitation can be summed up in one word: denial," Lanning wrote in a 1992 analysis on child sex rings.

"Most people do not want to hear about it and would prefer to pretend that child sexual victimization just does not occur," he wrote, urging professionals who deal with child sexual abuse to recognize and deal with this denial.

But the flip side of denial is public hysteria—and professionals must also be aware that there can be a lot of misinformation about the subject, Lanning said in his report.

"Some professionals . . . in their zeal to make American society more aware of this victimization, tend to exaggerate the problem," Lanning wrote. "Presentations and literature with poorly documented or misleading claims about one in three children being sexually molested, the $5 billion child pornography industry, child slavery rings, and 50,000 stranger-abducted children are not uncommon.

"The problem is bad enough; it is not necessary to exaggerate it," Lanning concluded.

Efforts have been under way to collect reliable data on missing and exploited children since 1984, when Congress passed the Juvenile Justice, Runaway Youth, and Missing Children's Act Amendments, creating NCMEC in Arlington, Virginia, and instituting the National Incidence Studies of Missing, Abducted, Runaway and Thrownaway Children (NISMART).

NISMART estimates that, each year:
- 450,000 children, most of whom are teenagers, run away from home and stay away at least one night.
- 354,000 children are abducted by a family member, typically a noncustodial parent.
- 127,100 children are "thrown away," that is, abandoned or eject ed from their homes.
- 114,600 cases of attempted abduction by a nonfamily member are reported.
- 3,200 to 4,600 children are reported abducted by nonfamily members.

Nonfamily abductors include persons who are known to the child (that is, a neighbor or family friend), or unknown, namely, strangers. But the most common scenario, according to NISMART data, involves someone using a weapon to force a child from the street into a vehicle.

Most of these nonfamily abductions last less than 24 hours, but two-thirds of cases involve a sexual assault. Half of the abducted children are teenagers, and 75 percent are girls. The highest percentage of victims appears to be girls aged 11–14 and boys aged 6–9.

Each year, between 200 and 300 children taken by strangers are gone for long periods. About half of the children are recovered alive, usually within two months. But each year, between 43 and 147 children abducted by nonfamily members are found dead, according to NISMART's review of data from 1976 to 1987.

Familiar Offenders

It's not only strangers who molest children, however. Sexual abusers include parents, grandparents, siblings, other family members, stepparents, family friends, and other responsible adults in close contact with children such as teachers, Scout leaders, clergymen, and coaches.

With abuse coming from so many directions, it's easy to assume that child sexual abuse is epidemic. Certainly, the endless parade of abuse survivors on daytime talk shows provides anecdotal evidence that the problem is "everywhere." And when the amount of unreported abuse is added in—an FBI document says that "only 1 to 10 percent of child molestation cases are ever reported to police"—it indeed appears that there must be a child molester on every block.

But it is frankly impossible to determine how extensive child sexual abuse is. The National Committee for the Prevention of Child Abuse said: "Retrospective surveys reveal great variation [in the national rate of abuse], with 6 percent to 62 percent of females and 3 percent to 31 percent of males reporting to have experienced some form of sexual abuse."

The Burden of Proof

Finally, it would be easier to toughen the laws against child molesting if more people were diagnosed as incorrigible child molesters. But those who try to prosecute child sexual abuse cases run into a vast array of hurdles.

In most instances of sexual abuse—three out of four documented cases, according to one reputable study published in 1994—there are no physical marks or signs of abuse.

This places the burden of proof on other signs of distress—for example, bed-wetting, sexual precociousness, and withdrawal. But these can be attributed to other causes.

Then there is the victim's testimony. But testimony from children is notoriously unreliable. They may be too young to talk or confused about what happened to them. They may be reluctant to betray the "special secret" they share with their abuser or may blame themselves, having been told "you wanted it" by the abuser. They also may be unduly influenced by their parents, therapists, law enforcement officials, or others and make allegations that are eventually recanted or discounted.

While most victims of abuse do not forget their molestation, some may repress such memories and not recall it until years later, either through some spontaneous event or through therapy.

Cases of such "recovered memories" have made sensational stories in recent years. Adult children have recalled being abused by their parents, and men have remembered being abused by their clergymen. Some of these cases have led to arrests, convictions, or multimillion-dollar lawsuits for damages. At least 21 states have extended the statute of limitations for sexual abuse so those who belatedly wish to take legal action against their abuser can do so.

But some cases have sparked a fierce outcry from those accused. In March 1992, a group called the False Memory Syndrome Foundation, located in Philadelphia, arose to help rebut what it said were distorted or confabulated memories contrived through incompetent therapy.

As a result of this and other controversies, convictions in sexual abuse cases are not only difficult to get but may be difficult to uphold.

For several years now, scandal has rocked the small town of Wenatchee, Washington, after dozens of adults were accused of participating in two child-sex rings. Nineteen people eventually pleaded guilty or were convicted of charges related to child molestation and rape. In February 1996, however, several of the adults who were acquitted sued state and local agencies for civil rights violations. In June 1996, seven adults and three children filed a lawsuit against law authorities charging them with coercing the children into making false statements against others.

"The reality," says David Beatty, a spokesman with the National Victim Center in Arlington, Virginia, "is that people victimize children because they feel like they can get away with it."

If society becomes better educated about sexual abuse of children, he said, it will at least increase the likelihood that predators will be caught and punished.

Pedophiles Are Gaining Easier Access to Children via the Internet

Catherine Edwards

Because Internet technology has rapidly outgrown the laws that regulate it, child molesters and pornographers are able to use the Internet to gain easier access to children, explains Catherine Edwards in the following selection. For example, she writes, many pedophiles set up seemingly innocent websites to lure children in, then proposition them for sex. Most law enforcement agencies lack the proper equipment and funding that would enable them to detect pedophiles who are using the Internet to exploit children, Edwards points out. As a result, law enforcement officials are finding it increasingly difficult to prevent on-line sexual predators from victimizing children. Edwards is a reporter for *Insight on the News*.

Every day Donna becomes a crime victim. Willingly. She turns on her computer and logs onto the myriad of chat rooms and bulletin boards available on the Internet. Chat forums with names such as "beaniebabeez" are listed right alongside "young gurlz" and "m4mbarely legal" (the "m" stands for men). Instead of using her regular screen name she chooses names such as "susieq86" and "brat13."

Posing as a 13-year-old, Donna does what many curious teens might do in her situation. She bypasses the "beaniebabeez" site and enters the "barely legal" site. Within seconds she is solicited for sex by older men—pedophilia, right in the comfort of her own home.

Accidentally or not, more than half of America's teen-agers have come into contact with obscene material on the Internet. For the first time ever, pedophiles intent upon seduction can tour the world, entering children's bedrooms at will.

Donna, who has asked that her last name remain confidential, happens to be a concerned parent and citizen activist who goes online posing as a teen so she can help local law enforcement nab sex criminals. Now she works closely with local cops. Her first target to be convicted was not a dirty old man in a trench coat, but a prominent and well-respected school principal. The FBI tells *Insight* that the average online pedophile is a white male age 25 to 40 with no prior convictions.

Many Parents Are Unaware

The problem is serious. Donna tells *Insight* that "most parents don't even know what a screen name is, but their kids do and that's the danger." Despite the best efforts of activists and law-enforcement officials to educate the public, many parents are unaware that their kids are viewing objectionable material and communicating regularly with people few would allow to cross the thresholds of their homes.

"I have worked on this issue for six years and my belief is that parents are still not understanding what the real dangers are to their children and families," says another Donna—Donna Rice Hughes, author of Kids Online and senior adviser to Familyclick.com. "They are not taking the initiative to implement tools to protect their kids, so we have children falling through the cracks. Pedophiles and pornographers are exploiting technology for their advantage, and they are way ahead of parents."

Internet technology has galloped ahead at a faster pace than the laws that regulate it. Law enforcement has been hard-pressed to keep up with the growing number of cybercrimes committed on a daily basis.

Take the Feds, for instance. The FBI set up an office in 1994 in New Calverton, Maryland, called Innocent Images. That office has a squad of 20 agents who go undercover online posing as children. The total number of staff in the Maryland office is more than 50, and Innocent Images now runs similar operations out of 10 field offices. Its annual budget is $10 million.

These agents strike up conversations with men and women in chat rooms. Sometimes both parties pose as kids. Some pedophiles reveal their age and ask for sex outright. If a meeting is requested, the agent goes to the arranged meeting spot and the online friend finds himself face to face with the FBI. "These guys show up with film, cameras and vibrators in a bag," says Special Agent Peter Gulotta. "We have evidence of their online conversations; it is not hard to convict them." Agents undergo regular psychological testing to ensure they are not mentally disturbed by their online activity, which can last as long as 10 hours a day. The FBI keeps these assignments short.

Transmitters and Travelers

The agents look for two types of criminals: transmitters and travelers. It is illegal to transmit child pornography over the Internet, and it also is illegal to travel across state lines to have sex with a minor. And it doesn't matter if the victim turns out not to be a minor when the pedophile gets there, explains Gulotta, the "traveling with intent" is crime enough. "We have no shortage of customers," he says, but many escape the net. In 1998 Innocent Images identified 702 instances of traveling or transmitting; in 1999, the number increased to 1,500. Since 1995 they've apprehended 478 people, with a 99 percent conviction rate.

Patrick Naughton, 34, a Disney executive on the West Coast, was charged with crossing state lines seeking sex with a 13-year-old girl after arranging to meet her via the Internet. In December 1999 a jury convicted him of possessing child pornography; he faces trial again in March 2000 on the traveling charges.

Despite lack of specialized funding some local prosecutors realize that they must be proactive in this area. Jeanine Ferris Pirro is the district attorney for Westchester County, New York. Elected as a Republican in 1994, she has made cybercrime detection a priority. Pirro established a unit to detect high-tech crimes and in late 1999 sought approval to convene a grand jury to seek indictments in these cases.

"Old crimes are being committed in new ways" Pirro tells *Insight*. "We used to tell our kids not to go to the park alone and not to talk to strangers. This is no different."

Despite paltry funding, Pirro's office has managed to convict 15 offenders for cybersex crimes during the last six months and boasts a 100 percent conviction rate. Like the Feds, the unit employs an undercover investigator who poses as a 14-year-old. "Sometimes it only takes two hours from actually logging on to the computer to the physical meeting," says Pirro. "These pedophiles are so desperate for sex with children they will do anything."

Underequipped

But most local law-enforcement offices lack even the equipment to detect cybercrime. "We are chasing the tail end of the problem," says Bob Flores, a former prosecutor and Justice Department official. "We don't take care of people until they are jumping off the cliff." Pirro agrees. "If we're not careful, we'll be investigating [resulting] homicides."

Flores works at the National Law Center for the Protection of Children and Families in Fairfax, Virginia, and is fighting for prosecution of obscenity and child pornography. He says he is frustrated that the Department of Justice has yet to convict even one person for online obscenity. "The Internet has become the sex-ed manual for the new millennium," he warns. "We saw the outcry after [the high-school shootings in Littleton, Colorado, at] Columbine. Those kids learned to make bombs online. I am convinced that if we don't do something soon we will have a tragedy on the scale of what took place in Littleton—except this time it would be a horrible sex crime performed by teens who were educated by graphic pornography on the Internet."

With the advent of the Internet, legislators realized that the obscenity laws already on the books had huge gaps and moved to update them. In 1997, the U.S. Supreme Court ruled that the indecency provisions of the Communications Decency Act, or CDA, were unconstitutional under the First Amendment. If upheld, the CDA would have protected children on the Internet from indecent materials, as the federal law prohibits such material on the airwaves while allowing states and localities to regulate porn behind brown wrappers in shops. Instead, the burden of regulating Internet reception was put on parents and adult supervisors of children.

But parts of the CDA were upheld. For instance, the act included a provision that seeks to protect children from online pedophiles and stalkers. And the Child Online Protection Act, introduced by former Indiana senator Dan Coats, mandates that commercial pornographers require verification of would-be vendors as adults before selling them porn.

Luring Kids In

Chat rooms and sexually explicit material from overseas are especially difficult to regulate. Dennis Perry, a law-enforcement agent in Naples, Florida, confirms this. He spends 10 to 50 hours a week of his spare time alerting authorities to illegal sites. "Some of these pedophiles put up sites to lure kids in to them. Sites like the Treehouse Kids Club look innocent enough until you look a little closer and find out it is maintained by boy lovers; Perry says. "Most often when Internet service providers are made aware that they are supporting pedophilia, they shut [the sites] down. But most pedophiles just set up sites overseas." So Perry writes the embassies. He says he chased one site from the United States to Germany and then Korea. It ended up being supported by a server in Russia, but he has had no reply from the Russian Embassy.

How harmful is pornography to children? The Cincinnati-based National Coalition for the Protection of Children and Families conducted a series of focus groups with teens in August 1998 in which 88 percent of males acknowledged that teens learn how to perform sex from porn. More than 70 percent of males and females agreed it is addictive. The coalition also found that 10 is the average age that children are being exposed to pornography.

"We think the Internet is a wonderful tool," explains coalition president Ray Schatz, and "we encourage people to use it, lest they be educationally deprived. But it is irresponsible not to talk about the dangers involved. It would be like telling someone about a beautiful woodland and not mentioning the grizzly bears inside."

Meanwhile, Internet-service giant America Online, or AOL, has background-checked staff monitoring every chat room it maintains. "We are designed as a family-friendly service," says AOL spokesman Rich d'Amato, "but parents must monitor what their kids do online." In other words, he says, parents must not use the Internet as an electronic baby-sitter, lest it turn out that the baby-sitter is a pedophile.

The Danger of "Buddy Lists"

"The scariest thing," explains activist Donna, "is how pedophiles can follow you around online without you knowing it." She tells *Insight* about a young child whose mother died. In her grief this child visited a chat room for other children who had lost a parent. A pedophile added her to his "buddy list," an online identification service that enables users to monitor Internet activities of friends. The man took notes on what the child said not only in that chat room but all the others she visited. After several weeks the pedophile contacted the child, posing as an Indian shaman who had made contact with her dead mother. Using his notes, he was able to pretend that he indeed was psychic and knew her thoughts. The little girl's excitement grew as the phony shaman recounted exactly what she had done the day before! Soon he lured her into a lesbian chat room and was forwarding her explicit material.

"People don't realize how dangerous it is for their kids," says Jo Ann, a mother who has helped authorities convict child molesters online. Her 11-year-old son has been molested, she explains. "I know what potential dangers there are for my kids and how this has destroyed my son." Her son now is terrified even to play on a baseball team, she says, lest his coach try to touch him. The family plans to move to another state "for a fresh start."

Gulotta of the FBI's Innocent Images program says he has been on the force for more than 30 years and has seen a lot but, when he refers to Internet pedophiles, his voice turns quiet and cold. "There is no more reprehensible a group than these people," he says.

THE UNDERESTIMATED DANGERS OF LONG-TERM NEGLECT

Deborah Blum

Because the immediate effects of neglect are subtle and not as obviously damaging as physical and sexual abuse, it receives less attention than other forms of child abuse, writes Deborah Blum. However, Blum notes, neglect accounts for more than half of all reported cases of child abuse and may be worse in its long-term impact on a child's psychological health than either sexual or physical abuse. She explains that physical and sexual abuse tend to be episodic, with periods of caring and nurturing following periods of abuse, but neglect is usually chronic. Also, Blum points out, the obvious nature of physical and sexual abuse often enables authorities to intervene quickly, while the invisible nature of neglect can allow victims to suffer for years before anyone takes notice. Blum is an author and a professor of journalism at the University of Wisconsin in Madison.

They were brothers raised in the same house—same parents, same school—but very separate hells. The mother adored the older son. She never walked by him without a touch on the head or a stroke down one arm. The father hated the sight of the boy; he could hardly walk by without taking at least one good punch at the child. The boy had his mother's fair coloring, but the father thought he saw another man's face in the boy's features. In his view, only the younger son was acceptable. Dark hair, olive skin like his; the boy looked right. The father never laid a hand on the second son. Yet neither, if she could help it, did the mother. She'd turn away when the little boy spoke, flinch when he touched her.

"It was as if she were taking out her anger on the child because he didn't have the hell beaten out of him like the older boy," says Bruce Perry, chief of psychiatry at Texas Children's Hospital in Houston. "She just ignored him. Wouldn't talk to him, tease him, hold him, comfort him. She'd say, Looks like his father, acts like his father."

Both boys were referred to Perry's clinic. They were ages 8 and 6 and already in trouble. They first appeared to be a matched set, united in their hostility, aggression, and determination to push others away. But over time, Perry and his colleagues began to see a difference. The older boy would occasionally smile back, meet their eyes. The younger boy just flat out wasn't there.

"The 8-year-old had better social skills to start with, and we were eventually able to make him see that the beatings were not his fault. With counseling and with some medication he got better. But the other boy never got better. He never had friends; he couldn't find pleasure in people. We couldn't get through."

Up until then, Perry, who is also a research professor in child psychology at the Baylor College of Medicine, had focused on the impact of violence and trauma on a child's brain, working with children from the most dangerous communities in Chicago and with children of the Branch Davidian cult in Waco, Texas. To study these brothers, watch them struggle, and see that the most damaged child was not the one who'd been physically beaten came as a surprise. "I thought, 'Whoa, I've been missing something here,'" Perry says.

Last on the List

The three great sins against children—those that invoke the law, bring down the wrath of the community and the hounds of child protective services agencies—have an unwritten hierarchy: Physical abuse and sexual abuse come first, and then, oh yeah, there's that neglect thing.

It's not that people don't take neglect seriously. More than half of the 3 million-plus children who end up in agency files every year are there because they were unwashed, unfed, untreated for illness, unwanted. Spectacular neglect cases even make headlines. "Remember that horrible case in Wisconsin last year, the little girl in the cage?" asks Susan Rose, a professor at the School of Social Welfare at the University of Wisconsin in Milwaukee. The parents, from the small town of Brillion, kept their 7-year-old daughter in a dog cage in their basement. Both are now in jail after their 11-year-old son walked barefoot through the snow to the police and turned them in.

But by and large, neglect is back-page news. In fact, the judge who handled the Brillion case handed down relatively light sentences, pointing out that, in his opinion, the child did appear difficult to handle. Rose has been investigating the way workers in child protective services view neglect, and why they seem less concerned about it than about other forms of abuse. "Part of it," says Rose, "is that they get inured to what they're looking at. It's more or less like being in a war zone. They see kids who are really severely neglected and, OK, that's bad, but it doesn't look as bad as the battered child they saw just before."

Yet a growing number of researchers, including Perry and Rose, are finding that neglect may in fact be worse in its long-term impact on a child than physical or sexual abuse. In a study published in the journal *Developmental Review,* Penelope Trickett, a childhood abuse expert at the University of Southern California, compared the developmental consequences of physical abuse, sexual abuse, and neglect. She looked at toddlers and elementary, middle, and high school students, studying learning delays, social problems, and hostile tendencies. Neglected children tended to be withdrawn and anti-social, not only with their parents but with other children. They weren't the angriest or the most aggressive, but even as toddlers, they were exhibiting signs of trouble ahead. Like abused children, neglected toddlers had learning delays, particularly in language skills. By elementary school, they had the lowest grades and test scores, the highest teacher ratings of learning problems, grade repeats, and school absences. More than that, they showed no signs of pulling ahead.

Trickett found the same pattern among the middle and high school students. "I was surprised that neglect was so much worse," she says. "Most of my work has been in physical and sexual abuse, and I just expected the bottom to be there. Perhaps we've been so focused on psychopathology, we haven't been paying attention."

Indeed, when Perry searched six major journals for articles on the consequences of neglect, a database of 7,000 articles, he found only 30 citations. "Does that make sense to you?" he asks. Pediatric textbooks, he points out, devote far less space to neglect, which affects hundreds of thousands of children, than to obscure genetic disorders, which may involve just a few thousand children. Ironically, neglect is the most common form of child abuse, accounting for 52 percent of all victims; physical abuse accounts for 24 percent, and sexual abuse another 6 percent. The remainder is a combination of medical abuse, emotional maltreatment, and unidentified factors.

Detection Is Difficult

The challenge is not simply recognizing that neglect is harmful but recognizing it at all. No one has to debate the definition of a broken arm or bruised eye. But even professionals wrestle over the many, subtle, and often varied ideas of what constitutes neglect.

"One of the issues that's held us back is the question of how to frame the issue," Perry says. "When we think of neglect we think of dirty kids who haven't been given enough food. We need to challenge people to think from another perspective. As children develop, they need different kinds of experiences—and I mean need—at different points in their lives. Neglect, simply, is the absence of those experiences at the time the child needs them."

Without affection, attention, social interaction, and a give-and-take between caregiver and child, the brain won't develop properly. A surprisingly small amount of parental indifference can generate surprisingly large problems.

"It is neglectful for an upper-middle-class family to take a 3-month-old, at the cost of holding and rocking and cooing, and put him in front of an educational videotape," Perry says. "That's neglectful, robbing that child of necessary somatosensory experience."

Perry offers another scenario of neglect: "You smile at your mother. She doesn't smile back. You want to be hugged. She pushes you away. You ask her a question. She won't look at you. And so you're taught that smiling gets you nothing, that people don't want to look at you."

He asks, "Have you ever talked to one of these neglected children? They don't know how to respond to you. It's as if where all that should be, where the brain should have stored that information, they're hollow."

Perry even has physical proof of this damage. He has a slide of the brain of a child whose parents completely shut him out—global neglect, he calls it. The ventricles, natural hollow chambers in the brain, appear as big black patches. They're meant to be small at this point in development, but in Perry's slide, they are tripled in size, filled with fluid because the surrounding brain didn't grow to its full potential.

He hopes such images will help solve the dilemma, pinpointing when a child is being harmed by his parents' indifference. Eventually, he says, we might be able to diagnose neglect by examining brain development.

Neglect and Dysfunctional Behavior

That possibility has given new energy to those arguing that neglect must be taken more seriously.

Researchers have long known that in social species a lack of parental care and affection creates a host of dysfunctional behaviors. Only recently have neuroscientists begun trying to work out the brain architecture behind such behaviors. Some of this derives from studies of rats, notably by William Greenough, a psychology professor at the University of Illinois at Urbana-Champaign.

Greenough showed that baby rats raised in a healthy but sterile environment—plenty of food and water and clean bedding but no companionship or toys—showed up to 25 percent less growth in their synapses (the connections between the nerve cells in the brain) compared with those rats that grew up with companions and an ever-changing menu of toys, puzzles, and mazes to figure out.

And this is exactly Perry's point. "The brains of children are use-dependent," he argues. They grow properly when given what they need. And that's a lot more than just clean clothes and food on the table.

One of the most provocative studies along this line was done recently by Geraldine Dawson, a psychologist at the University of Washington in Seattle, who looked at the children of severely depressed mothers—women who provided very little engagement or positive reinforcement to their infants. She found that, at 14 months, many of those babies had reduced brain-wave activity in the left frontal lobe of their brains. That region of the brain is associated with positive feelings such as happiness and curiosity. "When certain brain cells are stimulated," Dawson explains, "they become more responsive." By age 3-1/2, the children in Dawson's study whose mothers remained chronically depressed had a slew of behavioral problems, including withdrawal, aggression toward others, crying episodes, and disobedience.

A third study in Minnesota examined how these children fare over the long term. The Parent-Child Research Project began in 1975. Byron Egeland, Martha Farrell Erickson, and their colleagues enrolled 267 women who were in their last trimester of pregnancy. Their now-twentysomething children are still being tracked. Out of the group, the team of psychologists identified 24 mothers as being neglectful, 19 of whom stood out as emotionally remote, or what researchers call "psychologically unavailable." These women didn't like to cuddle, play with, or talk to their children.

And it was their children who stood out dramatically from the others. As part of the project, the psychologists spent hours interviewing preschool and kindergarten teachers. Erickson would ask about the children in the study, never saying who was neglected, abused, nurtured. Consistently, the children singled out as having learning problems—those the teachers considered inattentive, uninvolved, overly passive, anxious, or impatient—were the neglected children.

And there was something else. They were also the most unpopular children—and not only with their fellow students. The teachers didn't like them either. "They'd say, I'm always glad when he's not in class," Erickson recalls. "And they were talking about these emotionally neglected children. And so it starts looking like a cycle."

Erickson explains why the problem is so severe. "Other kinds of abuse are episodic," she says. "In between the bad episodes, the children usually get some attention and even some nurturing. But, from what I've observed in families, emotional neglect is chronic. And if children are emotionally neglected in the first two years—when the family is the child's whole world—then there are going to be striking consequences. It's hard to see because these children will eventually just act as if they are fine, as if they don't need anyone when, really, they've shut down."

The effects of neglect, it turns out, are cumulative. As Erickson points out, it's not the occasional TV babysit or late-night workday that has impact. It's when it happens every day. "Neglect just slowly and persistently eats away at the child's spirit until she has little will to connect with others or explore the world."

Poverty

According to Maureen Black, a professor of pediatrics at the University of Maryland in Baltimore, the greatest risk factor for severe neglect is poverty. But obviously, it's not the only one. Poor families get reported more often, not just because they lack resources but because they tend to be more visible to public service agencies. Other risk factors for children—parents who abuse drugs or alcohol, parents who are depressed, parents in bad relationships, parents who are just too busy to pay attention—can be found at any income level.

Yet neglect, she admits, is still a difficult issue for agencies to handle. It is, after all, an act of omission, making it near invisible. Without the obvious evidence that physical or sexual abuse provides, many people hesitate to intervene. One 1983 study found that hospitals failed to report more than half the cases of obvious neglect to child welfare authorities. "Bizarre as it is," Black says, "children are better served if something momentarily bad happens because they will get intervention. If a child gets a broken leg, some sort of injury, that child is going to get attention. The emotional problems, the lack of adequate care, the lack of supervision—it's very difficult to make a case."

When it comes to issues such as "psychological unavailability," says the Minnesota project's Egeland, child protective services criteria have failed to catch up with the current research. "We don't define [emotional] neglect in terms of long-term outcome because policymakers and politicians don't have the foresight to do that," he says.

Egeland is inclined to turn sarcastic over the gap between the researchers' findings and the country's social service policies. Imagine, he says, calling child protective services to alert investigators to an unsupervised toddler. Or imagine this call, beginning: "I've found a child who's watching TV for 16 hours a day, and I'm concerned that he's being emotionally neglected." Even with all the work by researchers showing such neglect matters, he says, he suspects the agency's response will be simple: "They'll hang up on you."

Adds Egeland, "Maltreatment is a huge risk factor for many kinds of pathologies—depression, suicide, conduct disorders, learning disorders—and it just blows me away sometimes that we don't talk about it in terms of prevention."

Perry has prevention on his mind as well. He's been tracking the troubled family, the two brothers, for more than five years now. The older boy continues to make gains, but not the younger one.

"The younger brother," says Perry, "is very distant, has no friends, is generally compliant but will have episodes of predatory and violent behaviors." Usually, he directs this anger toward younger children or animals, says Perry, and shows very little remorse afterwards. Perry notes that the boy has other problems, too. "He steals little things in school, he doesn't laugh very much—it's a pretty sad picture."

SPANKING: AN ABUSIVE PRACTICE

Alice Miller

Society has long held the mistaken notion that inappropriate behavior in children can be corrected by the use of corporal punishment, writes Alice Miller. In fact, according to Miller, corporal punishment simply reinforces aggressive behavior and discourages the development of empathy. Society's inability to recognize spanking as a form of child abuse, she maintains, has perpetuated a cycle in which children who are physically punished grow up to repeat the abuse with their own children. Moreover, argues Miller, a close examination of the prison population in America reveals that an overwhelming majority of criminals were physically abused as children, indicating that physical punishment does not help children become good citizens. Only by eschewing the use of corporal punishment will parents set a positive example for their children and contribute to the betterment of society, she explains. Miller is the author *of Prisoners of Childhood, For Your Own Good: Hidden Cruelty in Child-Rearing,* and *Thou Shalt Not Be Aware: Society's Betrayal of the Child.*

How did Evil come into the world and what can we do to combat it? While people have always had a diffuse, intuitive conviction that the seeds of Evil are to be sought in childhood, the ruling tendency has been to imagine Evil as the manifestation of innate destructive instincts, a congenital defect best transformed into goodness, decency, and nobility of character by corporal punishment.

This position is still frequently championed. Today, nobody seriously believes that the Devil has a hand in things, smuggling some changeling into the cradle and forcing us to employ strict upbringing methods to batter our diabolical offspring into submission. But from some quarters we do hear the serious contention that certain genes predispose some individuals to delinquency. The quest for these rogue genes has inspired many a respectable research project, even though the hypotheses behind it fly in the face of a number of proven facts.

For example, we know today that the brain we are born with is not the finished product it was once thought to be. The structuring of the brain depends very much on experiences undergone in the first hours, days, and weeks of a person's life. The stimulus indispensable for developing the capacity for empathy, say, is the experience of loving care. In the absence of such care, when a child is forced to grow up neglected, emotionally starved, and subjected to physical cruelty, he or she will forget this innate capacity.

The Effect Trauma Has on the Brain

In the last few years, neurobiologists have established that traumatized and neglected children display severe lesions affecting up to 30 percent of those areas of the brain that control our emotions. Severe traumas inflicted on infants lead to an increase in the release of stress hormones that destroy the existing, newly formed neurons and their interconnections. It's not just a coincidence that the number of children committing murders is on the increase, and that very many of them were born to adolescent, drug-dependent mothers. Extreme neglect, lack of attachment, and traumatization are the rule in such cases.

Of course we do not arrive in this world as a clean slate. Every new baby comes with a history of its own, the history of the nine months between conception and birth. In addition, children have the genetic blueprint they inherit from their parents. These factors may determine what kind of temperament a child will have, what inclinations, gifts, predispositions. But character depends crucially upon whether a person is given love, protection, tenderness, and understanding in the early formative years or exposed to rejection, coldness, indifference, and cruelty. Otherwise, how can advocates of the "congenital evil" theory explain why, thirty to forty years before the Third Reich, a sudden spate of children with "bad genes" was born ready at a later date to do Hitler's bidding?

The people who turned into Hitler's willing executioners had accounts to settle that dated back to their earliest days. In Germany in the 1860s, monstrous advice about "good" parenting was disseminated by self-styled educationalists; their advice manuals went into as many as forty editions, which has led me to conclude that most parents read them and did indeed act—in good faith—on the recommendations set out there. Parents beat their children from the outset because they had been told this was the way to make decent members of society out of them. Forty years later, the children thus treated did the same with their children. They didn't know any better. Born thirty to forty years before the Holocaust, those traumatized children later became Hitler's adherents, adulators, and henchmen. In my view, it was the direct result of their early drilling. The cruelty they experienced turned them into emotional cripples incapable of developing any kind of empathy for the suffering of others. At the same time it made them into people living with a time bomb, unconsciously waiting for an opportunity to vent on others the rage pent up inside them. Hitler gave them the legal scapegoat they needed to express their early feelings and their thirst for vengeance.

Change Comes Slowly

The latest discoveries about the human brain might have been expected to bring about a radical change in our thinking about children and the way we treat them. But as we know only too well, old habits die hard. It takes at least two generations for young parents to free themselves of the burden of inherited "wisdom" and stop beating their own children, two generations until it has become sheerly impossible to give one's child a slap "inadvertently," two generations before the weight of newly acquired knowledge gets in the way of the hand raised to deal the "unthinking" blow. Part of the reason change comes so slowly, however, is that, alongside the habits stored in our bodies favoring such misguided behavior, we also still listen to a host of "experts" who continue in the demonstrably false belief that the effects of corporal punishment are salutary. Because, in most cases, the experts in question inherited this opinion from their own parents when they were children themselves, their belief in it prevails over all the weight of scientific evidence pointing to the contrary.

We cannot reach adults who were subjected to abuse as children unless we return to the scenes of their childhood experience. As I argue in my latest book, *Paths of Life,* the experiences undergone by infants in the first days, weeks, and months of their lives are of immense significance in explaining their subsequent behavior. In no way do I wish to assert that later influences are completely ineffectual. On the contrary. For a traumatized or neglected child, it is of crucial importance to encounter what I call a "helping" or a "knowing witness" in its immediate circle. But such witnesses can only really help if they are aware of the consequences of early deprivations and do not play them down. It is in disseminating the information required by such potential knowing witnesses that I see my task.

For a long time, the significance of the first few months of life for the later adult was a neglected subject even among psychologists. In several of my books, I have tried to cast some light on this area by discussing the biographies of dictators like Hitler, Stalin, Ceaucescu, and Mao and demonstrating how they unconsciously reenacted their childhood situation on the political stage. Here, however, I want to turn my attention away from history and the past and train my gaze on our present practice. My conviction is that in numerous areas of practical life we could be more productive if we paid the childhood factor greater heed than is customarily the case. Consider the example of our current penal system, the area in which the willful neglect of the childhood factor is most apparent.

Abuse and Crime

Statistics tell us that 90 percent of the prisoners in American jails were abused in childhood. This figure is astonishingly high if we bear in mind how often individuals deny and repress childhood abuse. Probably the real figure is closer to a full 100 percent. A sheltered and respected child does not turn criminal.

Unfortunately little has been done to integrate this knowledge into the way prisons are organized and run. Outwardly, of course, today's prisons and penitentiaries have little in common with the grim fortresses of the nineteenth century. But one thing has stayed much the same: questions like what made an individual prisoner a criminal in the first place, what features of his early life set him off in that direction, and what could he do to avoid falling into the same trap over and over again are very rarely posed. In order to answer these questions himself, the prisoner would have to be encouraged to talk, write, and think about his life as a child and share these facts with others in a structured group setting.

In my latest book, I report on a program of this nature in Canada. Thanks to group work, a number of fathers who had sexually abused their daughters understood for the first time that their actions were criminal. Of crucial importance for them was that they were able to talk about their childhood to other people they trusted. That way they learned to grasp how they had automatically passed on something they had experienced themselves without realizing it.

We are accustomed not to say anything about the things we have suffered in childhood and frequently, instead of saying anything, we act blindly. But it was precisely the opportunity to talk about those things that released these prisoners from their blindness, gave them access to heightened awareness, and protected them from acting out. Programs like these are unfortunately still very much the exception. The only other one I know of is at a prison in Arizona where violent criminals can talk about their childhood and, with the help of the group, learn to decipher the covert meaning of their life histories. I have seen video recordings of these group sessions and I was impressed by the change in the facial expressions of these men after therapy. Proceeding in this way regularly would probably save a great deal of the taxpayer's money; programs like these are not expensive to organize and the danger of relapse is significantly diminished. It is thus doubly surprising that they have not found their way into most prisons.

The situation in prisons reflects a similar problem in the rest of society. On the political stage, the more nationalism threatens our world, the more frequently we must reckon with the emergence of unpredictable dictators. Dictators are simply a subgroup of people exposed to serious physical and mental jeopardy during childhood. To counteract their mania it is not enough to know that we are dealing with dangerous individuals who must be "taken out of circulation." We must instead understand the motives behind their actions on the basis of their life histories and not play their game, not be maneuvered into the role of their persecutor. We must trust to the productive fruits of direct communication instead of the destructive measures of direct confrontation.

The Denial of Human Dignity

As long as we are unaware of the degree to which the right to human dignity has been denied us in our own childhood, it is anything but easy to truly concede that right to our children, no matter how sincerely we may wish to do so. Legislators in Germany only a short while ago, in 1997, expressly conceded to parents the right to physical correction. In America, parents in poll after poll say they reserve the right to "spank" their children, and too many teachers still cannot imagine a school system without punishment and penalization. But we know beyond doubt that punishment has at best a short-term "positive" effect. In the long run, the exertion of force merely serves to reinforce aggressive behavior on the part of children and adolescents.

In schools, for example, if children from a background of domestic violence have to devote all their attention to averting danger, they will hardly be able to concentrate on the subject matter they are being taught. They may well expend a great deal of effort on observing the teacher so as to be prepared for the physical "correction" that they feel, fatalistically, to be inevitable. In reality as they see it, they can hardly afford to develop an interest in what their teachers are trying to tell them. Yet more blows, yet more punishments are hardly likely to allay this effect; on the other hand, understanding these children's fears could quite literally move mountains. But teachers who have themselves grown up with punishment favor punishment in the face of all the logic that militates against it because they learned at a very early stage to believe in its efficacy. Neither in their own childhood nor during their training as teachers have they had the opportunity to develop a sensibility for the sufferings of children.

Helping instead of punishing would be to the advantage of the teacher and his role as an instructor. We know that children who have faced physical punishment will be unable to defend their right to human dignity, unable to recognize physical pain as a danger signal and to act accordingly. Even their immune system may be affected. In the absence of other persons to model their behavior on, without knowing or at least helping witnesses, these children will lack the language to express themselves when they grow up because adults will normally elect to keep suppressed feelings of powerlessness in a state of suppression.

Protection and respect for the needs of a child—that is surely something we ought to be able to take for granted. But we live in a world peopled by individuals who have grown up deprived of their own rights. As adults they then attempt to regain those rights by force (through blackmail, threats, "physical correction," and the use of weapons). Thousands of professors at hundreds of universities teach all manner of subjects, but there is not one single university chair for research into child abuse and cruelty to children. How strange, when we recall that the majority of the people living on this earth are victims of precisely that kind of treatment!

Words Are Not Enough

As a priority commitment for the next decade, the United Nations has declared its allegiance to the implementation of "Education for Peace." This cannot be achieved by fine words alone. We need to set an example for our children as the people who will decide what the next generation will look like, and to show them that coexistence and communication without violence is possible. An ever greater number of parents are capable of setting this example and are aware of the far-reaching implications of their own behavior. Many of them agree that physical force against children should be banned by law. If this group succeeds in outlawing physical correction—as has already happened in nine European countries—then the next generation will grow up without spanking and beating, and that means growing up free of a legacy that can only set them off on a course that is fateful indeed. It is realistic to hope that this fact will lead to an increase in the number of knowing witnesses and a better world for us all.

THE DEVASTATING EFFECTS
OF SHAKING BABIES

Henry L. Davis

In the following selection, Henry L. Davis, a medical reporter for the *Buffalo News* in New York, examines the effects of shaken baby syndrome, an array of physical maladies that can result from injuries caused by violent shaking. When a parent or caregiver shakes an infant—most often in a fit of rage brought on by frustration with a crying child—the delicate veins in the baby's head tear and bleed, causing the brain to swell, Davis explains. This swelling frequently leads to blindness, paralysis, and developmental difficulties. Though shaken baby syndrome is the most common cause of abuse-related death among children, Davis asserts, it is difficult to detect because its immediate symptoms—vomiting, irritability, and lethargy—are often mistaken for other illnesses. However, he states, recent advances in medical technology are enabling doctors to diagnose the syndrome more readily.

It's standard procedure to teach couples what to do with their newborns once they leave the hospital. In Western New York, parents also are learning what not to do.

"Never, ever shake a baby." That is the advice now being drummed into the heads of tired new moms and dads at all area hospitals that deliver babies.

Medical personnel in eight counties are even asking parents to sign an affidavit, acknowledging they've received information about shaken baby syndrome, as part of a campaign to prevent the often-deadly form of child abuse.

The Buffalo physician behind the campaign envisions it as a model for the state and perhaps the nation.

"People are looking at us to see if we can do this successfully and make a difference," said Dr. Mark Dias, a pediatric neurosurgeon at Kaleida Health Children's Hospital. "I think we can make a big difference."

Shaken baby syndrome has received national attention because of a handful of celebrated cases, including the 1997 nanny murder case in

Boston, involving Louise Woodward. The fatal shaking also occurs in New York with regularity.

In 1999, Robin and Paul Vogel of West Seneca watched with anger and disbelief as a judge sentenced a once-trusted friend to prison for killing their son while baby-sitting.

For violently shaken babies who survive, life can change forever.

The father of Chelsea Bowes served a prison term for abusing her when she was 4 months old. Nine years later the Lockport, New York, girl still copes with the devastating injuries she suffered.

"It's hard," said Vicki Bowes, her mother. "I had a perfectly healthy child who will always be dependent on someone else."

There are no good statistics on the number of children injured or killed by shaking, although it is considered the most common cause of death and accounts for the most long-term disability from child abuse, authorities say.

Estimates range from 600 to 1,400 cases a year in the United States, according to a 1998 newsletter from the National Information, Support and Referral Service on Shaken Baby Syndrome. But experts say many incidents go unreported.

"Babies can't talk and, if parents abused them, which is usually the case, they aren't talking either," said Dr. Paula Mazur, a Children's Hospital child abuse specialist.

She and her colleagues investigate about 10 new cases a year. These are the children injured so badly, perhaps with seizures or left unconscious, that they end up in the region's pediatric trauma center.

No one knows how many undiagnosed shaken babies suffer disabilities, changed personalities or learning problems. Shaken babies may show subtle symptoms—lethargy, vomiting or irritability—that pass for other illnesses.

"Some symptoms can seem like an infection," Dr. Mazur said.

The Likely Abusers

Most abusers are parents or live-in boyfriends, and the effects of their abuse can last a lifetime, as Ms. Bowes learned.

In 1990, she was at work as a nursing home aide and the father of her daughter—they were not married—was watching Chelsea in their home.

Patrick J. Cannon called to say Chelsea needed help—she had hit her head on a crib railing—Ms. Bowes said. The trouble with the story is that it did not jibe with the magnitude of the injuries, including a fractured skull.

As is often the case with shaken babies, the child also suffered a hard impact to the head.

Cannon later pleaded guilty to attempted first-degree assault.

Ms. Bowes and her daughter continue to live with the consequences long after Cannon's prison sentence ended.

Chelsea is legally blind and uses a cane to get around. A plastic shunt implanted in her head drains fluid that otherwise would collect dangerously in her brain. Her attention span is short, making her easily overwhelmed in special education classes. She suffers headaches and seizures, too.

Ms. Bowes consoles herself by saying her daughter is doing better than expected. Still, she worries.

"Chelsea's a sweet girl," said Ms. Bowes. "She's making progress, but it's very slow."

Like Jell-O in a Bowl

Enclosed within the skull, the brain is a gelatinous material that floats in a protective sea of cerebrospinal fluid. This fluid supports the brain and acts as a shock absorber in rapid head movements.

When a child is shaken, delicate veins between the brain and skull tear and bleed, according to medical experts. Blood pools between the skull and dura mater, the tough membrane next to the brain, and forms a large blood clot called a hematoma.

Hematomas produce pressure that, along with the natural swelling of the bruised brain, causes irreversible damage to brain cells.

An estimated 25 percent of cases are fatal in the first few days after-injury, studies show.

Picture the brain as Jell-O in a bowl. Jiggle the bowl and the Jell-O will separate slightly from the sides. Jiggle the Jell-O hard enough and it will fall apart.

Similarly, experts say repeated whiplash forces slam and rotate the soft brain, tearing fragile blood vessels and cutting off needed oxygen to cells. Shake long and hard enough, and a brain can turn to mush.

"We call it black brain," said Dias, referring to the color of a badly damaged brain on a Computed Tomography (CT) scan.

Babies make especially vulnerable victims—57 percent are boys—because their heads are larger in proportion to their bodies and their neck muscles are weak.

Gentle shaking, such as the playful bouncing that babies love so much, is not harmful, experts say. It takes severe force to do damage.

"From interviews with child abusers and witnesses, we know that the shaking probably looks as though the baby's head is going to come off," Dr. Mazur said.

Crying Is a Common Trigger

The most common trigger for violent shaking is a crying baby, experts say. The Vogels aren't sure but they believe that's what led to the attack on their son.

Seventeen-month-old Paul Jr. was buried in 1997, but the grief remains fresh.

The Vogels haven't wiped their son's fingerprints from the mirror above their bed. His little snowsuit still hangs in a closet.

At the time of the incident, Mrs. Vogel dropped the boy off at the home of Linda and Paul Przystal, who had agreed to watch him. Mrs. Vogel and Mrs. Przystal had been longtime friends. Their parents had known each other. She had stood as a maid of honor in the Przystal wedding.

The friendship ended later that day.

In a fit of rage never publicly explained, and with his own sons in the house, Przystal shook the boy hard enough to leave him hopelessly comatose.

Three days later at Children's Hospital, Mrs. Vogel cradled Paul Jr. in her arms, the tubes that kept him alive dangling from his body. A priest prayed with them while a few family members stood by. Then doctors shut off life support and, shortly, declared the boy dead.

Mrs. Vogel struggles to hold back tears when she recalls what happened.

"I lost my son and someone I thought was my best friend," she said.

Detecting Shaken Baby Syndrome

The advent of CT and Magnetic Resonance Imaging (MRI) scans has advanced the detection of shaken baby syndrome, allowing physicians to confirm the presence of hematomas and brain swelling.

An eye exam is used to detect one of the other indicators—bleeding in the retinas.

These classic signs of shaking often are accompanied by injuries that help build a case of abuse, such as fractures and bruising. The Vogel boy, for instance, showed bruising on parts of his body that may have been used as "handles" for shaking, Mrs. Vogel said.

Dias said 68 percent of parents in abuse cases say they don't know how their children were injured. The next most frequent explanation is that the child fell off a couch or bed.

However, studies have shown the key injuries associated with shaken baby syndrome do not look the same as those from short falls.

"In most cases, the medical evidence is clear," said Dias, who in 1998, published the first study to use CT scans to establish the time of alleged cases of shaken baby syndrome, findings that one day may help identify perpetrators.

"Knowing when the shaking took place can pinpoint who was with the baby, and that's important information, given the legal uncertainties in this issue," he said. "You usually don't get a confession. People lie, and they can wait before calling for help."

Deliberately Making Children Ill: Munchausen Syndrome by Proxy

Nancy Wartik

In the following selection, Nancy Wartik examines a form of child abuse known as Munchausen syndrome by proxy (MSBP), a psychological disorder in which a parent—most often the mother—either fabricates or deliberately causes symptoms of illness in his or her child in order to attract sympathy and attention. Wartik writes that MSBP is difficult to diagnose because mothers who suffer from the disorder appear to be model parents who are extremely devoted to their ailing children. Mothers with MSBP also often have a background in medicine, she explains, which makes them adept at inducing certain disorders and fooling healthcare professionals. Though substantiated cases of MSBP remain rare, Wartik notes, medical experts are becoming increasingly suspicious of mothers whose children regularly suffer from unexplained health problems. Wartik is a freelance writer specializing in health and psychology.

To many who knew her, Ellen Storck, 41, seemed a caring and devoted parent. A single mother, she worked hard to raise her four children, Joshua, 16; Dana, 15; Courtney, 12; and Aaron, 9. The family lived in a well-kept home in East Northport, New York, a suburb with middle-class residents and good schools. At times Storck held three jobs at once, selling real estate and waitressing at two restaurants. When she wasn't working, she dedicated herself to her children.

Most of all Storck lavished attention on her youngest child. When Aaron was just six weeks old, she brought him to a hospital, reporting that he'd stopped breathing and she'd had to resuscitate him. Doctors suspected that the infant might have sleep apnea, a condition in which breathing stops for short spells, usually at least 15 seconds. They suggested that Aaron be admitted for observation. Storck demurred; she wanted to take her son home. Since the doctors didn't find an apparent cause of the apnea—a throat obstruction is

Reprinted from "Fatal Attention," by Nancy Wartik, *Redbook*, February 1, 1994. Reprinted with permission from the author.

common—Aaron was sent home with a monitor that would sound an alarm if he had difficulty breathing.

At ten months, Storck says, Aaron's apnea ceased, but it came back in full force when he was four. Once she reported that he'd had 226 apnea episodes in one month, and several times she rushed her son to hospital emergency rooms because, she told doctors, she'd had to resuscitate him. Storck also took Aaron to visit his pediatrician nearly 50 times between age four and eight. Yet despite repeated hospitalizations and extensive, painful testing, no doctor could explain why the child's problems were so severe.

Accusations

Then in July 1992 Mayer Sagy, M.D., chief of critical care medicine at Schneider Children's Hospital in Queens, New York, announced he'd discovered the cause of Aaron's mysterious illness. After his staff observed Aaron closely during a hospital stay and noted that he did not have a single episode of apnea in three days, Dr. Sagy claimed that the boy's mother was making him sick. "I'm one hundred and ten percent certain you did this," he reportedly told Storck, accusing her of fabricating her son's illness.

The doctor believed Storck had a bizarre psychological disorder called Munchausen's syndrome by proxy (MSBP). People with this disorder, almost always women, lie about symptoms of disease in their children or, in more severe cases injure them and then seek medical care. The doctor said Ellen Storck had abused her son by making him undergo a series of medical tests and treatments for an illness she knew he didn't have. After Dr. Sagy reported the case to county social workers at Child Protective Services, Aaron was placed in foster care and Storck was charged with neglect.

At the trial Aaron's foster mother gave the damning testimony that Aaron had not had a single apnea attack in the five months he was in her care. On February 22, 1993, Storck was found guilty of child neglect for routinely subjecting her son to unnecessary medical treatment. It was not determined whether she had fabricated or induced Aaron's apnea.

Storck was allowed to retain custody of Joshua, Dana, and Courtney; Child Protective Services would check up on them regularly. The judge ordered Storck to undergo psychotherapy and said that Aaron would remain in foster care until his mother's therapist felt it was safe for him to go home. One year later Aaron still had not been returned to Storck, who staunchly insists she's innocent. She and her lawyers are planning an appeal. "I worked my life around Aaron and his illness," she says. "We'll fight until the truth comes out."

Convincing Performers

A rare condition with only an estimated 400 to 500 cases diagnosed a year, MSBP is an off-shoot of Munchausen's syndrome, a disorder in which people seek medical treatment for self-inflicted illnesses. First described in medical literature in 1977, it is named for Baron Karl von Munchausen, an eighteenth-century German soldier who told tall tales about his exploits.

Mothers with MSBP can be extraordinarily convincing performers. "They look to all the world like wonderful, devoted parents, while they're slowly harming their children," says Herbert A. Schreier, M.D., chief of psychiatry at Children's Hospital Oakland in California, and coauthor of *Hurting for Love,* a book about MSBP. "The physician tries harder and harder to solve the medical puzzle instead of standing back and wondering why there is such a puzzle."

"We tend to like and trust the parents we see," adds Randell Alexander, M.D., a child abuse expert and associate professor of pediatrics at the University of Iowa. "We don't routinely assume they're lying."

More calculating than ordinary child abusers, who tend to lash out spontaneously, MSBP parents may falsely report that their children have apnea, seizures, bleeding, abdominal pain, or high fevers. In extreme cases they use laxatives, sedatives, or emetics (which cause vomiting) to create symptoms. Sometimes they even tamper with a child's blood samples or intravenous lines once treatment has begun, to make sure doctors believe the illness is real. The consequences of MSBP are tragic: Studies show most youngsters suffer psychological trauma, and up to 10 percent die.

In the last several years shocking incidents of MSBP have made headlines. Texas Children's Hospital in Houston caught a mother on a hidden video camera suffocating the infant daughter she'd brought in for breathing problems. A Westchester County, New York, woman fed her nine-month-old daughter laxatives for four months, almost killing her. Another child was treated for five years for ulcerations on his back; it was later discovered his mother was rubbing oven cleaner into his skin. And in 1991 Peggy Herzog, a 24-year-old Minnesota mother, was convicted of third-degree felony assault against her son, Michael, two. The little boy had been hospitalized more than 20 times for infections, pneumonia, and fevers; doctors had noticed puncture wounds but his mother said they were from pins in a quilt. Finally Michael told a family friend, "Mommy gave me shots." Police found syringes and tubes of sodium chloride in Herzog's home. Put in foster care, Micheal regained his health.

Herzog's attorney, Harold Kimmel, still marvels at his client's unassuming manner. "The first time I saw her in court I told a colleague, 'If you picked the least likely person here, it would be her,'" Kimmel recalls. "Her dress, everything—she looked like my mother might have looked."

"I still try to understand why I did it," says Christine Rupert, 36, speaking from the Minnesota Correctional Facility in Shakopee, where she is serving a seven-and-a-half-year sentence. "It's not like I had hurtful feelings toward my daughter, I love her with all my heart." But in 1990 Rupert put a near-fatal dose of Valium into her daughter's milk shake, then dialed 911. After police began questioning how the girl, then 12, had ingested the drug, Rupert finally confessed. Rupert's daughter, now 16, is living with her father.

At the time of the incident, Rupert, divorced since 1981, had just started a management job at a hospital. "I was under a lot of stress, and doing everything on my own. I had no family in the area. I remember being very lonely," she says. "It was like that was my way of reaching out for help. It's not a pleasant way, but that's how I did it."

When she tried to explain to her daughter what had happened, Rupert says, "I told her it wasn't because she was bad or I didn't love her. I told her I was sick and I needed help. What else could I say?" Today she and her daughter are in touch by phone and mail.

Denial

The fact that Christine Rupert confessed makes her case extremely rare; denial is a hallmark of the syndrome. Psychological tests to identify the disorder are usually inconclusive, and some MSBP mothers can seem so . . . normal. One method of clinching a diagnosis is to remove a child from the home and see whether his or her health improves. And some hospitals now secretly videotape suspected parents to catch them in the act. More often, in the absence of solid proof, doctors or psychologists base a diagnosis of MSBP on how well a suspected mother fits a certain profile.

Experts say many MSBP parents have a medical background or are married to someone in the profession, which makes them experts at fabricating symptoms. They often grow very friendly with doctors or nurses treating their kids. Sometimes they have other children who've experienced unexpected illnesses. Many were ignored, neglected, or physically abused as children. As adults, they may be isolated, lonely, or married to men who are often absent or emotionally distant. And usually they have an excessively intimate relationship with their child.

"The physician may be one of the few people who really notices this woman and appreciates how she cares for her children, particularly when the child is ill," says Dr. Schreier. "When she discovers she's valued by such a respected figure, she may find herself taking steps to continue the relationship—at the expense of her child."

In many ways Ellen Storck, a petite, green-eyed, articulate woman, neatly matches the MSBP profile. She has ties to the medical profession: Aaron's father was a doctor and Storck has earned most of the credits toward a nursing degree. She was friendly and on a first-name basis with Aaron's pediatrician, Vincent Palusci, M.D. Storck also testified in court that her father physically and sexually abused her when she was young, a charge her family denies. And she was unusually close to Aaron: She and her son slept in the same bed for several years, she says, so she could shake him awake from his apnea attacks.

But Storck claims her resemblance to a typical MSBP parent is an unlucky coincidence. "These stereotypes are very dangerous," she says. "They put every parent with a child who's chronically ill in jeopardy."

Caught Lying

During lengthy court testimony, however, the prosecution caught Storck in several lies. She claimed to be a nurse when she had never gotten a degree, and said she was married to the father of her first three children when she was not. It was also pointed out that Storck's son Joshua had been underweight as a child and had undergone extensive testing, including some for seizures. Although a court-appointed neurologist confirmed that Joshua might have a seizure disorder, the judge's notes state that when Joshua was once treated for seizures, "the hospital did not feel the seizures were real and questioned Ms. S.'s emotional well-being." Courtney, Aaron's sister, had been tested for several disorders as well.

Dr. Palusci came to Storck's defense, saying he'd seen "no evidence" she was fabricating Aaron's illness. "We have a disease [referring to Aaron] that makes sense," he said. Dorothy Kelly, M.D., a professor of pediatrics at Harvard Medical School, appeared as an expert witness and said she'd studied rare cases where apnea problems appear and disappear as Aaron's did. Nurses from one hospital where Aaron had been tested said they'd seen his apnea monitor go off when Storck was not around. And although medical records also showed that Aaron was treated for numerous other complaints, including pneumonia, asthma, a blood infection, infected pelvic bone, and muscle abscesses (the latter three extremely rare in children), experts could not explain how Storck might have caused those medical problems.

In her defense Storck said that she never considered it a lie to call herself a nurse—she'd worked for several years as a medical assistant in an internist's office—and explained she fictionalized a marriage for her children's benefit. And in testimony given in the judge's chambers, Aaron said his mother had not harmed him. Storck's other three children also say that Aaron does have apnea. "Sometimes I was up there just by myself with him and his monitor would beep," says Courtney.

Ellen Storck now sees her son during weekly two-hour visits held at a social services agency near her home and during weekly family therapy sessions. Her son, she says, has been traumatized by being wrenched from his family. "The longer this goes on, the greater the damage will be."

Meanwhile those who know Storck remain polarized in their opinions. "She's a very good mother and her children are taken care of in every way," says Sally Stark, a family friend. "She'd drive Aaron to school because she didn't want to let him cross a busy street." A Long

Island therapist who has treated Storck in the past insists, "It's just not within her capacity to consciously hurt her children."

But two of Aaron's former teachers, who requested anonymity, say that when Aaron was their student, they started out believing in his illness, then grew to suspect it was fraudulent. Both teachers were told by Storck that Aaron was seriously ill and that if he ever dozed off, he might stop breathing and die.

Yet when it came time for routine school checkups, says one teacher, "[Storck] didn't want any doctors to examine him." The other teacher recalls that when she asked Storck to accompany the class on a field trip because no one would be able to perform CPR on Aaron if it became necessary, Storck said Aaron would be fine without her. "For me, that was it," she says. "I knew no mother would let her kid go on that trip if he was truly in danger."

A Fashionable Disease?

In the 1980s hardly anyone had heard of MSBP. Today it has hit the talk-show circuit, been featured on popular shows like *L.A. Law,* and is the subject of a best-selling novel, *Devil's Waltz.* Some experts are disturbed that the disease has received so much attention. They're concerned that doctors or state authorities are finding evidence of MSBP where none exists. "Munchausen's by proxy is a fashionable disease right now," says William Sears, M.D., a nationally renowned pediatrician based in San Clemente, California. "And for an innocent family, the consequences of a misdiagnosis are tragic."

Dr. Sears is serving as a consultant, free of charge, to Michele Beideman, 31, a Henderson, Nevada, mother who has spent more than two years trying to win her son Corbin, 4, back from foster care. Authorities took him away after accusing Beideman of trying to starve him and possibly induce infections.

As Beideman tells it, Corbin was frail from birth. He wouldn't eat and grew too slowly, a condition doctors call failure to thrive. He was also prone to ear, nose, and throat infections. In his first two years Beideman took Corbin to a pediatrician 48 times; she consulted at least two specialists. None could find the cause of Corbin's illnesses. Finally physicians referred her to UCLA Medical Center where Corbin was examined by David Charles Beck, M.D., a hospital psychiatrist, and a medical team. They concluded that Corbin was a "completely healthy and normal" child and accused Beideman of MSBP. Corbin was small for his age, they said, because his mother may have underfed him. They even said it was "quite possible" she'd been giving him appetite suppressants: During his stay, caffeine—a common diet aid ingredient—was found in his urine. Beideman claimed it was from chocolate Corbin had eaten at the hospital.

This isn't the first time child abuse charges have been leveled at Beideman. In 1987 she was investigated for abusing a son by a previous marriage, who now lives in Florida with his father. Though Beideman admitted hitting the child with a wooden spoon, charges were never filed. A psychological report made at the time said Beideman, "willingly exploit[s] others" and "is not likely to be sensitive to the needs of her children."

Having reviewed Corbin's medical records, Dr. Sears notes that Corbin may be underweight because "a child with frequent infections diverts energy he'd otherwise use to grow into healing." Corbin's throat infections continued to occur after he was put in foster care, Dr. Sears says, and he had to have a tonsillectomy in 1993. Though at last report Corbin had grown nearly five inches and gained seven pounds, Sears points out that he is still small for his age, despite the fact that he is no longer under his mother's care. In testimony, however, other doctors noted that Corbin has had "only normal childhood illnesses" in foster care, that he now has a good appetite, and is gaining weight more rapidly than he did at home.

Beideman is currently in treatment with a court-appointed psychotherapist; Corbin is still living in a foster home, and a court hearing is pending. A source close to the case says that today Corbin is a "very troubled little boy" who doesn't like to eat around his mother.

Although some experts say MSBP is in danger of being overdiagnosed, others maintain the disorder is more widespread than previously believed. "Physicians are still very slow to suspect Munchausen's by proxy," says Dr. Alexander. "I think we're missing plenty of cases out there."

"Some of These Parents Are So Charming"

Therapy for MSBP parents has had mixed results. "At least fifteen percent of mothers try to do the same thing again," says Dr. Schreier. Numerous questions about MSBP continue to stump the medical community. Doctors don't know why MSBP affects mainly mothers; it may be because women are the primary caretakers or that fathers with MSBP simply aren't getting caught. They also suspect this disease has always existed and has gone unrecognized. In fact, experts are now saying that an undetermined number of sudden infant death syndrome casualties may actually be intentional suffocation.

Since early 1992 the FBI has been alerting local law enforcement officials and medical personnel to the warning signs of MSBP. In the future, authorities say, doctors will need to tread a fine line between being alert to signs of MSBP and not jumping to conclusions. It's not going to be easy.

Dr. Alexander says he has twice been fooled by MSBP mothers. "In one instance, it was someone feeding a child Ex-Lax [a laxative], in another, Valium. And probably, I could be fooled again," he says. "Because some of these parents are so charming and convincing."

CHAPTER 2

THE CAUSES
OF CHILD ABUSE

SUBSTANCE-ABUSING PARENTS ARE MORE LIKELY TO ABUSE THEIR CHILDREN

Joseph A. Califano Jr.

An epidemic of parental drug and alcohol abuse has caused a catastrophic increase in child abuse that has pushed the child welfare system to the brink of collapse, writes Joseph A. Califano Jr., president of the National Center on Addiction and Substance Abuse at Columbia University in New York City. According to Califano, parents who abuse drugs and alcohol are three times more likely to physically or sexually assault their children, and children of substance-abusing parents are four times more likely to be victims of neglect. If there is to be any hope of preventing child abuse and preserving the natural family unit, he maintains, child welfare workers must be trained to detect substance abuse. Moreover, Califano argues, parents who abuse drugs and alcohol must be offered a comprehensive rehabilitation program that centers on substance abuse treatment, parenting skills, job training, and physical and mental health care.

Consider the following for a measure of national self-indulgence in the midst of the longest and greatest economic boom in our history. We Americans spend more on cosmetic surgery, hairpieces and make-up for men than we do on child welfare services for battered and neglected children of substance-abusing parents.

A tornado of drug and alcohol abuse and addiction is tearing through the nation's child welfare and family court systems, leaving in its path the wreckage of abused and neglected children, turning social welfare agencies and courts on their heads and uprooting the traditional disposition to keep children with their natural parents.

There is no safe haven for these abused and neglected children of drug- and alcohol-abusing parents. They are the most vulnerable and endangered individuals in America. That is the grim conclusion of an exhaustive two-year analysis by The National Center on Addiction and Substance Abuse at Columbia University [CASA].

Reprinted from "The Least Among Us: Children of Substance-Abusing Parents," by Joseph A. Califano Jr., *America*, April 24, 1999. Reprinted with permission from the author.

Drugs and Alcohol Are Fueling an Epidemic

Parental alcohol and drug abuse and addiction have pushed the nation's system of child welfare to the brink of collapse. From 1986 to 1997, the number of abused and neglected children in America has soared from 1.4 million to some 3 million, a stunning 114.3 percent jump, more than eight times faster than the 13.9 percent increase in the overall children's population. The number of reported abused and neglected children who have been killed has climbed from 798 in 1985 to 1,185 in 1996; the U.S. Advisory Board on Child Abuse and Neglect sets the actual number much higher, at 2,000, a rate of more than five deaths a day.

Alcohol, crack cocaine, methamphetamine, heroin and marijuana are fueling this population explosion of battered and neglected children. Children whose parents abuse drugs and alcohol are almost three times likelier to be physically or sexually assaulted and more than four times likelier to be neglected than children of parents who are not substance abusers. The parent who abuses drugs and alcohol is often a child who was abused by alcohol- and drug-abusing parents.

Eighty percent of professionals surveyed by CASA said that substance abuse causes or exacerbates most of the cases of child abuse and neglect they face. Nine of 10 professionals cite alcohol alone or in combination with illegal or prescription drugs as the leading substance of abuse in child abuse and neglect; 45.8 percent cite crack cocaine as the leading illegal substance of abuse; 20.5 percent cite marijuana (which can hardly be considered a benign drug in this situation).

Parental substance abuse and addiction is the chief culprit in at least 70 percent—and perhaps 90 percent—of all child welfare spending—some $10 billion of the $14 billion that Federal, state and local governments spent simply to maintain child welfare systems in 1998. This $10 billion does not include the costs of health care to abused and neglected children, operating law enforcement and judicial systems consumed with this problem, treating developmental problems, providing special education or lost productivity. Nor does it include the costs attributable to child abuse and neglect that are privately incurred. These costs easily add another $10 billion to the price of child abuse and neglect.

The human costs are incalculable: broken families; children who are malnourished; babies who are neglected, beaten and sometimes killed by alcohol- and crack-addicted parents; eight-year-olds sent out to steal or buy drugs for addicted parents; sick children wallowing in unsanitary conditions; child victims of sodomy, rape and incest; children in such agony and despair that they themselves resort to drugs or alcohol for relief.

Alcohol and drugs have blown away the topsoil of family life and reshaped the landscape of child abuse and neglect in America. Parents addicted to drugs and alcohol are clever at hiding their addiction and are often more concerned about losing their access to drugs and being punished than about losing custody of their children.

Motivation

For some parents, holding onto their children can provide the motivation to seek treatment. But for many the most insidious aspect of substance abuse and addiction is their power to destroy the natural parental instinct to love and care for their children. Eighty-six percent of professionals surveyed cited lack of motivation as the top barrier to getting such parents into treatment. As Alan Leshner, director of the National Institute on Drug Abuse, has observed, the addicted parent sometimes sees the child as an obstacle to getting drugs.

Parental drug and alcohol abuse and addiction have overwhelmed the child welfare system. By 1997 some caseworkers were responsible for 50 cases of child maltreatment at any one time and judges were handling as many as 50 cases a day, giving them less than 10 minutes in an uninterrupted eight-hour day to assess the testimony of parents, social workers, law enforcement officers and others in determining a child's fate.

Child welfare agencies have been forced to allocate more time to investigations, gathering evidence of neglect and abuse of children by alcohol- and drug-involved parents. This shift in focus has changed the way parents and children see caseworkers and the way these caseworkers view themselves. This shift also threatens to criminalize a process that should be driven by treatment, health care and compassion for both parent and child. The frantic response of many in Congress and the Clinton Administration is to add felonies to the Federal criminal code and throw more parents in prison—actions likely to do more harm than good for the children of these parents, who need stable and secure homes.

Few caseworkers and judges who make decisions about these children have been tutored in substance abuse and addiction. There are no national estimates of the gap between those parents who need treatment and those who receive it, but Federal Government surveys show that two-thirds of all individuals who need treatment do not get it. There is nothing to suggest that these substance-abusing parents fare any better than the general population.

As the role of substance abuse has increased, the age of the victimized children has gone down. Today most cases of abuse and neglect by substance-abusing parents involve children under five. Alcohol use and binge drinking during pregnancy are up, with at least 636,000 expectant mothers drinking and 137,000 drinking heavily. Some 500,000 babies born each year have been exposed in their mother's womb to cocaine and other illicit drugs (and usually alcohol and tobacco as well). Each year some 20,000 infants are abandoned at birth or kept at hospitals to protect them from substance-abusing parents. The proportion of children whom caseworkers place in foster care at birth jumped 44 percent from the 1983–86 period to the 1990–94 period.

Drug and alcohol abuse has thrown into doubt a fundamental tenet of child welfare workers: the commitment to keep the child with his or her natural parents. While terminating parental rights has long been viewed as a failure, alcohol, crack cocaine and other forms of drug abuse have challenged this time-honored precept.

Lost Opportunities

There is an irreconcilable clash between the rapidly ticking clock of physical, intellectual, emotional and spiritual development for the abused and neglected child and the slow-motion clock of recovery for the parent addicted to alcohol or drugs. For the cognitive development of young children, weeks are windows of opportunity that can never be reopened. For the parent, recovery from drug or alcohol addiction takes time—and relapse, especially during initial periods of recovery, is common.

Bluntly put, the time that parents need to conquer their substance abuse and addiction can pose a serious threat to their children who may suffer permanent damage during this phase of rapid development. Little children cannot wait; they need safe and stable homes and nurturing adults now in order to set the stage for a healthy and productive life.

The cruelest dimension of this tragedy for children abused by parents using drugs and alcohol is this: Even when parental rights are terminated in a timely way for such parents who refuse to enter treatment or who fail to recover, in our self-indulgent society there is no assurance of a safe haven for the children. There are not nearly enough adoptive homes. Being in foster care, while far better than being abused, rarely offers the lasting and secure nurturing for full cognitive development—and appropriate foster care is also in short supply. More caring, responsible adults need to step forward to care for the least among us, children of substance-abusing parents.

Child welfare systems and practices need a complete overhaul. Social service providers, from agency directors to frontline child welfare workers, judges, court clerks, masters, lawyers, and health and social service staffs need intensive training in the nature and detection of substance abuse and what to do when they spot it. In all investigations of child abuse and neglect, parents should be screened and assessed for substance abuse. Caseworkers and judges should move rapidly to place children for adoption when parents refuse treatment or fail to respond to it. We need to increase greatly the incentives for foster care and adoption and the number of judges and caseworkers.

Comprehensive Treatment Is a Must

Comprehensive treatment that is timely and appropriate, especially for substance-abusing mothers, is essential to prevent further child abuse and neglect. Treatment must be part of a concentrated course that would include mental health services and physical health care; literacy, job and parenting skills training; as well as socialization, employment and drug-free housing. Since most fathers have walked out on their responsibilities, such treatment must be attentive to the fact that most of these parents are women. Where the only hope of reconstituting the natural family for the abused child rests in comprehensive treatment for the parent, it is an inexcusable and vicious Catch-22 situation not to make such treatment available.

Of course, this all costs money. Can we afford to do these things? In the most affluent nation in the history of the world, the answer is a loud and clear yes. Failure to protect these children and provide treatment for their parents who fall prey to drugs and alcohol is more likely than any other shortcoming of survival-of-the-fittest capitalism to bring the harsh judgment of God and history upon us.

In recent years, Pope John Paul II has repeatedly reminded capitalist nations to soften the sharp edges that cut up the least among them. What better way to heed that admonition than to give the needs of these parents and their children first call on the burgeoning Federal budget surplus and the money that the states are picking up from the tobacco settlement.

The Foster Care System Exposes Children to Abuse

Timothy W. Maier

Despite research that indicates that children in the foster care system are ten times more likely to be abused than children in the general public, Timothy W. Maier writes, the number of children placed in out-of-home care has risen dramatically. In the following selection, he describes a number of cases in which overzealous Child Protective Services (CPS) workers have taken children from their nonabusive parents and placed them in nightmarish foster homes where they were physically and sexually abused. Because child abuse occurs at an alarmingly high rate in the United States, the mere suspicion of abuse is often enough for a social worker to remove children from their homes, Maier points out. Moreover, he explains, CPS workers often coerce children into implicating their parents even when no abuse has occurred. More care should be taken to ensure that children are not removed from their homes unnecessarily and that foster parents are not abusing the children in their custody, he concludes. Maier is a reporter for *Insight on the News*.

"Mommy, Mommy, they're raping me!" Then click and a dial tone. The desperate call had come in the dead of winter 1994 at 2:30 A.M. to Alma Kidd. Her 14-year-old daughter, Norma "Hope" Robbins, was trapped in a Washington state foster-care home. Kidd immediately reported the incident to police, but no charges were filed. The rape was described as consensual lesbian sex.

This story seems almost unbelievable, but *Insight* has reviewed hundreds of pages of documents, depositions, videotapes and internal Child Protective Services, or CPS, field investigations confirming this and other sadomasochistic sexual assaults.

While in foster care, Hope became a heroin addict, dropped out of school and grew so despondent that three times she tried to commit suicide. Records show she ran away at least 11 times, only to be brought back to her torturers. Medical reports indicate that she sustained such deep cuts to her arms that doctors called it satanic ritual abuse.

A Strained Relationship

Hope was placed in foster care in March 1993 after CPS claimed Kidd abused her. The mother never had the hearing that Washington state law requires within 48 hours.

Evidence shows mother and daughter had a strained relationship. Kidd objected to her daughter associating with boys involved in drugs and opposed Hope's desire to adopt a lesbian lifestyle. Hope once attacked Kidd with a knife, and another time told her, "You're not my mother. You're just someone who laid down and out I came." Hope clearly wanted to shock and hurt her mother, but reports also indicate that the girl recanted stories that her mother abused her, and wanted to go home.

In 1994, Kidd was granted custody of her child under a court order. That order came after three separate investigations found the allegations that the mother had abused Hope were false. But after the custody hearing, Kidd was severely beaten outside the courtroom by a "mob of lesbians," some of whom worked for the state and previously had guardianship over Hope, according to court records and witnesses. The attack now appears to have been a premeditated tactical move between Hope's attorney, CPS, and the lesbian foster-care providers, which gained time for CPS secretly to transfer custody of Hope to an alternative residential placement run by yet another lesbian. The move only could have been filed by Hope herself, or her state-appointed attorney, and approved by a judge. In Hope's case, both her state-appointed attorney and judge were pro–gay-rights activists.

At the new home, witnesses reported, Hope and other girls were seen naked in the apartment with chains around their ankles and wrists and a dog collar looped around their necks. When the distraught mother learned of this, she again filed a criminal complaint. She claims police officer Marlene Goodman pointedly told her: "Ms. Kidd, you're in Washington state now. They can chain her 24 hours, seven days a week, and there is nothing you can do about it. It's a lifestyle, a romance. We will tell them to tone it down."

"There Is Nothing You Can Do"

A few months later, Hope was tossed down two flights of stairs while in her underwear. Neighbor Carrie Songerez approached the girl and asked, "Can I help you? Is there anything I can do? Should I call the police?" Hope responded tearfully, "There is nothing you can do. They'll just get me again, and again and again."

Hope's case had been placed under the authority of Washington's State Sexual Orientation Initiative program, which puts allegedly gay children with homosexual role models and promotes hiring of homosexual social workers and foster parents. Never mind that there is definite ambiguity about Hope's sexual preference, according to court records and her own writings obtained by *Insight.* At times she pleaded for relief from those pushing a homosexual lifestyle upon her. "I think I'm sick for becoming gay," she wrote. She filed a complaint, stating, "I want someone to answer for this mess" and requested to be "returned to [her] family." Her own writings speak of a desire to be placed in a "normal foster home," explaining "I don't want to be in a lesbian foster home," because "all lesbian foster homes are political weirdos and pushy."

The tragic story of this rebellious adolescent and others triggered state protests, prompting the Washington state Senate's Law and Justice Committee on Civil Rights to hold hearings in 1997, and some state senators have urged a federal investigation. No such probe is under way—and Hope now is reported missing. Child Protective Services has "lost her."

Hope's case represents what critics charge is the basic problem: CPS spends too much time investigating well-meaning parents and too little time investigating children at risk. The result often is that innocent parents lose their children to state-sponsored hellholes and abusive parents get their children back.

Solutions?

The solution is not so apparent as the problem. Some experts call for a national program where all caseworkers and social workers are credentialed and licensed. Congress wants to dump more money into the system to terminate parental rights and speed adoption so the child can find a permanent home. Still others support funding for family reunification, and some have reached the point of wanting to contract the entire problem to the private sector.

Historically, the system's trouble can be traced back to when it began in the 17th century in England with creation of the Poor Laws. These helped the rich to adopt poor orphans, but the laws often were abused as adopted children were sold as servants or forced into manual labor. In 1912, the Children's Bureau was formed in the United States and it pressed to have the government take control. Within a decade, many local jurisdictions had passed laws allowing social workers unlimited power to intervene in cases of abuse. In the 1960s, California passed the first law requiring doctors to report child abuse, and other states began to follow with similar laws. In 1973, Democratic Senator Walter Mondale of Minnesota held hearings on child abuse, and five years later millions of federal dollars were available for jurisdictions that created mandatory reporting laws, provided legal process for prosecution of parents and put children declared to be neglected and abused into state care. It looked to be necessary and good. It turned out to be a trap for millions—and an unspeakably nightmarish experience for children like Hope.

Still, "you are always going to find bizarre cases that are messed up," says Ann Coyne, a professor of social work at the University of Nebraska in Omaha. "But if you step back and realize that a state may have dealt with 6,000 cases you will find that in the vast majority they did okay."

Others see it differently. "These are not isolated cases," says George Wimberly, founder of Colorado-based Victims of Child Abuse Laws, or VOCAL. "It happens more often than not." Wimberly says he receives dozens of calls every day from children recanting stories of parental abuse and begging for help to return to their parents.

False Accusations

Nearly 3 million cases of child abuse and neglect are reported annually. Of those, 60 percent either are deemed false or lack credible evidence to move forward, according to the Department of Health and Human Services, or HHS. This means more than 1 million people a year could be falsely accused.

"Kids are being sequestered from their families," Wimberly says. "They are actually being held hostage. That's what it is. They're being told they have to say things against mommy or daddy or they won't ever come home again. They are so quick to place a kid in foster care that sometimes the child is held for months before there has been a hearing."

"The one thing that really bothers me is that on a juvenile and criminal level there is never any consideration as to relative or family placement," Wimberly adds. "We have cases all over the country right now where relatives are availing themselves to care for these children." One such case is in Louisiana with Betty Maddox, who lost both of her children to CPS, even though charges of child abuse were dismissed. Maddox says her relatives are willing to take the children but CPS won't turn them over. She explains: "They can't be placed in our blood line if our relatives believe in our innocence."

Liz Richards, executive director of the Virginia-based National Alliance for Family Court Justice, pins the blame on CPS bureaucrats who fail to look at the evidence and instead retaliate by going after the accusers who report the abuse. "We're finding out that child protectors end up losing their kids," she says. "Now, we tell people, whatever you do, don't call CPS. Keep your mouth shut or you will lose your kid."

The OK Boys Ranch Scandal

Retired Seattle attorney Robert A. Nord says even pedophiles working in state youth centers are escaping justice in the mad drive by bureaucrats to control children. Nord complained about the OK Boys Ranch sex scandal that rocked the Evergreen State. More than two dozen boys were abused at the youth center, but no charges ever were filed. A state investigation could not be completed because officials in the attorney-general's office destroyed confidential records regarding 326 allegations of abuse, according to investigators in charge of the probe. Finally the boys' families successfully sued Washington state and won $18 million in damages for what was described as a "jungle of molestation."

In a letter a former Seattle police sergeant circulated to state officials, he says, "People in this county who publicly complain about the sexual abuse of children have their heads handed to them. They lose their jobs. They have their children taken away by CPS. They have criminal charges cooked up against them. They are harassed and intimidated by rogue police officers. If they have the temerity to accuse a protected pedophile—someone with establishment protection—the roof really falls in on them."

Retaliation also may fall upon parents who complain against school administrators or psychologist, as Italian immigrant Joe Paolillo found out. He lost his 11-year-old son, Joseph, to the foster-care system in Washington state when the child confided to a school psychologist that he didn't get along at home. He claimed his parents abused him—a charge he later would recant. But the psychologist reported the incident to CPS after the father complained about lack of school discipline and the school's failure to tell him his son was seeing a psychologist.

CPS took the child after the psychologist and a caseworker made statements referring to the Paolillo family as "culturally backward" and "old New York Italians" who want their son to go into their "family business," records allege. In 1994, Joseph was placed in eight homes in 10 months and, the following year, three homes in 40 days. He was molested and so distraught that he engaged in a petty-crime spree that landed him at Echo Glen Youth Center, a juvenile-detention facility.

Paolillo later learned that this center hired a private group to counsel teens on sexually related issues. One session includes asking teenagers, "What do you think caused your heterosexuality? Is it possible that your heterosexuality is just a phase you may grow out of? A disproportionate number of child molesters are heterosexual. Do you consider it safe to expose your children to heterosexual teachers?" Officials at the center offer no explanation for the questions. Frustrated with how CPS was "brainwashing" his child, Paolillo contacted the Italian Embassy, which helped him get his son out of the system and placed in a private facility in Missouri.

Lauriano LaBrecque

James C. LaBrecque, formerly of New Jersey, also experienced how powerful CPS can be. In 1996, LaBrecque lost custody of his 11-year-old mentally disabled child, Lauriano, because CPS claimed he was not giving the boy seizure medication. At the time Lauriano was averaging one seizure per month, according to medical records; that rate rocketed to 60 times a month while under foster-care supervision. Medical records obtained by *Insight* suggest that the increased trauma the child suffered in the hands of the state may have occurred as "a result of his removal from his biological parents."

While Lauriano initially was placed in a foster-care home, he soon was transferred to the New Jersey Shore Medical Care Center because he was experiencing seizures that the foster parents couldn't handle. At the medical center he was placed in a cage-like crib with a top over it because the facility didn't have enough staff to monitor Lauriano.

"He was petrified," says LaBrecque, who sneaked into the medical center and observed his son trapped in the cage. "He needed to pee. He is absolutely not violent. He is the most sensitive and tender-loving child you could ever meet. And now the child is in medical chaos. They have seriously damaged my son."

After showing a photograph of his child trapped in the cage to a judge, LaBrecque still didn't get immediate custody. "I'll tell you what the problem is with the system," he says. "It's not the social workers. It's the courts and the judges. The courts allow them to do this. It's called junk justice."

Finally, in November 1997, the state was ordered to return little Lauriano to his father. And, like so many parents furious at such official abuse, LaBrecque plans to file a lawsuit against the state for failing to conduct proper investigation. In fact, as of November 1997, 22 states are being sued in class-action litigations for failing to protect children in their custody. Many other actions have been filed against caseworkers and CPS agencies but few ever go to trial. When they do, CPS often ends up paying thousands of dollars in damages.

The parents filing these suits find fault in every aspect of the system that seized their children. Enraged, some speculate on widespread conspiracies that drive away the mainstream press, though once in awhile the evidence supports the theory. For example, in Washington state, there was the Wenatchee child-abuse case in which dozens of parents were accused of child molestation. It all was proved to be false when investigators learned that dozens of social workers and psychologists coerced the children to claim abuse.

"For the Good of the Child"

But highly publicized cases, such as that of New York's 5-year-old Elisa Izquierdo, who died of torture allegedly inflicted by her mother, place tremendous pressure on CPS agencies to act quickly.

They know that five American children die every day of abuse, and the Number 1 killer for children under age 2 is child abuse. This leads them to step on parental toes whenever they think it is necessary "for the good of the child."

The general rule is for CPS agencies to remove the child first, says Colorado author Brenda Scott, who wrote *Out of Control: Who's Watching Our Child Protection Agencies?* "They call it how they feel it," Scott tells *Insight.* "It's on the hip. They err on the side of what they think is safety."

And as long as there is a suspicion of abuse the child can be removed. It can be from an anonymous complaint as minor as someone reporting a mother spanking a child in public. Some schools even are urging children to turn in their parents. "The schools are teaching kindergarten children they have rights," Scott says. "Children are learning they don't have to be spanked. By doing this you just gave an immature child a way to send their parents to the principal's office."

The agencies also have become more aggressive. In 1995 the government put 715,743 children in out-of-home care, such as foster homes, group homes, juvenile facilities and mental wards. The number of children in out-of-home care has increased by 74 percent from a decade ago. Likewise, the number of children reported as abused or neglected has increased in the last decade by 42 percent, from 33 per 1,000 in 1986 to 42 per 1,000 in 1995.

About 40 percent of these children put into out-of-home care facilities never return to their parents. More than half will be away for at least one year and the majority will have multiple placements, some in as many as 15 different homes. "The trauma and the damage and the incredible harm comes when the child is taken away from their home," Scott says. "They suffer what we call a 'kidnap syndrome.'"

In 1986 a survey conducted by the National Foster Care Education Project found that foster children were 10 times more likely to be abused than children in the general public. A follow-up study in 1990 by the same group produced similar results. And when the allegedly abused child leaves the system at age 18, the prognosis is not good. For example, in Massachusetts 60 percent of the state's criminals come from foster homes or state institutions, while in California that number is closer to 69 percent.

A Cottage Industry

A 1992 San Diego grand-jury probe suggested that some foster-care parents are more interested in the dollar than the child. The grand jury found that, for many, foster care is a livelihood and that foster parenting has become another part of the child-abuse industry. Foster care was referred to by one witness as "the largest cottage industry in America today." It costs $10,000 to $15,000 a year to keep a child in foster care, but conditions can be grim and *Insight* discovered some foster homes to be in extremely poor condition. Social workers described one to a court as a large, sanitary house with a pool. Photographs showed a firetrap with garbage all over the kitchen. The pool was ripped and appeared not to have been used in years.

To reform the system, Congress is considering two measures. Michigan Republican Representative David Camp's $1.7 billion bill passed the House overwhelmingly in 1997, but has hit a snag in the Senate. It would limit the time a child can spend in foster care to about a year, speed the process of deciding who the child will live with permanently and expedites adoption procedures. The Senate bill, sponsored by West Virginia Democrat Senator Jay Rockefeller, is similar but requires the federal government, instead of states, to pay $2.3 billion for special-needs adoptions of children from nonpoor backgrounds. It also reauthorizes Family Preservation Services for the next five years by endorsing "kinship care," which places foster children with members of their extended family—a practice that opponents say delays adoption.

Patrick Purtrill, director of government relations for the National Council for Adoption, is one who says the Senate bill hampers adoption. "There is a professional culture that views adoption as a failure," Purtrill says. "All the programs view family reunification as the answer. But when you see the children become victims of violent sexual molestation, broken bones, starvation and unbelievable things, the emphasis has got to be on child safety and not rehabilitating the abusive parents."

Promising Results

Nonetheless, some communities are having good results encouraging parental rehabilitation. These programs teach parenting and job skills—and offer drug counseling. A recent General Accounting Office study noted that more than 70 percent of children in foster care once lived in homes where there was substance abuse.

Families First in Michigan has reported an 80 percent success rate in keeping families together through instruction and rehabilitation. Louvenia Williams, who runs a similar program in Washington, D.C., called the Edgewood-Brooklyn Family Support Collaborative, observes, "The bottom line is that most of these children don't want to leave their families. Children love their families no matter what these parents do to them. We put money into systems to deal with the children after the fact but not into the systems that deal with the family. Why can't we put money into the communities at risk?"

THE RELATIONSHIP BETWEEN POVERTY AND CHILD ABUSE

Leroy H. Pelton

In the following selection, Leroy H. Pelton cites a number of studies that have found a strong link between poverty and child abuse. Most impoverished parents are not abusive, Pelton notes, but children of impoverished and low-income families are disproportionately represented in the data concerning the overall rate of child abuse. According to Pelton, research has also revealed that the severity of abuse suffered by maltreated children is directly linked to the degree of poverty the family lives in, with the worst abuse occurring in the poorest families. The form of child abuse most associated with impoverished families is neglect, Pelton writes, because the material hardship associated with poverty makes it difficult for poor parents to provide their children with basic necessities. Furthermore, he explains, because poor families tend to live in dangerous areas, some parents may resort to physical violence or emotional abuse to control their children's behavior in an effort to keep them away from neighborhood hazards. Pelton is a professor in the School of Social Work at Salem State College in Salem, Massachusetts. He is the author of *For Reasons of Poverty: A Critical Analysis of the Public Child Welfare System in the United States*.

There is overwhelming and remarkably consistent evidence—obtained across a variety of definitions and methodologies, and from studies performed at different time periods—that poverty and low income are related strongly to child abuse and neglect and to severity of child maltreatment. Even though most impoverished parents do not abuse or neglect their children, children from impoverished and low-income families are *vastly over-represented* in the incidence of child abuse and neglect. This strong relationship holds not only for child abuse and neglect in general, but for their every identified form, including emotional abuse, emotional neglect, and sexual abuse.

Every national survey of officially reported child abuse and neglect incidents (most of which were made by the American Humane Association [AHA] between 1975 and 1987) has indicated a preponderance of reports involving families from the lowest socioeconomic levels. Data collected by AHA for 1976, for example, showed that the median income of families involved in validated reports was $5,051. The 1976 poverty level was $5,815 for a nonfarm family of four, which contrasts with a median income of $14,958 for all American families in that year. About two thirds of the families in validated reports had incomes under $7,000, and only 9 percent had incomes of $13,000 or more. Reports of neglect only were almost twice as numerous as reports of abuse only. In neglect only reports, the median income was somewhat lower ($4,250) than for abuse only ($6,886). These low-income trends continued over time in a stable fashion. The proportion of reported families who were receiving public assistance when the incident occurred remained between 42 percent and 49 percent throughout the AHA survey years in the 1970s and 1980s.

Poverty and the Severity of Abuse

There is substantial evidence that the strong relationship between poverty and child abuse and neglect is not merely an anomaly of reporting systems (that is, of public surveillance biases), or of personal biases in the identification or reporting of child abuse and neglect. First, while greater public awareness and new reporting laws led to a tremendous increase in official reporting over the years, the socioeconomic pattern of these reports has not changed appreciably. We might have expected an expanded and more vigilant public watch to produce an increased proportion of reports from "above" the lower class, but this has not happened. Second, studies indicate that even among families living in poverty, child abuse and neglect are related to *degrees* of poverty, that is, to the extent of material hardships encountered by those families. Third, studies have found that, among the reported cases, the most severe injuries resulting from child maltreatment have occurred within the poorest families. Thus, poverty is not only related to child abuse and neglect, but to the severity of maltreatment. Moreover, child homicide studies have consistently indicated that the vast majority of the victims of the most severe and least easily hidden child maltreatment—that which results in death—were from poor families. Severity of the behavior or the injury is certainly an important consideration. While definitions of abuse and neglect can be arbitrarily stretched to include even the occasional spanking of a child, the origins of our attention to child abuse and neglect are tied to concerns about children who have been placed in serious danger of severe harm or who have been severely harmed.

The Westat National Incidence Study was designed to gather information beyond that provided by the officially reported incidents of child abuse and neglect known to child protective service agencies. The study gathered additional information on abuse and neglect incidents directly from other agencies (e.g., police and public health departments) and professionals in hospitals, mental health facilities, other social service agencies, and public schools. The study found that in the year beginning May 1, 1979, and ending April 30, 1980, the annual income of the families of 43 percent of the victims was under $7,000, compared with an estimated 17 percent of all American children who lived in families with this income level. (The poverty level for a nonfarm family of four was $7,412 in 1979.) Fully 82 percent of the victims were from families with incomes below $15,000, in comparison with 45 percent of all American children. Only 6 percent of the victims were from families with incomes of $25,000 or more. The relationship between low income and child maltreatment was less pronounced for abuse than for neglect, but still was strong. The study concluded that the strong relationship between poverty and child abuse and neglect is not largely explainable in terms of reporting biases because the relationship "is almost as strong for unreported cases as for those which are reported to Child Protective Services."

The second National Incidence Study showed that in 1986 the relationship between low income and child abuse and neglect continued to be strong. In fact, the incidence rate of child abuse and neglect was more than five times higher among children from families with annual income below $15,000 than from families with incomes of $15,000 or more. (The poverty level for a nonfarm family of four was $11,203 in 1986.) In only 6 percent of cases was the family income $30,000 (roughly the median income for all American families) or more. (The term, "incidence rate," refers to the ratio of abused and neglected children in a particular income category to all children within that category. Thus, a child in a family whose income was below $15,000 was more than five times as likely to have been abused or neglected than a child in a family whose income was $15,000 or more.)

The Funneling Effect

Both the National Incidence Studies and the AHA surveys reveal a dramatic funneling effect in regard to income, with the poorest children being at greatest risk of child abuse and neglect (having the highest incidence rates) and the wealthiest children being at least risk (having the lowest incidence rates). This funneling effect is very fine tuned. The AHA data for 1977, for example, revealed a perfect inverse relationship between income bracket and the percentage of validated reports an income bracket accounted for, moving up the income scale through a dozen brackets, most of which were no more than $2,000 to $3,000 in width. Such a finding would be truly difficult to explain in terms of personal biases in the identification and reporting of child abuse and neglect; it is highly unlikely that prejudices are so fine tuned.

The National Incidence Studies clearly show that strong income-related differences hold for all specific forms of abuse and neglect. For example, in 1986, the incidence rate of physical abuse was three and a half times greater among children from families with an annual income of less than $15,000 than from families with an income of $15,000 or more; and the incidence rate of emotional abuse was four times greater. The incidence rate of physical neglect was nine times greater and that of emotional neglect almost five times greater within the lower income group than within the higher income group. Even sexual abuse, which had already been found in the first National Incidence Study to be strongly related to poverty and low income, demonstrated in 1986 an incidence rate six times greater within the lower income group than within the higher income group. In fact, in this second National Incidence Study, family income was the only factor found to be consistently related to risk for all categories of child abuse and neglect.

Most impoverished parents do not abuse or neglect their children. The only personal differences that have been found that tend to distinguish those who do are depression, low self esteem, and low sense of control of one's life. These personal differences are directly relevant to the ability to cope with poverty, its stressors, and its material hardships.

The Relationship Between Poverty and Neglect

Neglect is the most frequent form of child abuse. Also, neglect is involved in the majority of incidents. Most incidents of neglect involve "deprivation of necessities" or "inadequate supervision." Both of the latter concepts make direct reference to material conditions, but implicate the responsibility of the parents as well. That is, there is little doubt that poverty is characterized by limited money available to purchase necessities, and by dangerous and hazardous conditions in and around the home. Under these circumstances, any less-than-optimal management of money or supervision of one's children can indeed contribute to potential severe harm. Such a contribution can be characterized as neglect, and often is under current definitions. In addition, many families on public assistance run out of money before the end of the month simply because public assistance grants are insufficient. Thus, these families are exposed to the potential of being called neglectful.

The less money parents have, the better money managers they must be in order to avoid depriving their children of necessities. The more dangerous the environment in and around the home, the more diligent parents must be in the supervision of their children, and the more possible it becomes to implicate the parents for not preventing danger.

It should be noted that sexual abuse should be included among the dangers of the neighborhood environment. In 58 percent of sexual abuse reports, the alleged perpetrator is someone other than a parent or stepparent, and the child is unrelated to the alleged perpetrator in 35 percent of sexual abuse reports. It is probable that because of the recent intense public and professional focus on sexual abuse, many incidents that used to be called neglect are now called sexual abuse.

Moreover, as D.A. Tertinger, B.F. Greene, and J.R. Lutzker suggest, even physical abuse may be related directly to material deficits in the environment, in that parents may resort to physical abuse in their anxious attempts to keep children away from safety hazards. Indeed, dangerous neighborhoods and living environments may elicit from parents an extreme fear for the well being of their children. They may, ironically, be driven by intense concern for their children's safety to physically or emotionally abuse them in attempts to control their behavior.

Coping with Poverty

People vary in their ability to cope with poverty and its stressors. Both evidence and logic suggest that the relationship between poverty and child abuse and neglect is mediated by an interaction between individual differences in the cognitive ability to cope with poverty and the extent of the dangerousness and inadequacy of the material conditions of the family's environment. For people living in poverty, adequacy of child care is dependent upon their ability to cope with poverty. But adequacy of care is also relative to the adequacy of the environment. What is adequate care in one environment may be inadequate in a more dangerous one. The diligence of care necessary to protect a child in a dangerous environment is greater than in a safer one.

To the extent that environments and living conditions are made less dangerous, the quality of care given by those parents with the least ability to cope with poverty will be less inadequate, even though essentially the same as before. Such parents will be less susceptible to a judgment of neglect, and will be less likely to resort to abuse of their children in desperate attempts to control their behavior to keep them away from the hazards of their environment.

The unavoidable conclusion is that the most effective way to reduce child abuse and neglect is to reduce poverty and its attendant material hardships and dangers. At the very least, if child abuse and neglect are to be reduced, material supports and concrete services must be provided to impoverished and low-income families.

Of course, in the long term, we must increase the individual competencies and inner resources of all citizens. But this is less likely to be achieved through therapy, parenting skills classes, self-help groups, and the like, than by opening up opportunities for decent education, jobs, and careers, and through ensuring the health and safety of children so as to allow them to take advantage of these opportunities as they grow up. In short, we must address the poverty-related conditions that leave children abused, neglected, or otherwise harmed in the short run, if we are to increase individual competencies and inner resources in the long run. The pervasive presence of material hardship in child abuse and neglect cases argues clearly that any strategy aimed at reducing significantly the incidence of child abuse and neglect must centrally address this bedrock context in which harm to children thrives. Without a key focus on material hardship, other additionally desirable approaches will not succeed in significantly reducing the incidence and severity of child abuse and neglect.

THE GENERATIONAL CYCLE OF ABUSE

Tom Ito

Research has indicated that a large proportion of adults who abuse their children often suffered abuse at the hands of their own parents, writes Tom Ito in the following selection. Because they grew up in a violent atmosphere, these abusive parents never learned any alternatives to violence for coping with stress and relating to children, Ito explains. In addition, he points out, many abusers do not want to face the emotionally wrenching fact that their own parents treated them badly. These parents seek to justify the abusive treatment they received by physically abusing their own children in the same manner, thereby repeating the cycle of abuse. Ito is a freelance writer living in Los Angeles.

Research has shown that many adults who physically, emotionally, or sexually abuse children were themselves abused as children. The trauma of this mistreatment often results in severe emotional or psychological problems in adulthood. Adults who were victims of child abuse may carry intense feelings of repressed anger toward their abusers which they vent on their own children through cruel or violent behavior.

Some experts believe that this cycle of abuse is caused by the adult's need to justify the brutal behavior of his or her own parents. In their book *Straight Talk About Child Abuse,* Susan Mufson and Rachel Kranz state that many adults who abuse their children do so because they are unwilling or unable to admit that their own upbringing was abusive and wrong:

> For many parents who were abused as children, their reason for abusing their own children is that they need to prove that their parents were right. They do this by treating their children exactly as their parents treated them. . . . Many children find it easier to pretend that they are somehow responsible for the abuse, or that their parents are acting out of love, rather than to hold their parents responsible for acting badly. When those children grow up, they still don't want to admit their parents acted badly. So they act just like their parents,

because they reason to themselves their parents were acting out of love.

Experts also suggest that some adults who were abused as children imitate their parents' behavior out of a misplaced sense of duty to carry on the child-rearing practices from their own painful childhood. According to Mufson and Kranz, such parents were taught as children that they deserved such abuse, and they may communicate a similar message to their own children. Mufson and Kranz write: "Sometimes these parents decide that their children 'deserve' to be abused like they 'deserved' it when *they* were kids. Sometimes these parents identify with their own parents: 'He got to beat me, so now I get to beat you—it's my turn now.'"

Patterns Are Hard to Break

In some cases an abuser simply does not know that there are other ways of relating to a child. That abuser might never have seen healthy interaction between a parent and child. In *Straight Talk* Mufson and Kranz explain: "Some people . . . are simply unaware of any other way of acting. They may believe that it's normal to beat a child or to vent one's anger with harsh insults. They may believe that it's normal to engage in sexually abusive behavior since that's the way they grew up."

Some abusers have witnessed how people in other families relate to each other. But patterns set in early childhood are hard to break. An adult who was abused as a child often repeats the only behavior he or she has experienced. In her book *Toxic Parents,* Dr. Susan Forward discusses the cycle of abuse:

> Physical abusers themselves often come from families to which abuse was the norm. Much of their adult behavior is a direct repetition of what they experienced and learned in their youth. Their role model was an abuser. Violence was the only tool they learned to use in dealing with problems and feelings—especially feelings of anger.

Experts continue to research why adults mistreat young people in the hope that increased understanding of the roots of abusive behavior will result in its prevention. Although experts do not yet know all of the factors causing child abuse, they have concluded that many abusive parents lack self-control and fail to see the damaging effects of their own behavior toward their children. Dr. Forward states that abusive behavior is often an automatic, unthinking reaction to stress:

> We can only speculate why, but physically abusive parents seem to share certain characteristics. First, they have an appalling lack of self-control. Physically abusive parents will assault their children whenever they have strong negative

feelings that they need to discharge. These parents seem to have little, if any, awareness of the consequences of what they are doing to their children. It is almost an automatic reaction to stress. The impulse and the action are one and the same.

Many abusers never recognize their behavior as problematic and many do not see the recurring patterns within their own families. For those who do, the realization is often painful. In *Toxic Parents* one abusive parent reveals her horror at seeing herself repeating the abuses of her own childhood:

> I'm so ashamed of myself. I've slapped him in the past, but this time I really went berserk. That kid makes me so damned angry. . . . You know, I always promised myself that if I had kids, I'd never raise a hand to them. . . . I know what that's like. It's horrible. But without realizing it, I'm turning into that crazy mother of mine. I remember one time she chased me around the kitchen with a butcher knife!

The high incidence of child abuse committed by individuals who were themselves mistreated as children has provoked numerous child care experts to stress the necessity of breaking the cycle of abuse. Many adults who are survivors of child abuse have become increasingly more vocal and active in their efforts to raise the public consciousness regarding the need for professional treatment and counseling of abuse victims.

THE DANGER OF GRANTING CUSTODY TO ABUSIVE PARENTS

Tucker Carlson

In the following selection, Tucker Carlson examines family reunification laws and the danger they pose to the children of unfit parents. Federal law requires social workers to make every effort to prevent the removal of abused children from their homes and to work toward the reunification of families that have been separated due to parental abuse, Carlson explains. Most states adhere to this law in its strictest form, Carlson points out, making it almost impossible for child welfare workers to permanently remove an abused child from his or her biological mother—even if that mother has seriously injured or killed one of her other children. Carlson is a staff writer for the *Weekly Standard*.

One Friday morning in June 1992, six-week-old Nakya Scott woke up in an apartment in southeast Washington, D.C., and began to cry. Nakya's mother, 19-year-old Latrena Pixley, gave the girl a drink of water, but the crying continued. Frustrated, Pixley put the baby back into her crib. As Pixley later told police, "This is when I put the blanket over her face. I just killed her."

In fact, it wasn't that simple. Nakya Scott's murder took a long time. While her 2-year-old son played with his toys in the other room, Pixley smothered the girl for half an hour, pulling the blanket away periodically, then pressing it down again on the child's face. Autopsy photos show Nakya's lips mashed against her gums from the force of her mother's hand.

Once she finished killing her daughter, Pixley stuffed the little girl's body into a plastic trash bag, threw it into a dumpster outside her apartment building, and went back upstairs to sit in her bedroom. Her boyfriend (who is not Nakya's father) came home that afternoon. The two had dinner, then went to a relative's house to play cards. They stayed until after 2:00 A.M.

The next morning, Pixley had breakfast and watched television. Sometime before noon she woke her sleeping boyfriend and told him what she had done to the baby. Pixley's boyfriend checked the dumpster.

"I can't believe that you did that," he said when he returned. Then he called the police.

Much has been written about what happened next. The following June, Pixley pleaded guilty to second-degree murder. Judge George W. Mitchell of the D.C. Superior Court sentenced her to probation and ordered her to spend weekends in the city jail for three years. A few months later, Mitchell reduced Pixley's jail time, and she took a clerical job at a vocational training center in Washington. In the spring of 1995, it was discovered that Pixley had been stealing Social Security numbers from office personnel files, applying for credit cards in the names of co-workers, and using the cards to buy VCRs and stereo equipment. Pixley was fired and later convicted in federal court of mail fraud. But she had no problem landing a new job. (Nor did her mood seem darkened by her brushes with the law. In July 1995, she wrote a bubbly fan letter to *Ebony* magazine praising Aretha Franklin. "I have her whole collection of music on tapes and CDs," said Pixley. "I sing them all the time. Aretha, keep up the good work and keep singing. I love it.") Jerome Miller, the head of the city's child welfare agency, hired Pixley as a receptionist in his office. "This agency is about offering care, concern, and help," Miller said.

Cornelious

In January 1996, Pixley had another child, Cornelious, her fourth by four boyfriends. (Pixley's oldest child, now 8, has lived with relatives since infancy; the second, the boy who was playing when Pixley killed Nakya, is in a foster home.) Pixley might have drifted off into obscurity from there, had she not been interviewed that month by a local television reporter doing a story about young mothers on welfare. The story that aired said nothing about Pixley's murder conviction. But it did catch the attention of an assistant U.S. attorney who remembered Pixley and was infuriated to see her on television with another child. A brief media storm followed, during which Pixley's credit-card scam was reported in the papers. Before long, Pixley wound up back in George Mitchell's court for violating the terms of her probation.

Under heightened public scrutiny, Mitchell sent Pixley back to jail in May 1996, only to release her eight months later to a group home in Washington called Hannah House. Pixley, however, never bothered to show up at Hannah House, and the judge was forced to send her back to the lockup. He released her for good in November 1997.

During her time behind bars, Pixley left Cornelious with a casual acquaintance, a 25-year-old intern at the Public Defenders Service named Laura Blankman. Blankman, who is now a police trainee in the Washington suburbs, has cared for the boy, at her own expense, since he was four months old. Eventually, she filed papers to adopt him. Pixley accused Blankman of trying to "steal" Cornelious and challenged the adoption in court. In December 1997, Michael D. Mason, a circuit-court judge in Montgomery County, Maryland, awarded full custody of the child to Pixley, explaining that Cornelious would be best off in a black household (Blankman is white) and in the care of his biological mother.

Judge Mason's decision made the front page of the *Washington Post* and was widely denounced as outrageous. Laura Blankman is appealing the decision, partly on grounds that there is no evidence that transracial adoption harms children.

Postpartum Psychosis

How did a child-killer wind up with custody of another child? The answer begins with a group of psychiatric experts who have worked on Pixley's behalf since her first arrest. Asked by homicide detectives the day after the killing why she had murdered her daughter, Pixley answered, "I don't know." (Nor did she know how old her daughter was when she was killed.) By the time Pixley was sentenced a year later, an explanation emerged. Latrena Pixley, her lawyer argued, had been suffering from postpartum depression. The most severe, and rare, form of postpartum depression can result in psychotic episodes, during which a new mother experiences hallucinations. Had Pixley been afflicted with postpartum psychosis, she might plausibly have pleaded insanity. She might also have wound up in a mental institution.

Instead, Pixley's court-appointed lawyer argued that her client had been pushed into killing her child by a combination of economic desperation and a form of non-psychotic depression linked to giving birth. The diagnosis never got much more specific than that, nor could various experts even agree on what the diagnosis was. In a subsequent hearing, at least one therapist testified that Pixley suffered from "post-traumatic stress." But that was enough for Mitchell. At sentencing, Mitchell said that he had special sympathy for Pixley, who, not being "some high-class society woman," had been unable to mount a sophisticated defense. "People understand those psychological phenomenons in high-level people, but it becomes ununderstandable in a poor person sometimes," explained the judge, who is head of the D.C. Superior Court's family division. "I don't want to be victimized by that kind of thinking."

Actually, the public defenders who represented Pixley assembled a team of court-savvy psychiatric experts that would have been the envy of many rich criminals. One of the first experts Pixley's lawyers hired, for instance, was Dr. Nuha Abudabbeh, a forensic psychologist well known for her "stress disorder" defenses of accused murderers. Abudabbeh's evaluation of Pixley was not made public, though in a recent interview she described her perceptions of the defendant. "This was not a child murderer," Abudabbeh says, but instead a woman who acted "under duress, under certain conditions. This was a baby she didn't even want. Her boyfriend made her keep the baby. She ended up having to take care of this child. You have to weigh all of these circumstances." Plus, Abudabbeh says, the murder "was understandable because [Pixley] was mentally ill."

The Mental-Illness Defense Falters

The mental-illness defense worked well enough initially, but it presented an obvious difficulty later when Pixley tried to convince Mitchell that she should be released from jail to take care of Cornelious. In the spring of 1995, Pixley was arrested for physically assaulting her boyfriend. In May 1996, a psychological evaluation determined that Pixley still had difficulty managing her anger. Pixley's lawyers were forced to explain how and when her violence problem had been solved. In addition, there was the question of the fraudulent credit cards—was that the result of depression, too?

Pixley's excuses began to get tangled in one another. "Suffice it to say that I declined to be involved in the second case," says Carol Kleinman, a Washington psychiatrist who has testified in a number of cases related to postpartum depression, and who first diagnosed Pixley as having the disorder. Stealing money, says Kleinman, "is not part of postpartum depression." Moreover, she says, "I found some of [Pixley's] behavior outrageous, beyond the postpartum business. I felt I had reached my limit. It was just enough for me."

Ever resourceful, Pixley's public defenders turned to a Yale-trained psychiatrist named Susan Fiester for help. Fiester had become famous in 1994 during the Lorena Bobbitt trial, when, in gripping televised testimony, she argued that years of abuse and "poor self-esteem" had led Mrs. Bobbitt to "attack the instrument that was the weapon of her torture—that is, her husband's penis." At various times, Dr. Fiester has described herself as an expert on premenstrual syndrome, and on the "epidemic of nicotine addiction among women." In Pixley's case, Fiester testified as an authority on postpartum depression.

At a hearing in January 1997, Fiester testified that Latrena Pixley was now perfectly sane. Fiester then gave her definition of postpartum depression: "Postpartum depression in and of itself is often thought to be a fairly biologically based disorder that's related to, to at least in part some of the significant hormonal changes that women go through during the postpartum period. . . . So there may be an independent sort of biological piece and also some pieces in the social environment that can affect the, you know, whether the disorder occurs or not and make it worse in essence."

In other words, no one is sure exactly what postpartum depression is. Nevertheless, after evaluating Latrena Pixley for less than a day, and performing no psychological testing, Fiester produced a diagnosis. "It's my professional opinion," she testified, "based on a reasonable degree of medical certainty, that she is not currently a danger to herself or others, and that specifically that she would not be in any danger of harming children, either her own or other people's children, were she to reside in the community." Pixley, Fiester added, has "worked on improving her self-esteem."

It was an authoritative performance. Outside the courtroom, however, Fiester's "medical certainty" doesn't seem quite so certain. Asked if Pixley's son will be safe once he and his mother move into their own apartment, Fiester admits she doesn't know. "I'm giving my opinion about this point in time," she says. "If you want my opinion about what happens two years from now, I'd have to see her again and see how things went when she was in the transitional housing facility. Assuming things go well and there's no problem, I don't think [the child] would be at high risk."

What happens to Cornelious two years from now hardly seems the most pressing issue on Fiester's mind. But she is happy to reel off a list of the programs she has appeared on to talk about the Pixley case: "*The Today Show, CNN, Talk Back Live.* I've been on radio, WTOP, Channel Four, NBC News." Going on television, Fiester explains, has given her "an opportunity to educate the public about psychiatric issues as relevant to criminal stuff and about these disorders: How frequently they occur, how serious they are, and what they can lead to." How frequently *do* they occur? Fiester pauses, then admits she isn't sure. "Call the American Psychiatric Association," she suggests.

The Judge's Confusion

Fiester and her fellow therapists are easy to mock, but they had a profound effect on Judge Mitchell, who often seemed lost in the fog emitted by Pixley's hired shrinks. At one May 1996 hearing, the judge explained to Pixley why he had been so lenient with her: "I tried to understand the drama that the—your life had been very bad. You had gone through the kind of crisis that would cause a person to do things, and your mind get warped, and you get depressed, you get down, you get oppressed and you do things."

Even with a roomful of helpful experts, Mitchell never appeared to fully understand what was going on in his court. Years after he ruled in the Nakya Scott murder, the judge was still wondering why Pixley had killed her daughter. "I don't know why these women put these children in these trash bags," he grumbled. "That's a phenomenon that I would like to understand." At one point, he turned to Pixley's lawyer for illumination. "But how," the judge asked, "does one, how does one come to kill—the basic nature, as I understand it, of, of the, of the—even the syndrome that they described derives itself out of being a woman—how does she come to kill her child? That's what is my first hard thing to overcome. And I, obviously, at some point I decided that I would accept certain propositions about this postpartum syndrome."

And not just postpartum syndrome. Mitchell seemed open to just about any theory Pixley's therapists felt like tossing out. In January 1997, the judge interrupted Susan Fiester in the middle of her testimony to ask a question: "Is there any punishment, if you will, from a societal point of view in the nature of the crime itself, that is the killing of one's child, of one's own child, is there, is there a form of punishment that comes about as a result of being involved in that wherever you be? Whether you be in prison or you be on, in the community?"

An ordinary witness might have asked Mitchell to repeat the question. But Fiester didn't miss a beat. "Yes, your honor," she answered. Killing one's own child "is, I think, one of the most severe sorts of internal punishment that any woman can have to live with. . . . I think society at times takes a very simple sort of punitive view toward it and lacks an understanding of some of the underlying factors that can be involved." Mitchell was sold. Before letting Pixley out of jail yet again, he speculated aloud about the nature of baby killing: "Isn't that the kind of crime, isn't that the kind of crime that has a punishment in it itself?"

The assistant U.S. attorney on the case, Deborah Sines, countered Fiester's testimony with an eloquent plea that Pixley be kept away from her children. Sines pointed out that one of Pixley's older sons had been assessed by a psychiatrist and found to be "an extremely psychologically messed up little kid."

The judge was unmoved. At a final hearing in late January 1997, Mitchell concluded that "it would be in the best interest of the youngest child that this mother continue the bonding process that she has started with this baby," and he let Pixley out of jail so the two could be reunited. Even before he came to his decision, however, the judge explained that there was little he could do to keep Latrena Pixley from her son. "The law in this area works towards reunification of mothers and families if at all possible. As a matter of fact," Mitchell said, "our Court of Appeals seems to put its fingers, its hands down on judges who even consider taking children from drug-abusing mothers, and you are likely to be reversed as the trial judge if you start taking babies from mothers who have a little drug problem, as they say."

Mahala Irene Page

Latrena Pixley doesn't have a drug problem, but Judge Mitchell was right about one thing: Thanks to the philosophy of "family reunification," enshrined in federal law since 1980, it is frequently next to impossible for the state to take children away from their biological mothers, no matter what those mothers do or have done. Consider another case: that of Mahala Irene Page.

On the same day in 1992 that Latrena Pixley was being arraigned in Washington for her daughter's death, police less than 20 miles away, in Prince George's County, Maryland, were in the process of charging a woman named Mahala Irene Page with a similar crime. Firemen responding to a call at Page's house in suburban Forest Heights had arrived to find Page standing in the doorway of a second-floor bathroom. Behind her, according to the police report, a fireman "noticed a placenta on the floor and an umbilical cord leading to the toilet. Inside the toilet was a baby wedged in the water canal. Applying pressure to the skull, the baby was extracted." Doctors later determined that the child, a boy, had been under water for 25 minutes. There was evidence that Page had attempted to flush him down the toilet. "The defendant also stated she had touched the infant and saw movement," says the report, but gave him "no assistance."

Rushed to the hospital, the boy survived. A grand jury indicted Page for assault with attempt to murder, and four other felonies. Page's only explanation for her behavior was that she had not known she was pregnant. The boy, however, was close to full term at birth; Page is 5'1" and normally weighs 125 pounds. It seemed like a sure conviction. Then, in April 1993, a county circuit court judge, Audrey Melbourne, inexplicably let Page off. She received 21 days in jail for second-degree child abuse (all of which she had already served), two years of probation, and was ordered to attend parenting classes.

Page's Poor Prognosis

According to her lawyer, Page completed the parenting classes and "initiated therapy" at the local department of social services. Yet it was obvious that Page still wasn't equipped to handle the demands of motherhood. A confidential state psychiatric evaluation conducted in July 1993 suggested that Page remained mentally unstable. Her "prognosis," the report concluded, was "poor to guarded." Subsequent events confirmed the diagnosis. In 1995, Page, who was and is unemployed, was rearrested and jailed for failing to pay less than $100 in court costs.

Nevertheless, Page was allowed to keep her children. According to court documents filed by her lawyer, by early June 1993, less than two months after she was convicted of child abuse, Page had custody on weekends of the child she abused "with the hope of one day attaining full custody of that child." Some time after that, Page did indeed get full custody. Most records pertaining to juveniles are hidden from public view, so it's not clear when or why Page's son was returned to her. "I wouldn't give you the information if we had it," says Karen Lynch, acting director of the Prince George's County social-services department. Reached at her home in January 1998, however, Page confirmed that all three of her children, including the son she left in the toilet, live with her, and have for years.

How did this happen? County officials don't know or won't say. Ron Povich, who oversees foster care and adoptions in Prince George's County, says he has never heard of Mahala Page, but he does concede that it is not uncommon for children to be returned to parents who have abused them. The federal Adoption Assistance and Child Welfare Act of 1980 requires that before placing a child in foster care, state agencies make "reasonable efforts" to "prevent or eliminate the need for removal of the child from his home, and to make it possible for the child to return to his home." The statute has been modified in the years since it became law, but in most states it is still interpreted strictly.

An Obstacle to Adoption

Before attempting to place a child in an adoptive home, Povich says, social workers in Prince George's County are required to prove they have done everything possible to make the negligent mother a better parent. It's a difficult standard to meet. To unfit parents who insist on keeping their kids, Povich's agency offers daycare, therapy, counseling, and subsidized housing. "In some situations," he says, "we've transported the parents to and from therapy sessions, to and from different types of treatment. We even have some funds to purchase supplies for families—bedding, clothing, things of that nature."

And Povich's agency is not unusually generous by the standards of other states. Several years ago, a Rhode Island couple beat their young daughter so badly that by the time the girl was placed in foster care, she had suffered severe brain damage. Yet even when the couple's younger son began showing signs of neglect, the state's child-protection agency did not remove him from the home. Instead, according to Richard Gelles, a child-welfare researcher who has written a book on the case, social workers simply made arrangements to provide the family with a housekeeper to allow the mother to get out more often. The boy was murdered by his parents soon after.

How Long Should Children Wait?

Defenders of family reunification argue that a few well-publicized tragedies don't by themselves warrant wholesale changes to the country's child-welfare system, and they have a point. Making strong efforts to reunify families isn't a bad idea. Most of the time it's probably the right thing to do. Even abused children generally want to live with their biological parents. And the state should always hesitate before removing a child from his home. The problem is that many parents take a long time to straighten out. Others will never be capable of raising children. How long should children wait—in foster care or in dangerous circumstances at home—before their biological parents are fit to take care of them?

It's a question responsible social-service agencies have asked for a long time. Or did. Increasingly, the theology of family reunification allows therapists and social workers to avoid making such difficult judgments. If a child is always better off living with the woman who bore him, then any biological parent is a potentially good parent. Even Latrena Pixley.

Nuha Abudabbeh agrees wholeheartedly. "Of course" a mother who has murdered one child could be a good parent to her other children, says Abudabbeh, one of Pixley's many psychologists. "People are always assuming that because a person is mentally ill or has been incarcerated, she can't be a good mother," Abudabbeh complains. "There are schizophrenic mothers who could be very good mothers. Who decides what's a good mother?"

As it turns out, sometimes nobody does.

The Incidence of Child Abuse by Stepparents

Colin Tudge

Stepparents are one hundred times more likely to abuse their children than are biological parents, writes Colin Tudge, a science writer and research fellow in the Centre for Philosophy at the London School of Economics. Citing research conducted by Canadian psychologists Martin Daly and Margo Wilson, who studied this phenomenon in light of Charles Darwin's theory of natural selection, Tudge explains that the high rate of abuse by stepparents can be attributed to the lack of a biological relationship between stepparents and their stepchildren. According to Darwinian theory, he writes, stepparents have little evolutionary interest in ensuring the safety of a child who does not share and will not perpetuate their genetic makeup. Most stepparents do not abuse their stepchildren, notes Tudge, but compared to other risk factors for child abuse, the presence of a stepparent is statistically a significant threat to a child's safety.

Tell any group of people that stepparents are about one hundred times more likely to fatally abuse their children than are "true" parents and you can't expect an easy audience—especially if you suggest that the key factor could just be the lack of a genetic relationship. So the questions rained down thick and fast on Canadian psychologists Martin Daly and Margo Wilson when they floated these conclusions (gleaned from their twenty years of research) at a Darwin Seminar at the London School of Economics. The questions were as varied as the audience of scientists, historians, undergraduates, and interested passersby that these provocative seminars invariably attract.

"How can you know such a thing?" people asked. "What makes you think that genetic relationships play a part, as opposed to a hundred other possible confounding variables, such as the poverty of the parents and the duration of contact between parent and child?" "What about adopted children?" "What use is such information, anyway?" "Aren't you just stirring things up for no good reason?"

Darwinian Theory

Daly and Wilson, from McMaster University, Hamilton, Ontario, did not arrive at their conclusions casually. In the 1970s, about ten years after the "battered child syndrome" had been officially recognized, they set out to see if children were more likely to be abused by step-parents than by biological parents. In addition, they wanted to explore a specific Darwinian hypothesis. There had been new developments in Charles Darwin's idea that human behavior, as well as our physical appearance, has been shaped to a significant extent by natural selection. In particular, in the 1960s, William D. Hamilton, now professor of zoology at Oxford University, had put a new construction on the phenomenon of altruism—the process by which individuals apparently sacrifice their own self-interest, and even their lives, to benefit others.

Hamilton showed that natural selection could and would favor genes that promoted altruistic behavior, provided that the individuals who benefited from the altruism had a high chance of containing the same genes. In fact, such altruistic behavior is not altruistic at all, in the sense that moral philosophers use the term, but is entirely selfish. The gene that promotes the apparent self-sacrifice is simply promoting its own replication, by enhancing the survival of copies of itself—albeit copies contained in other individuals. Thus, said Hamilton, we might expect individuals to compromise themselves if doing so benefited their own kin, who would indeed contain copies of the gene that promoted the self-sacrificial behavior. The final twist is that parental care, and the self-sacrifice that goes with it, are merely special examples of the altruism that any organism might be expected to show toward its own kin.

Although stepparents in some societies are related to the children, Daly and Wilson reasoned that stepparents are not generally kin to their stepchildren, at least not in most Western societies. Therefore, we might expect that they would show no predilection to sacrifice themselves (in large or even small ways) on a stepchild's behalf. They sought to find out if this hypothesis, based on Hamilton's extension of Darwin's ideas, was true.

Wilson says, "We were astonished to find that it was not easy even to begin to explore this hypothesis. Official statistics from the United States didn't reveal whether parents who abused children were step or biological. It just didn't occur to criminologists that the nature of the relationship was important, so they generally didn't bother to record it." She and Daly had to look beyond the official statistics, to the raw data of case histories. By 1980 they had demonstrated that children under three years of age are at least seven times more likely to be abused by stepparents than by biological parents.

Stepparents and Homicide

Daly and Wilson believed, however, that statistics for child abuse in
general might be biased by underreporting or incomplete reporting.
After all, parents don't want to admit that they have beaten their children; there are plenty of ways to conceal abuse or to explain away
injuries. To gain a truer picture, the researchers decided to focus specifically on a form of abuse that is exceedingly difficult to cover up:
homicide. Once again—even more astonishingly—most official statistics, including the FBI's Supplementary Homicide Reports, the U.S.
national archive, did not differentiate between killings by stepparents
or by biological parents. But Statistics Canada from 1974 to 1990 did
contain relevant data.

Its figures showed that children under the age of two were at least
one hundred times more likely to be killed by stepparents—particularly
stepfathers—than by biological parents. "Of course," Daly stresses,
"most stepparents take to the task extremely well, and generally make
loving substitute parents. The incidence of abuse is low." Nonetheless,
for stepparents the homicide rate comes out at about 600 per million
parent-child groups living together, compared with just a handful for
biological parents. Further examination of records in the United States
and Britain revealed an increased risk for children with stepparents.
Moreover, a closer look at the case histories reveals that while biological parents who kill their children are often severely depressed and,
Daly and Wilson reported, "may even construe murder-suicide as a
humane act of rescue," stepparents who are homicidal "are rarely sui-
cidal and typically manifest their antipathy to their victims in the relative brutality of their lethal acts."

That there is a difference in incidence of fatal abuse between stepparents and genetic parents seems undeniable, but what are the reasons for it? Daly and Wilson have explored all the obvious, possibly
confounding variables of the kind that their Darwin Seminar audience
seized upon. Is poverty the real cause? Certainly, it is a risk factor in
child abuse. And the breakup of previous marriages that often lies
behind stepparentage obviously can be costly, reducing economic status. But, according to Daly and Wilson, the case histories show that
child homicide is vastly greater among stepparents than biological
parents at all levels of wealth. Poverty emerged as an independent,
additional factor, but a relatively weak one.

Well, is remarriage itself then a factor, suggesting some fickleness of
personality that might predispose a person to abuse? Apparently not.
The case histories show that people who remarry typically continue to
treat their own children well even when they abuse their stepchildren.
Or does the difference lie in early opportunities for bonding? Are biological parents conditioned to respond well to their children because
they are exposed to them from birth? "There isn't much evidence on
this," says Wilson, "because not many stepparents see their stepchil-

dren at a very early age, so it is hard to make a direct comparison. The few cases there are—although not statistically significant—suggest that stepfathers are at least as likely to abuse their stepchildren even when they are present at the actual birth."

Adopted Children

Don't adopted children provide a cogent comparison since, as with stepchildren, they are generally unrelated to their substitute parents? In fact, their risk is roughly the same as with natural parents. Surely this negates the notion that the added risk of stepparentage has genetic origins? "It might seem to," Daly acknowledges, "but there are two big, additional factors in adoption. First, adopting parents are obviously highly motivated and extremely closely monitored before they take on a child. Second, they tend to return children to adoption agencies far more often than is generally appreciated." This would weed out "unbonded" adoptive parents. So, although the data from families with adopted children appear to contradict the Darwinian idea that lack of genetic relationship reduces the likelihood of care, confounding variables make direct comparison impossible.

To test the genetic hypothesis to the full, Daly and Wilson asked their own question in reverse. Why is it that the overwhelming majority of stepparents treat their stepchildren well? After all, parenthood is a huge investment, an enormous burden to shoulder for the genetic offspring of somebody else. In Darwinian terms, at least, parenting means one thing only: perpetuating yourself by reproduction. But Daly says, "We know that when some other male animals take over a new family they will kill any existing offspring of previous matings—as male lions will do. It's easy to see why: it is in their own genetic interests to impregnate the females themselves, and existing cubs simply get in the way. Not all male animals behave this way. Incoming male baboons, for example, treat existing children well. This seems to be part of the mating effort; the females will not accept males that do not demonstrate parenting skills. This model seems to fit the human case as well. But, although stepparents do take on the task, Darwinians would predict that the full expression of parental feeling is liable to be buffered. Sometimes it's buffered too much."

Daly and Wilson reiterate that the overall rate of homicide by all parents of their children is low, and that most stepparents treat their new families well. Nevertheless, stepparentage emerges not only as a key risk factor in parental child abuse and homicide, but as the biggest factor. The Darwinian hypothesis—that the explanation may lie in the lack of familial relationship, and not primarily in economic or social factors—has stood up so far to the more obvious criticisms.

Finally we can ask—as the Darwin Seminar audience did—"Of what use is such knowledge? After all, most stepparents are good parents, so what good does it do to target them?" Margo Wilson answers, "In general we feel that it is better to know than not to know. It must be bad in principle to shy away from discovery just because the knowledge gained may seem uncomfortable. In fact, we can envisage good, practical reasons for this kind of knowledge. For one thing, social workers worldwide are invariably overworked. Anything that might help them to focus their efforts more accurately has to be worthwhile. And it can't be good that everyone has been overlooking the biggest risk factor for so long.

"We might also suggest that a mother who is thinking of remarrying should bear in mind that she cannot take her new partner for granted; she cannot expect that he will automatically treat her children as if they were his own. Actually women know this already of course—but perhaps the point needs more emphasis."

In short, if Wilson and Daly's ideas are applied sensibly and humanely (and are not used to make stepparents feel bad), then, in principle, they could save much human misery and perhaps human life. If this proves to be so, then those who object to this kind of insight should acknowledge that by objecting, they are allowing human suffering to take place unnecessarily—and they should take moral responsibility for so doing.

SOME PARENTS USE SCRIPTURE TO JUSTIFY PHYSICAL BEATINGS

Maija Elina

According to freelance writer Maija Elina, religious teachings concerning corporal punishment are used to justify child abuse in some fundamentalist Christian households. Child abuse in religious homes is difficult to confront, explains Elina, because child welfare agencies, law-enforcement officials, and politicians are reluctant to infringe upon the rights of parents and the Constitution's guarantee of religious freedom. In addition, she notes, children who are raised in religious homes are taught to accept their parents' authority unconditionally; as a result, they seldom report the abuse inflicted upon them by their parents. If child abuse committed in the name of religion is ever to be brought to the public's attention, Elina concludes, its victims must find the courage to break their silence and tell their stories openly.

Finally, the Catholic church is being forced to take action against its sexually abusive priests rather than just moving them to new parishes to prey upon other unsuspecting children. Spurred on by the courage and determination of the victims, public attention has put pressure on the church hierarchy to stop protecting its own reputation at the cost of the most vulnerable members of its flock.

While we are relieved that the old practice of child sexual abuse behind the facade of religion has been exposed and the first steps taken to stop it, this is just one area where abusive power over children is being applied under the mantle of religion. Physical and emotional mistreatment, condoned—and often even demanded—by dogmatic teachings, are equally ancient customs. We read occasionally about the abusive treatment of students in a fundamentalist Christian school or about some fanatical father beating his infant to death to drive out the devil. But we hear very little about the countless children who are routinely subjected to abuse by authoritarian mainstream churches. This tragedy remains hidden in the darkness of ignorance and fear.

Reprinted from "In the Family of God," by Maija Elina, *The Humanist*, July/August 1996. Reprinted with permission from the author.

"Train up a child in a way he should go: and when he is old, he will not depart from it," says Proverbs 22:6. Those who believe in a literal interpretation of the Bible and the innate badness of children find many biblical passages that advise using physical force to make the young good for God. One of the most commonly quoted verses ties hitting children with love: "He that spareth his rod hateth his son: but he that loveth him chasteneth him betimes" (Proverbs 13:24).

Divinely Sanctioned?

Parenting books which advocate corporal punishment as God's way of raising children—and which even describe the proper biblical method of doing it—are available in Christian bookstores across the country. Their authors seem to agree that, as long as the stick is the weapon, the bare bottom the place, and love the motive, physical punishment is divinely sanctioned. These particular Christian educators say they abhor child abuse but, in the same breath, tell parents to start as early as six months, when children first show their own will, and spank as long as it takes to break that stubbornness. And don't let them be angry or cry for too long, they counsel: children have to learn to control their feelings early.

Why has child abuse in the name of God and in the guise of love not been addressed? Because religion and family are the two sacred cows of our society. Many still believe that all religious teachings and practices—as long as they are not "cult related"—are holy, as if designed by God, and should not be questioned. Even when we find abuse, many people often conclude that Christian intentions are good or their actions follow biblical guidelines.

We also remember that freedom of religion is guaranteed by the First Amendment of the U.S. Constitution and fall silent. For instance, the director of a Christian day-care center in North Carolina appealed the ban on spanking in such institutions, saying, "It is against the scriptures." He won his case, and the superior court judge ruled that the ban was an infringement on religious freedom. It is not surprising, then, that even some child-protection agencies overlook child abuse done in the name of religious freedom. Freedom of religion can become freedom to abuse, and the separation of church and state becomes the wall behind which the perpetrators hide.

We are also reluctant to point a finger at the family, saying that it's nobody's business what happens in the privacy of someone else's home. There are fundamentalist parent groups which oppose the work of child-protection agencies, maintaining that no one has a right to interfere with their families. Child rights are not sanctioned by the ~~word of~~ God, and child-abuse laws undermine parental authority, they say. Unfortunately, those laws rarely reach the battered children of religious fanatics. The "family of God" isolates itself from the secular community and remains, by and large, outside of social and legal scrutiny.

Difficult to Detect

Child abuse that takes place in a religious home is difficult to detect. To an outsider, the family appears pious and respectable. Its members are god-fearing churchgoers who would vehemently deny that their child-rearing practices are abusive. The children show no overt signs of abuse. Their emotional wounds are camouflaged by a compliant, ready-to-please appearance; a shy smile hides their fear and pain just as the physical bruises are hidden on the backside of their bodies.

Uncovering any child abuse is difficult, but children beaten as a punishment from God very rarely tell anybody because they are taught that they themselves are to blame. A woman raised in a fundamentalist home told me an incident that illustrates the collective approval of this phenomenon. As a little girl, her mother's regular whippings gave her horrifying nightmares and panic attacks. "Once I fell asleep during Sunday school and the teacher wanted to know why I was always so tired. I told her. She said I should be more obedient to my parents and to pray harder."

In cases where abuse is reported, children themselves often deny or minimize it. There is a strong tendency in all of us to protect our parents; but for those raised under the commandment "Honor thy father and thy mother," the necessity to preserve the illusion of righteous parents is continually impressed upon their minds. Even after leaving the church, the adult survivors of religious child abuse are reluctant to tell what happened to them. Like a woman I know who was raised as a missionary child, most of them say, "I don't want to make my parents look bad. They thought they did the right thing because they believed children are born evil and must be made good for God." My friend was beaten several times a week to break her will and make her obedient to her parents and God. She was indoctrinated with a lasting fear of God's wrath, demon possession, and eternal damnation. "Even now, 15 years after leaving the church, I'm afraid that God will strike me dead if I tell what was done to me as a child," she says.

Denial

Others have to break through a wall of denial. The daughter of a fundamentalist Christian college professor was regularly subjected to the "rod of correction" and kept isolated from the "evil world," yet she believed in an illusion of a perfect Christian home. "'This is for your own good. If we didn't love you, we wouldn't do this,' my parents told me. I believed I deserved the beatings. The most difficult part of telling my truth has been the death of a fantasy that my family was good and loving."

As a result of "good intentions" and obedience to divine orders, untold suffering is inflicted on innocent, powerless children in many mainstream Christian homes, schools, and day-care centers. In them, the Christian message of love has been distorted and twisted into a most insidious form of cruelty: the hurting and damaging of children in the name of God. It is my hope that, like those molested by clergy, the victims of childhood religious abuse will find the courage to tell their stories publicly so that the silence about this taboo subject will finally be broken.

CHAPTER 3

CHILD ABUSE:
PERSONAL NARRATIVES

Contemporary Issues
Companion

My Mother Made Me Sick

Mary Bryk, as told to Laura Berman

In the following selection, Mary Bryk, a nurse and mother of two, describes the abuse she experienced as a child. According to Bryk, her mother suffered from Munchausen by proxy syndrome, a form of child abuse in which parents—most often mothers—seek attention by inducing illness in their children. In Bryk's case, her mother deliberately broke her bones and created massive infections in her arms and legs by contaminating her wounds with foreign substances. By the time she was ten years old, Bryk had endured twenty-four surgeries and numerous hospitalizations, transfusions, and bone and skin grafts and transfusions as a result of her mother's actions. She explains that the abuse ended only when she was old enough to threaten to reveal what her mother was doing. With the help of a skilled therapist and a loving husband, Bryk writes, she eventually overcame the psychological scars left by her mother's abuse.

"No one will believe you," my mother used to warn. "They'll say you're crazy and lock you up." As a child, her threats terrified me. As an adult, they continued to hold power over me, keeping me silent out of fear and shame. Even my husband, David, knew only pieces of the truth.

Who would believe that a mother could mutilate her own child? Bruise her, break her bones, cause infection deliberately and methodically? Despite a head full of nightmarish memories and a career in nursing, I could make no sense of my past. I remembered my childhood as if it were a movie about someone else's life—when the lights went back on, I put the story out of my mind.

Then I became a mother and experienced the awesome love and joy a baby inspires. Sitting in the kitchen with 3-month-old Elizabeth, holding her close, I knew I would do anything, risk anything to protect this tiny, helpless infant. My mother never held me like this, I thought, tears streaming down my cheeks. I realized then that I had never felt the loving touch most children take for granted. With my mother, every kiss, every hug was suspect, a prelude to fear and pain.

Reprinted from "How Her Mother Hurt Her . . . in the Name of Love," Mary Bryk's story as told to Laura Berman, *Redbook*, February 1998. Reprinted with permission from Laura Berman.

Cuddling Elizabeth that day, I knew I didn't want to taint my children's futures with the secrets so deeply embedded in my psyche. Lies and deception may have been a way of life in the family in which I grew up, but I wanted a different kind of home for my children, my husband, and myself. At 30, I was finally ready to begin opening doors that had long been sealed shut.

In the summer of 1997, eight years after my journey toward understanding the truth began, the medical journal *Pediatrics* published my account of growing up as a victim of an insidious form of abuse: Munchausen by proxy syndrome, in which a parent invents symptoms or causes illness in a child. It was the first such detailed account ever to appear in medical literature—testimony to how dangerous and frightening a task it is to unmask a parent's distorted love.

Real Sickness, Real Terror

My mother—a nurse, a physician's daughter, a woman loved by many in our hometown—deliberately created massive infections in my arms and legs throughout much of my childhood. Beginning with my toddler years, I was hospitalized 28 times. I underwent 24 surgeries and submitted to many blood transfusions and incision and drainage procedures, as well as skin and bone grafts. Despite massive doses of antibiotics, my wounds never seemed to heal. On the days when I wasn't hospitalized, I often hobbled to school on crutches or used a wheelchair. I still mourn the early schooling I missed, the friends I never made, the childhood I lost.

To her friends and large extended family, my mother was a wonderful woman, practically a saint, whose life was filled with constant sacrifice because of her sickly, invalid daughter. Although she was a nurse, my mother didn't hold a job outside our home: I was her patient. To the well-meaning doctors who treated me, and who noted their bafflement about my chronic infections on my arms and legs, my mother was a model caregiver. They even allowed her to dress my wounds and give me medication in the hospital, and sometimes released me early for treatment at home. Although she wasn't on staff at the hospital, she was so trusted by the doctors that her handwriting appears in my hospital charts.

To me, my mother was someone entirely different: a cold and terrifying person whose anger I feared and whose love I sought desperately, hopelessly. She showed one self to adults and the outside world and another to the daughter she needed to hurt to love. I learned to be suspicious of people's false fronts and appearances, to choose friends slowly and carefully, to guard my emotions.

My medical record begins when I was 2 years old, 16 years before Munchausen by proxy syndrome was recognized by the medical establishment, and at a time when doctors didn't suspect child abuse in "nice" families like ours. It was 1961 and, according to the hospital records, my parents reported that I'd fallen down a flight of stairs, twisting an ankle. Six weeks later, my condition had deteriorated—I was limping, my foot was swollen, and there was a large bruise over my ankle.

By the time I was 3, I'd been hospitalized nine times. The nursing notes from the ninth stay are in my mother's handwriting, and say that I "started to walk, took a couple of steps, when a crack was heard and leg hung. Doctor notified." My right femur, the thighbone, was fractured, and I was placed in traction with a pin through my right heel, a wound that failed to heal for the next seven years.

What the doctors didn't know was that my mother's at-home nursing sessions were methodical, consistent, and often brutal. Before I was old enough for school, she scheduled my "treatments" three times a week, always after Paul Harvey's noon radio broadcast, when my father and grandmother were at work and my older sister was in school. To this day, I have a sinking feeling whenever I hear that commentator's trademark sign-off, "Good day."

The doctors also didn't know that my mother tied me to a chair or sat on me, then hit my leg with a hammer. Or that she probed my draining wounds with sharp objects—a knitting needle, a roofing nail—to prevent healing, and contaminated them further using potting soil and coffee grounds. "I'm doing this for your own good," she would say when I fought her. "The doctors want me to do this treatment for you to get better."

As I got older, I missed so much school that I needed a tutor to help with my lessons, which enabled my mother to pick me up early from school for a "treatment" before the tutor arrived—and before my sister got back from school. When I grew bigger and stronger, she would pin me on the linoleum kitchen floor, sitting on me with her back to my face, "treating" my infected leg. Many times I was hysterical. Sometimes, I thought if I was really good and didn't fight back, maybe the pain wouldn't last as long. Other days, I would run from her or hide, which only made her angry and more frightening. She was so powerful and I was so weak: After all, look what she could get away with.

An Unanswered Plea for Help

Gradually, I lost faith that anyone would rescue me. We lived with my grandmother (on my mother's side), but she was a cold and remote person, not someone I could turn to. Like most young girls, I idolized my father, who worked long days at a pharmaceutical company and often took on carpentry jobs that kept him away from home until late in the evening. In my fantasies, my father was the white knight who ultimately would save me. As a 6-year-old, still hopeful that my mother's torture could be stopped, I directly reached out to my father for help.

It was Sunday, the only day our family was usually all together. I was in the car with my father and sister, waiting for my mother to come out of the house, when I seized my chance. "Daddy, why does Mommy hit me with a hammer?" I asked him, explaining what she did to me. After my mother got in the car, he asked her, "What is Mary talking about?" and mentioned the hammer. My mother was, and is, a force to be reckoned with: Tearfully, she refuted my story. She sacrificed her life to care for me, she insisted, and here I was, accusing her of horrible things. In the backseat, my sister, her hands clasped over her ears, was screaming and crying, unwilling to hear anything bad about Mommy. My father chose to believe my mother that day, and on others to come.

But even then, I clung fiercely to the truth. Unlike my sister, who must have heard my screams, who even shared my room, yet repeatedly shut her eyes and ears, I knew my mother was wrong and I was right. Looking back, I think my recognition of my mother's abuse was a lifeline: She could hurt me but she couldn't get me to believe her lies or that her sickness was real love. Somehow, I instinctively knew not to let her win that way. My belief is that a strong sense of God's love (even at an early age) and the good role models I saw in my extended family gave me the strength to survive and to keep my mother from triumphing over me in any meaningful way.

The Abuse Ends, but the Struggle Goes On

By the time I was in fourth grade, I couldn't stand the routine any more. The anxiety I felt, the dread and anticipation of pain, had become worse than the actual physical suffering. In school, I worried about what would happen when I got home. Can a 10-year-old know that she's being driven crazy? I think I did, just as I knew that no one was coming to rescue me. One day I simply said: No more. In the strongest voice I could muster, I warned my mother that I would tell the doctor and my teacher the truth if she didn't stop. No more.

Amazingly, it worked. The physical abuse ended. My health improved immediately, and for the first time in eight years, I had full use of both my legs. Everyone thought there had been a miraculous "cure," as if I had had cancer or some other real disease.

My "recovery" didn't end the suffering in our household. Soon after, my 3-year-old brother began to have symptoms very similar to those that had afflicted me for so long. I felt guilty and helpless, fearful that my mother had turned her attention to my brother, yet equally fearful of interfering. One day, I walked in on my mother as she sat astride my brother just as she had done to me. The hammer was poised in her hand as I screamed for her to stop. "Get back outside," my mother yelled. I pleaded with her to stop, until she sent the hammer flying past me and into the wall behind me, barely missing my head.

She stopped abusing my brother after two years or so, perhaps because she worried that the doctors were growing suspicious. As an adult, my brother admitted to me that he too had been abused, but he has not talked to others in the family about it; he is not yet ready to confront what happened to him. Why my mother chose the two of us and not our older sister is a question that only my mother can really answer. I think, though, that my mother bonded with my sister, her firstborn, in a way she didn't with my brother and me.

My struggles with my mother did not end when the abuse did. My high school years were full of angry conflict, as I continued to try to prove to both my parents that I was worthy of their love and approval. Although I was shy and self-conscious about my body—especially about the deep scarring on my arms and legs, the legacy of all those operations—I finally had a few close friends of my own. The power struggle with my mother intensified, though, as she tried to control me by belittling and criticizing me. In school, I studied hard, trying to make up for the years of learning I'd lost because of illness, trying to prove to my parents that, yes, I was smart and capable.

Despite graduating fifteenth in my high school class and winning an academic scholarship to college, my parents dissuaded me from becoming a veterinarian. I'd never get into vet school with my grades, they said. Instead, still trying to please my mother, I decided to become a nurse, as she had. Once in college, and away from my parents, I steadily gained self-confidence, gathering the strength I needed to become an emotionally healthy person.

I know that it is hard to believe that today I have a loving, normal family. My husband, David, has been, almost from the moment we met at a singles party 13 years ago, my best friend, my confidant. Before we married, I'd told him only a little about my history. He said, "When you're ready to talk about it, I'll be here to listen and support you." David, who's a dentist and a great father, is my other half—he can express emotions freely, and I'm sure that is part of what drew me to him: He could do the feeling for both of us.

Setting Out on the Path to Understanding

The cliché is that an abused child grows up to repeat the parent's behavior, but nothing in me seeks to repeat the pattern of my mother's abuse or to be abused myself. This is simply how I am. When I left for college, I wanted to find the kind of acceptance and love I didn't have as a child, and I ran from any relationship that reminded me of my mother or her manipulative, controlling ways. That is a healthy, strong part of me that I'm grateful for.

After Elizabeth was born in 1989, I went into therapy for four years with a wonderful woman, Mimi Becigneul, who specializes in working with victims of physical and emotional trauma. Already married, a mother, and a nurse with a career, I was still painfully shy and self-conscious, and I didn't open up in therapy for a very long time. The memories were clear, but the emotions were buried. Finally, after almost a year, I broke down in a convulsion of tears, letting go of some of the hurt and loneliness and fear I'd felt as a child. That was so hard for me to do: I felt very ashamed and embarrassed. When you've suppressed so much shame and guilt for so long, releasing them is very scary.

One night in 1991, the baby was asleep and David was watching TV in the family room while I cleaned up in the kitchen. "Mary, you've got to see this," David called. He was watching an interview on NBC's *Dateline* with Dr. Herbert Schreier, an expert on Munchausen by proxy syndrome, a little-understood condition that even my therapist was not aware of at the time. As I listened to Dr. Schreier ticking off the characteristics of mothers who secretly make their children sick to get attention, I realized, "Oh my God, he's talking about my mother."

Hearing that what my mother did to me had a scientific name, an explanation, made me feel suddenly free, and frightened. It also gave me another push toward the truth—and, painfully, away from my parents.

In June 1993, I invited my parents, brother, and sister to meet with me and my therapist. My brother, with whom I'm only intermittently in touch, chose not to come. In Mimi Becigneul's office, I confronted my family directly, telling them my mother had deliberately abused me as a child; she fit the profile of Munchausen by proxy syndrome, I said, handing them articles on the subject. By that time, I knew, my mother had developed Munchausen syndrome—she'd begun hurting herself. I had even shown my father the hammer she kept hidden in a dresser drawer. So I wasn't surprised when she denied everything, nor that my father and sister believed her and not me. My mother is a very intelligent, very manipulative person who can be extremely convincing, and my father and sister had always wanted to believe her, no matter what. After they all left the office, my therapist said, "Boy, your mother is something."

"I Am Not My Mother"

The only contact I've had with my family since then was a letter from my sister, telling me that she no longer wanted any contact with me. My parents have not seen their granddaughters, Elizabeth, 8, and Annie, 6, in almost five years.

I am haunted by what I saw in my mother's eyes in our last meeting— a sadness and loneliness that I'm not sure others recognize. Imagine living your life as a lie; imagine denying who you are for your entire life. While I cannot excuse my mother's behavior in any way, I still feel love for her.

In these last few years, I have had to mourn the loss of my parents, especially my father, who I'd always believed would one day recognize me for the person that I am. But because he cannot accept that I was abused, he cannot see me. I think it is easier for my father and sister to deny what happened, to go on with the life they know, rather than face a truth that would tear their lives apart.

There is no such choice for me. I can never forget what happened, because the physical evidence is always there as a very visible reminder. My right arm is scarred and shriveled and my legs are riddled with surgical scars. As a teenager, these physical imperfections humiliated me, and even as an adult, I've felt very self-conscious about them. One of the ways that I knew David truly loved me was when I asked him if the scars bothered him. "I never really thought about them," he answered. My children know only that "my mommy wasn't very nice to me"; when they're old enough to understand, I'll tell them more of the story.

My mother and I look very much alike. Even now, staring at myself in the mirror, I sometimes hear myself saying, "I am not my mother, I am not my mother." Telling the truth is a way for me to enforce the separation. She may deny who she is and what she has done, but I cannot.

Memory Meets Fact

About the time that I was ending therapy, I was introduced to Patricia T. Siegel, Ph.D., a pediatric psychologist at Children's Hospital of Michigan in Detroit and an expert on Munchausen by proxy syndrome. She encouraged me to explore the medical facts of my story, the 400-page hospital record of the childhood that I lost. Reading the first entry—at 2 years old—was the most upsetting: I had been a whole person, an unscarred baby like my own daughters, when the hospital records began. Leafing through the records, I broke down in tears.

But the bulging package of records also offered me a new kind of hope and strength. It wasn't only my word against my mother's. Here sat evidence, the corroboration of memory with fact. The broken hip in the hospital, while in my mother's care. The bacterial infections that, doctors have confirmed, could have been caused by coffee grounds and potting soil. Myriad bruises and sprains the doctors could not explain. And my sudden, complete recovery that dovetails with the moment I threatened to tell authorities if my mother didn't stop abusing me.

Telling my story publicly is yet another step in my journey toward the truth. I am not seeking revenge against my parents. But after a lifetime of being so controlled by fear and the desperate longing to be loved by my mother and father, I want others to know they can find a path away from abuse. Or help recognize a child who needs to be rescued. If anyone had ever directly asked me: "Does your mother hurt you?" I would have answered with the truth. But no one ever did.

My beautiful daughters, Elizabeth and Annie, are showing me how innocent and happy a childhood can be. Through them, I am experiencing some of what I missed. At the moment, our house is filled with animals, including Buck, the floppy-eared gray rabbit, and a litter of four orphaned kittens we rescued from a haystack in the country. We laugh a lot. Being Annie and Elizabeth's mother, a good and loving mother, is for me the greatest healer.

I Was Sexually Abused by My Guidance Counselor

Donna Covello

In the following selection, Donna Covello recalls the years of sexual abuse she suffered at the hands of her high school guidance counselor, who took advantage of her emotional state when she was an insecure and lonely teen. The trauma of sexual victimization caused her to attempt suicide and contributed to later marital and health problems, Covello reveals. After undergoing therapy, Covello decided to confront her abuser, taking a concealed tape recorder with her to gain proof of the abuse. Her recordings of her conversations with her abuser ultimately resulted in his removal from his job by the New York Board of Education, she writes. Although Covello admits her dissatisfaction with the lenient punishment her abuser received, she explains that she does not regret confronting him because it has helped her to overcome her emotional troubles. Covello is the president of Survivors of Educator Sexual Abuse and Misconduct Emerge (SESAME), a victims advocacy group dedicated to increasing the public's awareness of sex abuse by educators.

Would confronting him—21 years later—help heal the wounds? Would it help me get on with my life?

On June 13, 1994, I found myself sitting across a desk from the man who nearly destroyed my life. It was a hot, sticky day, and I trembled as I gripped my pocketbook, with a tape recorder hidden in it. I needed information, but I had to compose myself and keep my anger and hostility inside. It gave me a shock to see how old he had become. Gary Landau, dean of guidance at Lafayette High School in Brooklyn, New York, was 32 when I first met him. Now he was 53, mostly bald, with some white hair.

"Do you remember me?" I asked him.

"Boy, do I remember you," he answered, and he leaned forward, looking me over. "My goodness, you look the same," he said.

Reprinted from "I Was Abused by My Guidance Counselor," by Donna Covello, *Good Housekeeping,* February 1996. Reprinted with permission from the author.

All the terrible memories came flooding back. Suddenly, I was a 14-year-old freshman again.

No One Had Much Time for Me

I grew up in a working-class Italian neighborhood in Brooklyn, the youngest of three children. My mom suffered from clinical depression. And my dad drove a taxicab and wasn't around much. So I spent most of my time tagging along with my sister, Carol, who was 12 years older and like a mother to me. It was Carol who took me to the beach, movies, and museums.

In my Catholic elementary school, I was made fun of because I wore braces and my words came out all fuzzy. I always felt ugly and awkward. When it came time for high school, I chose Lafayette, a public school, because I thought it would be freer and friendlier.

Around the time I was starting high school, Carol found out she had Hodgkin's disease, and would need surgery to remove her spleen and a tumor on her lung. No one had much time for me, and I felt neglected. I couldn't wait to start school because I wanted a chance to make new friends.

The first week of school, Mr. Landau approached me in study hall and asked if I'd like to do some filing for him. I said yes. He was very charming and popular, and being chosen by him made me feel important.

Three weeks later, when we were alone in his office, he grabbed my rear end. I was totally taken aback. When I left school that day, I felt confused.

A few days later, as I was trying to leave, he grabbed me and kissed me and started fondling my breasts. I remember feeling very shaky but also flattered. The next day, I found it hard to concentrate in class. I started obsessing about Mr. Landau. I had no experience with boys, and I had no idea what was appropriate or what was supposed to happen.

Before long, he wanted me to help with filing after school too. One afternoon, when the building was emptier than usual, he opened his personal cabinet and pulled out a pornographic magazine with brutal images of women being violently abused. After showing it to me, he turned out the lights and did a lot more fondling. He took off my clothes and groped me all over. Then he penetrated me with the handle of a hairbrush, and I lost my virginity. I started to bleed, and it really hurt. I didn't know what had happened. I was scared, and I started crying.

He tried to convince me that everything that had happened between us was normal, even though I hadn't felt any pleasure. His approval meant so much to me, and I was so afraid of losing him, that I continued to do whatever he asked. Sometimes he pulled me out of class early so I could be with him. He had keys to different rooms all over the school, and he always seemed to know which rooms were empty. He was very careful not to get caught.

When I look back now, I actually think some teachers suspected. But they felt like it wasn't their business, so they kept quiet.

Keeping the Pain Inside

Even when I began to realize something was wrong with this picture, I didn't say anything. My mother was so fragile, I was afraid she'd fall apart if I brought it up. And I worried that I'd be kicked out of school.

I never had much of a chance to socialize with kids my own age. During my junior year, I remember, a guy in my class invited me to a big party at his house. I noticed that a lot of kids there were going steady, wearing school rings and ankle bracelets. I really felt left out. I was so shy; I felt like I wasn't good enough for anyone.

My grades weren't very good either, and I didn't have a lot of confidence in myself. Whenever we talked about my future, Mr. Landau would put me down and tell me I wouldn't amount to anything.

The sexual abuse continued until I graduated in 1977. He asked me to work for him that summer at a newsstand he ran, but I said no. I knew in my heart it was time to be free of him.

I got a job as a file clerk, but I continued to live at home. That first year out of high school was hard, partly because of the pain I was keeping inside.

One day when I was home alone and feeling depressed, I snatched a handful of my mother's tranquilizers. I remember I just wanted to die. My father found me on the floor, unconscious, and I was rushed to the hospital, where I had my stomach pumped.

When my sister came to see me, she wanted to know why I had done it. I finally confided in her, telling her everything that had happened with Mr. Landau. I told her how much I hated myself for what I had done. Carol was devastated. She told the rest of the family, but they never asked questions. No one wanted to talk about it. They just wanted me to forget and move on.

Trying to Move On

Slowly, I began pulling myself together. I attended a community college for a couple of years and then enrolled in Brooklyn College, where I took physical education courses. There, I met my future husband, Donald, who was my physiology professor. He was very distinguished looking, with salt-and-pepper hair and a beard. Toward the end of the semester, we met for coffee and he asked me out.

After that, we dated casually for a few years. He was the first really nice guy I'd met. We visited museums and went hiking and running together. At the time I was in my 20s and he was in his 40s. But he was very kind and respectful, and nothing about him reminded me of Mr. Landau. Our relationship started slowly; at first it was like a friendship.

I got my bachelor's degree in 1985 and started teaching preschool. Four years later, Donald and I decided to get married. By this time, I had my master's degree in occupational therapy, and I'd found a job I loved: working at a hospital with HIV-positive children who had all kinds of physical and developmental problems.

Donald and I never discussed what had happened with Mr. Landau. But my memories haunted me. Two years after I got married, my world came tumbling down. I began an affair with a coworker— someone who was abusive like Mr. Landau. I guess it was what I had come to expect in a relationship. I began intentionally starving myself, and my weight plunged to about 78 pounds. I stopped functioning.

Thankfully, I had a wonderful supervisor at work who saw I was in trouble and encouraged me to get help. I checked into the eating-disorder unit of a local hospital, where I stayed for nearly a month. That's when my recovery really started. I began to open up to Donald, and for the first time I told him about Mr. Landau. Though he was upset, he said his biggest concern was that I get help. And he let me know that he'd be there for me.

Reopening Old Wounds

While I was hospitalized, I got a phone call from Carol, who was in remission from Hodgkin's disease and living in California with her husband and two children. She said she thought I would feel better if I could go back and confront Mr. Landau.

I told her I didn't think I had the courage, but I promised to consider it. In the hospital, I talked to counselors and began creative art therapy, drawing pictures to help me express my feelings. I felt a wound had been reopened, and the poison started coming out. I spent a lot of time just crying.

Gradually, I came to understand my relationship with Mr. Landau. For the first time, I was using words like childhood sexual abuse and molestation. And I stopped blaming myself.

When I got out of the hospital, I needed to take some time off work. I started seeing a therapist, and I got involved in a support group. I was able to talk with other women who were sexually abused during childhood, either by a family member or a trusted authority figure. At first, I just listened. When you hear all the stories, you learn you are not alone.

Confronting the Abuser

I knew the final step was confronting Gary Landau. But though my support group assured me I could do it, I resisted. Then something happened to change my mind. In January 1993, my sister Carol died of cancer. I felt like I had lost a parent. But I kept thinking that she had wanted me to face him.

During the fall of 1993, I started composing a letter to school authorities, describing what had happened. It took me months just to write a paragraph. Finally, I met with investigators from the Special Commissioner's Office for the New York City School District. My hope at that time was to press criminal charges, but I was warned it was probably too late, because New York State's statute of limitations for sex abuse cases runs out after five years. I decided to go forward anyway.

In order to prepare me, the investigators drove me past the high school and gave me an up-to-date picture of Gary Landau. They called the principal to tell her I was coming, but they didn't want me to alert Mr. Landau. The idea was for me to just drop in and explain that I was now an occupational therapist doing home-care visits in the neighborhood.

It was late afternoon when I arrived. At first, I was taken aback because Lafayette looked and smelled the same as I remembered. I was really nervous when I walked into the office of the dean of guidance.

Mr. Landau was a little surprised to see me, but he just fell right back into his old role: cocky, relaxed, very much interested in me. It all felt strange and overwhelming. I felt safe, though, because the investigators were waiting in a car outside and could hear our conversation on a remote transmitter.

After the small talk, I brought up some of the things we used to do. "Do you remember the oral sex?" I asked.

"Oh, baby, if you continue I'm going to jump on you," he said, as he lunged for me.

"Don't," I said firmly, and the moment passed. I wanted to scream and curse at him, and tear his eyes out. But I had to contain myself, and focus on what the investigators told me to do.

We made plans to meet again at a neighborhood diner. Once again, I had a tape recorder. At one point, he told me he was getting excited. He also said he was angry at me because during the years we were involved, he couldn't go home afterward and touch his wife. And he said he hoped we could still be close. It was really hard to hear him talk that way, and I just kept praying I would stay calm.

By the time I got home after that second meeting, I wanted to explode. I collapsed on the couch, sobbing. I told Donald I just needed to rest, and he didn't push me. All he said was, "Thank God it's over."

That night, I went to treat one of my home-care pediatric patients. I did it because I needed reality brought home to me: I was 35, a grown woman with a life and a job I loved; I was not a 14-year-old high school girl.

Stronger and Better

My colleagues at work knew about the confrontation. The next day, they hugged me and told me I seemed different—more alert, more relaxed. A few weeks later I told my mother. Though she didn't press me for details, she let me know she was proud of me. She hadn't been able to give me what I needed when I was younger, but I'd come to terms with it.

I'm furious, though, that Mr. Landau cannot be sent to jail. Based on the transcripts of my conversations with him, he was removed from his job and reassigned to work at the New York City Board of Education. But in the summer of 1995, he was allowed to take early retirement and collect his pension. He chose to surrender his New York State teaching certificate rather than face disciplinary hearings that could have resulted in the certificate being revoked. I don't think that's a strong enough punishment, considering all the damage he caused me. And he can still work with children or volunteer at a community center.

Still, I'm glad I did what I did. I'm a lot stronger now. Every morning before work, I run about four miles, and on the weekends I do ten-kilometer road races. I use the time to meditate and pray. I used to think about Mr. Landau's wife and his two children, who are now grown. Part of me felt for them. But I know now that is not my responsibility.

Recently, I became a victim's advocate, and I often lobby the state legislature in Albany, urging the elimination of the statute of limitations for sex abuse cases. I also belong to a support group working to increase awareness of sex abuse in schools.

Confronting Mr. Landau turned my life upside down. But it's given me my spirit and my power back. Each day, I feel a little better.

Struggling with the Psychological Scars Left by Abuse

Joan Bryce Crompton

In the following essay, freelance writer Joan Bryce Crompton recalls the horrific abuse she suffered at the hands of her mother during her childhood. The beatings and sexual torture that Crompton's mother inflicted on her left not only permanent physical scars, but lasting psychological damage as well. The author explains that although she built a fulfilling life as an adult, she could not completely overcome her emotional scars. Despite the support of her father, husband, and children, Crompton reveals, her life was darkened by overwhelming feelings of worthlessness and despair. She describes how the long-term effects of her childhood ordeal led her to attempt suicide three times—and how the love of her family ultimately inspired her to choose life over death.

Suicide. Not just a word or a statistic, but for me three times almost a reality.

To know me, you would not suspect this. I love life and all God's creation. I laugh easily. I have a wonderful husband and three highly engaging children. My sister and brother are my best friends, and my father means the world to me. I have many close friends. I have a good life.

I am also a survivor of eighteen years of extensive child abuse— physical, emotional, and sadistic sexual abuse at the hands of the woman who bore me.

Fear and Pain

I never ever stopped loving my mother, or wanting so much for her to love me. But from my earliest days, she vented on me all the anger and pain she had suffered in her own horrendous childhood. I could do nothing right. She thwarted my talents, ridiculed my thoughts and words, inflicted pain on every part of my body, and fused fear onto my soul.

Reprinted from "To Choose Life: A Survivor's Story," by Joan Bryce Crompton, *The Other Side,* July/August 1999. Reprinted with permission from the author.

My head ached constantly from being banged against the wall and having my hair yanked. I was beaten black-and-blue, choked so hard that her hand prints remained on my neck, and scratched until my face ran with blood. I went to school with instructions to say that I had fallen down the stairs or been scratched by the cat.

From time to time, my mother dangled me from my second-story bedroom window. Once she dropped me. As a result, I have permanent back injuries that required three surgeries in my early twenties. Even now, I am in pain every day and need an army of specialists to keep me going.

The woman who gave me life would hold pillows over my face until I was about to pass out from suffocation, then remove them, laughing like the wicked witch in *The Wizard of Oz,* scornfully calling me "My pretty." She hid in my closet at night, and jumped out at me wearing dark robes. In those same robes she took me to the attic, laid me on a table surrounded by candles, held fire to my feet, and hurt me sexually.

Once she took me to our pediatrician to be treated for anal bleeding. She laughed derisively, knowing the doctor would never say a thing. She was right. No one ever said anything.

A black-and-white photo faces me from my writing journal. The woman is attractive but has about her an aura of craziness. The little girl sits close to her, submissive and scared. The picture was taken on a family trip through the Blue Ridge Mountains, where my mother took me alone to a high ridge and urged me to jump off. "Jump for Jesus," she whispered harshly, "jump for Jesus." I was only four, but I turned away. The survival mechanism was already in place.

Overwhelmed by Worthlessness

As I grew older and bigger, I tried to protect myself from her attacks. When I did, my mother forced me to kneel at my her feet, take all the blame, and beg for forgiveness.

She would tear me from my bed in the middle of the night, shaking me until I thought I could feel my brains rattle. Her rage was so great that my father could barely restrain her even by sitting on her.

A brilliant, beautiful, highly educated woman, my mother was extremely clever about choosing her times and concealing the sexual abuse. She would wait until my father was away, and even keep me home from school. Afterward, I would stagger through the next weeks numb, as if some crucial part of me had been torn out. I lived a childhood permeated with shame and pain, overwhelmed by worthlessness, still aching for my mother's love.

My desperate father sought help everywhere, but received nothing. It was the fifties, that time of Ozzie-and-Harriet perfection. Child abuse was not acknowledged; the term *sexual abuse* did not exist. So my father went to court and sued for custody. But my mother and her lawyer instructed me to lie, to deny my father's testimony and take the blame for my mother's "discipline," saying that I was a "difficult child."

The court gave me to my mother.

Attempting Suicide

In 1997, I was living near the South Carolina shore with my husband and three children. On Labor Day weekend, in the deep, dark, and late hours, I stood at the ocean's edge in a cotton nightgown, oblivious to the water's warmth and the fuzzy foam playing between my toes.

Only once before had the pain been so consuming. Ten years previous to this balmy Southern night, I had faced a sub-zero Midwestern midnight, agony gnawing at my body and soul. Standing on the edge of the back porch in a heavy flannel nightgown—oblivious to the thirty-below wind chill—I gazed with irrational longing at the deep snow drifts and thought how comforting it would be to sink into them, surrendering myself to the freezing white powder, just to stop the pain. Barefoot, I stepped out, my only thought to numb myself forever, when from inside the house came baby Emma's hungry cry.

That night seemed both far and near as I walked into the ocean, testing my intentions, lying face down in the shallow water. I could not believe this time had come again. So many years of therapy, so much progress. Always I had functioned, persevered, produced and pushed way beyond my limits. It was my way of proclaiming my survival, a coping mechanism no child should ever have to devise and carry through adulthood. And then, only weeks before, I had begun to unravel.

I rose and moved further out, yearning for whatever small solace the waves might bring. Instead, the ache and shame bit harder, and I went eagerly into the ocean's open arms.

From behind me, a light flicked on, illuminating the water. I turned instinctively. A beach house about thirty feet from the shore was lighting up, window by window. One person stood staring on the porch. I panicked.

It was an odd thought, but it was enough: I was horrified that I would be pulled by strangers from the ocean without my underwear. This bizarre notion drove me from the sea. I ran for my truck and sped off. Fear and loathing now crawled into the morass of pain. I wanted no one to know of this. I would slip in the back of the house, into the shower, and into bed.

Driving down the highway, crying and shivering, the distance from my former strength seized me. I was coming apart at the seams, and I knew it.

I made it home. Bill was there as I walked in the door. He quickly saw what had happened, then everything became a blur. Somehow he managed to protect the children and make all the right phone calls.

Soon I was in bed, sobbing and sedated, wishing I would sleep and never wake up. Bill spent the night on the floor, blocking the bedroom door with his large frame. The next morning I gave myself up to hospitalization.

Post-Traumatic Stress Disorder

The hospital was a nightmare. I had entertained vague hopes of comfort and nurturing; instead I felt the familiar sting of punishment, and a loneliness that only made me hate myself more for such a stupid action that separated me from those who actually love me. The only "outside" available to me was a small yard, heavy with smoke and gossip—a far cry from my neighbor's farm where I loved to spend hours with my friends, my animals, and my children. I retreated to my room to tremble and sob, longing for the thick, red curls of my youngest and the warmth and smell of my horses.

In the midst of this despair I met my psychiatrist—a tough, compassionate, brilliant woman who broke every preconceived mold in the business. She was direct, clear, even funny. She also gave a whole new dimension to my diagnosis of Post-Traumatic Stress Disorder (PTSD).

"You are more than a survivor of child abuse and are affected by more than the triggers that set off PTSD," she explained. "You are a trauma survivor. You probably have no serotonin left. The neurotransmitters in your brain have been damaged by the extensive abuse. This breakdown was probably inevitable. You are going to need medication to compensate for the damage to your brain."

Finally I understood why I had come apart. I was greatly relieved to have reasons for my behavior. I only wished that this disability had some outward sign so that people would understand my fragility, my limitations. I had made so much progress over the years. The sweat-drenched nightmares were gone and the fears that ruled my life had faded over time. I had even gone to my mother's deathbed two years before, and experienced some sort of reconciliation.

But now the barometers were smashed, and the compass was bobbing erratically. I had heaped on guilt the way some people pile their plates at a buffet. I was a magnet for pain, taking in every needy soul and critter that found its way to my wounded-healer heart. No matter how bad they were, the pains and scrapes of others were far easier to face than my own.

My trust levels were askew. I panicked easily. My psychiatrist explained, "Every possible conflict you encounter puts you right back dangling from that window, waiting to fall." And although I had heard the phrase for twenty-five years, her words "You need to take care of yourself" still did not sink in.

Grandmother Oak

They sent me to Springbank, a religious retreat center—a place of beauty, wisdom, and peace. Once there, I ached to participate fully, but could not. I watched as women young and old sang and danced and told their stories with strength and authority. Not so long ago I had been one of them. Now I could barely whisper my name.

Unable to bear my brokenness, I went along the path to the ancient oak tree the nuns had named Grandmother Oak, and curled beneath her branches. In times like this I had never been able to find God in church. Why should I? The institutionalized church, which could deal with everything from polishing brass to AIDS, could not bring itself to deal with survivors of abuse and violence. With few exceptions, churches' concerns over sexual abuse are still limited to ensuring that their clergy behave themselves so their denominations do not get sued.

I thought, "We survivors are like the pauper Lazarus, catching the crumbs dropped from a heavily laden table." I prayed as best I could, but mostly felt the age-old wisdom of the oak, just as I had absorbed the grace so freely offered by my horses. I gathered a dozen acorns from the gnarled tree and retreated to the solitude of my room.

Our program centered on creating various art forms. My art was awful—full of chaos and twisted darkness, always ending in great heaving sobs that threatened to pull my guts right up my throat and out my mouth.

"Be gentle with yourself," the staff encouraged. *Be gentle?* I blurted angrily to myself, *What in God's name does that mean?* Sister Carol was more specific: "Go take a long, hot bath."

It had been years since I had taken a long, hot bath. When I was fifteen, my mother had yanked me from the shower, sexually assaulted me with a steel pipe, and smashed my head against the cold tile floor until I lost consciousness. When I awoke I had to clean up the blood, barely keeping up with what I was losing.

So bathtubs were not exactly a place of consolation.

This one was different, though. It felt safe. So take a long bath I did, and it melted a tiny opening in my soul.

I Had to Stop Running

The last day at Springbank I learned a great truth. In spite of all the years of therapy, the workshops I had led, the sermons I had preached, and the healing services I had designed; in spite of all my efforts to act as if none of this had affected me, to please, to function, to continuously produce, to put it all behind me—in spite of all these things, I had never learned to sit with my pain. I had to stop running. I had to stop doing. I had to stop taking care of everyone else. I had to sit and own my pain. I had to retrieve my soul. This, it seemed, would be the hardest task of all.

I came home and potted the seeds from Grandmother Oak. They were a reminder of the length and promise of the process.

And as I sat and struggled, God dropped a great gift into my lap. After a year of searching, some dear friends told us about a perfect place in the country for my family to live and keep our horses in our own backyard. A new dimension was added by my father, whose sorrow was great not only over the plight of his daughter, but over the loss of his second wife to a severe stroke and a nursing home she would never be able to leave.

When my dad saw the gorgeous country home, the pond, and the stunning twenty-five acres, so close to the Pee Dee River on which he had grown up, he decided to buy into the property. He put up his own home so he might live to see his daughter grow well, be amongst his grandchildren, and spend his final years fishing on the lakes, the pond, and the old familiar river.

It was a grand plan, though my therapist was nervous that it might be too soon for such a major life change. But the beauty of the place and the opportunity to fulfill so many dreams at once, perhaps the chance to taste normalcy, turned my head.

Soon I was back in the old productive mode, packing up, selling our house, and buying a country dream. Blind to all the dangers, I convinced myself I was fine. We moved in. Announcing that I was taking a break from therapy, I began to clear the four-acre pasture with a vengeance.

The Panic Returns

But I was not fine. More than once I sobbed into the mane of my horse, Express, who followed me. He would gently nuzzle me back to reality, bringing my focus to the wild sounds, the egrets, the great blue heron, the courting turkeys, and the primitive pond.

The rains were fierce that winter. The children and I would walk to the river and watch its coal-black waters rising, whirling angrily, ripping at trees, then washing its stolen bounty downstream. They loved this sight and begged daily to "go check on the river." To me it was a chilling spectacle.

Around Christmas—a crazy time even for normal folks—the panic slowly seeped back in. Choirs of angels did not bring glad tidings; I heard only a sinister chorus that reinforced my failures, my worthlessness, and sneered at me that I did not deserve this country dream. The demons had returned, and I was too far gone to ask for help.

So one day, when my son and husband were out and the girls were playing upstairs, the predators took hold. Using my favorite paring knife I made five deliberate cuts, long and deep, on the top of my forearm. As blood gushed over the kitchen counter, I took a hammer and repeatedly smashed the bleeding arm, punishing myself for my shame, my worthlessness, my inability to get well. Then, lapsing into my functioning mode, I noted coolly that I had just committed a typical survivor's act: self-mutilation.

I dialed the local hot line and demanded they find my psychiatrist. Instead, they traced the call. Just at the point when my daughters found me and I was babbling something about mommy being fine, the sheriff and the ambulance roared into the driveway, my son and husband behind them.

Bill was white, my girls were crying, my son was cleaning up my blood, and the sheriff was making sure no one else had done this. All these people, all this chaos, all this pain—all my causing. If I were not strapped to a stretcher, I would have reached for a bigger knife and hacked at the other arm.

Closing the wounds took forty-seven stitches, all accomplished with skill and kindness by a lovely woman who never once made me feel shameful for what I had done.

I spent the next few weeks in a Haldol haze, lower and more hopeless than I had ever felt. My arm throbbed, my spirit was shredded, and I felt as if I had blown out part of my brain.

I struggled to find places of peace where the pain did not follow. I spent hours at a farm where some friends grew herbs and flowers that they transformed into gift items for their shop. I took delight in watching them create beauty with the flip of a wrist.

At home, I groomed the horses and rode Express. With the kids, I sloshed through the puddles and pond after the endless rains. Slowly I dared to hope that I might, at some point, have one good day. But so far there were only moments, and they were not enough to keep me going.

One night, after yet another great rain, I lay in bed unable to sleep. I was ever so weary, so tired of trying. Even the curls had left my hair, as if they could not bear my presence.

All the failures of the past months crowded my spirit, and before I knew it, the demons were upon me, ready with a fresh plan. My brain swirled with all that I had caused myself and others, and the black waters of the raging river joined these thoughts to form a whirling beckoning mass.

The river. It was close. It was cold. It was a rapid torrent. It was not my friend. I tried to think of my family, but the release that the rushing waters offered squashed what remnant of rationality I had left. A voice inside me said, *If you kill yourself, your mother wins.* I answered, *She won years ago, I'm too tired to fight anymore.*

Express

I stepped outside into the light of a full moon. Even before my eyes could adjust, I saw him. Standing tall behind the fence was my horse, Express. Ears forward, he watched my every move.

I turned toward the river, but he nickered. Fearful he would wake someone, I sloshed back to the paddock. His wise Arabian eyes were wide and alert. I went to the fence to pet him, but he pulled back, prancing and nickering. I reached toward him, but he backed away further. Any minute he would wake the dogs and everything would go awry. I opened the paddock and went in next to him.

The great Anglo-Arab stood firm and large in the moonlight. He studied me, his eyes reproachful, and would not let me touch him. I shivered, and suddenly longed for the warmth of his broad back and the smell of his mane. Again he backed away, and in frustration I let out a cry that soon became a hard and desperate sob. He came, nuzzling me, placing his body so that I could hold him and weep into his mane.

For twenty minutes or more he did not move a muscle, his feet planted firmly in the muddy paddock, while I cried my exhaustion and despair. When I calmed down he licked my face, making me laugh, and soon I noticed how the moon sat in glory over the pond. The spring peepers had just begun to sound, the puddles glowed, and moths danced in the moonbeams. Nothing I had ever felt was as soft and warm as Express's muzzle.

I looked at him evenly and quoted Deuteronomy as best as I could remember: "I offer you this day the choice of life or death, blessing or curse. Choose life, and you and your descendants will live; love the Lord your God, obey God, and hold fast to God: that is the life for you."

I Chose Life

I kissed Express on the nose, thanked him profusely, and turned back to the house. He watched me from the corner of the fence, and was standing there still when I went to bed. As I came in the door I noticed the pot where I had planted Grandmother Oak's acorns. One of them had sprouted. I sat down at the kitchen table. I chose life.

I chose life in spite of the pain, and because of the joy; in spite of a mother who tortured me, and because of a father who would die to save me; in spite of those who would never understand, and because of those who cared; in spite of the church, and because of the grace of God.

I chose life so my mother would not win and I might help others who suffer as I do. I chose life for my sister, my brother, my husband, and my children. I chose life for my friends and my animals, for guardian angels that masquerade as horses, and for all of God's great and glorious creation. I chose life for myself and for God who had called me back three times. I chose life, and then went off to bed.

I Used to Hit My Kids

Jean Evans with Sally Stich

Jean Evans (a pseudonym), a Colorado housewife and mother of three, details the difficulty she encountered in attempting to control her abusive behavior toward her children. An abused child herself, Evans found herself following in her own mother's footsteps, often resorting to verbal intimidation and physical abuse to punish her children when they misbehaved. After kicking one of her daughters in a fit of rage, Evans writes, she realized that she needed professional help. At the suggestion of the local social services department, she enrolled in Parent Aide, a national program that trains people to work one-on-one with abusive parents. Evans explains how her Parent Aide counselors helped her to control her anger and explore more effective ways to discipline her children. The following selection was written with Sally Stich, an author who frequently writes about parental issues.

"Stop bugging us," I yelled at 3-year-old Julie and 2-year-old Jennifer, who had interrupted the conversation I was having with my husband, Jay, for what seemed like the millionth time. I was trying to tell him how the girls had gotten into his shaving cream, how Julie kept wetting her pants, and how the baby, Jeremy, hadn't napped much.

"Mommy!" Julie screamed. "She took my . . ."

"Shut up!" I said. Then I kicked her.

As her legs flew out from under her, she screamed again, but this was a different scream from before. I kicked her once more, her shriek still ringing in my head. "I hate you," I thought. "I'm sick of you, sick of everything."

Jay grabbed Julie and put her down on the rug out of range of my foot. She wasn't hurt, but she was scared. Realizing what I'd done, I threw my arms around Jay, sobbing, "I'm my mother all over again."

"Mommy's Having Some Trouble"

He patted my back until I calmed down, and then I picked up Julie. "I'm so sorry," I said. "Mommy's having some trouble." She snuggled into me, and we all sat on the sofa and watched TV. We probably looked just like any other family, but I knew that I needed help.

It wasn't hard for me to call social services: I'd called them two years earlier, when Jennifer was a newborn. I'll never forget the day I stood over her crib after she had been crying for hours. I was exhausted. Suddenly I pictured myself picking her up and throwing her across the room; I saw her little body shatter against the wall. And then I started to cry. "My God," I whispered to myself, "what am I doing?"

Making the call then was terrifying. I was afraid the kids would be taken away from me. I even imagined myself behind bars. But I forced myself to dial the number. As it turned out, the girls were not taken from Jay and me. I saw a social worker for about eight months, and after a while I felt more in control.

We moved to a bigger apartment on the outskirts of Denver, and I thought the extra space would make my life easier. But the garden-level apartment was pretty depressing.

Jay was working more than ten hours a week of mandatory over-time as a draftsman, so he wasn't around much. I was stuck in a dark apartment with two toddlers and no car. I also became pregnant short-ly after the move, and was overwhelmed with fatigue. Sometimes I slapped the girls when they disobeyed me. But my real specialty was screaming.

One day I caught them "playing" with Jay's razor. "If you get cut I'll have to take you to the hospital, and they'll take you away," I yelled. They responded just as I had when my mother yelled at me: They lowered their eyes and looked at their hands. My chest hurt as I watched them. They reminded me of me as a scared kid.

I tried to tell myself that I only blew up when the girls were really naughty, or when I was really tired. I think I truly believed that everything was basically okay—until I kicked Julie.

Parent Aide

When I called social services the next day and told a social worker what had happened, she said I had two choices: I could join a self-help group made up of other parents like myself, or I could take part in a program called Parent Aide. This national program trains people, most of them volunteers, to work one-on-one with abusive parents. The aides meet with the parent in her own home for three hours a week, talking with her about parenthood issues and teaching her better ways to deal with daily problems. I decided this program would be the most helpful for me.

The first aide and I just didn't click. I was eventually paired with Jim and Char, a couple in their 40s whose children were grown. I knew I had to tell them all the things I'd done to my kids. So I told them about kicking Jennifer, about wanting to throw Julie across the room, and about the yelling.

Then I found myself talking about my own childhood, something I had never discussed with anyone except Jay. As I told them how my mother was quick to swing and slow to talk, how my sister and I were blamed for everything that went wrong, I felt scared. Even though I was an adult, I was still afraid of my mother's wrath. When I finished, Char said, "Maybe your mother didn't know better, but I'm sure we can help you."

One of the first areas that Jim and Char focused on was housework. By now the baby was 13 months old, and his diapers and bottles seemed to be everywhere. Our apartment was always a mess, and the worse it got, the more uptight I got. If I stepped on one of the girls' toys, I'd scream. Sometimes I'd slap them too.

I told Jim and Char that I always started cleaning in the bathroom, which was the easiest room, and finished in the kitchen, which was the biggest mess and the destination for much of the kids' junk.

"Start in the kitchen," Char said, "and put everything away first. Then work your way to the bathroom." It sounded too simple, but after a week or so, I was able to get the house in order.

Changing my housekeeping methods helped, but I knew this wasn't the most important issue. Now it was time to focus on learning better ways to cope with the kinds of situations that triggered my abusive behavior.

Difficult Dinner Hour

The first half hour of my time with Jim and Char was always devoted to problems that had arisen during the past week. One week we talked about our disruptive dinner hour. The girls and Jeremy usually played with their food and refused to sit at the table. Sometimes a food fight would erupt.

Char asked me what I did when the kids misbehaved. With great shame, I told her I'd yell, "Damn it, why can't you be good?" I'd also threaten to send them to bed without dinner the next night, but I never held to it.

Jim suggested that as soon as Jeremy and the girls acted up, I should remove their plates and say dinner was over. I squirmed at the thought, remembering how many times my mother had sent me to bed with no dinner for things I'd done—and things I hadn't.

"I'm uncomfortable with that," I said, explaining why.

"Your mother took dinner away as a punishment for everything," Char said. "You're taking it away for bad behavior at the table."

"You'll probably have to do it only once," Jim added.

He was right. That night, when Jeremy started throwing his food, I warned him to stop. He turned over his plate. I scooped up his food and his plate and put them in the sink. I put him, screaming, in his room. The girls were shocked into silence, but they've all behaved much better during mealtimes ever since.

Jim and Char's support and understanding were as important as their suggestions. They knew what a struggle it was to stifle my yelling, to keep my hand at my side when I wanted to raise it against my kids. They appreciated the pain I still felt about my own childhood and about what I had done to my children. They made me see that it was okay to make mistakes.

Although Jim and Char came every week, I still felt isolated from other moms. So I joined a mothers' group organized by a local interfaith social-service agency. We met once a week at the community center in town; transportation and child care were provided. The group wasn't therapy—it was a way for me to meet other moms and talk about problems we all faced as parents. Sometimes we even went on field trips with our kids.

I looked forward to each Friday's meeting. I never talked about abusing my children, but I did talk about my frustration with my husband's long hours. "He's not doing it to hurt you," one woman said. "It's mandatory." Jay had been telling me that for years, but I never really believed him. Now, when someone else said the same thing, I realized that his working late had nothing to do with me.

Learning by Watching Other Moms

I learned a lot by watching certain moms. When one little girl got all wet and dirty playing in a puddle on one of our outings, her mother said, "Looks like we'll have to rinse you out when we get home."

I always came unglued when my kids got so much as a spot on their clothes. "Look what you've done to that outfit," I'd yell, yanking it off and throwing it into the washer.

That day, I saw a more realistic reaction: It's okay for kids to get dirty. In fact, it's fun. A few weeks later, Jennifer was playing with bubbles and spilled the soapy liquid on her shorts. She looked at me and said, "I'll go change."

I bit my tongue. Instead of yelling, I said, "Don't worry. We probably won't need much soap to wash those shorts." She giggled.

After I'd been going to the group for about a year and a half, I had a particularly bad day. I sat around the apartment feeling sorry for myself. Even though I'd made great progress, there didn't seem to be much recognition of my efforts. I knew it would be years before I could tell if there was a payoff. After all, you don't know how your kids are going to turn out until they're grown.

Then the phone rang. The leader of the group said she'd chosen me "mom of the month." She explained her choice by saying, "I've seen a real difference in the way you treat your kids." After the shock came a high so high I was floating. How did she know what I'd been feeling?

When the award was announced, the other mothers in the group were surprised to learn that I'd been struggling to control my impulses to hit my kids. I'd known these women for more than a year and had never once mentioned anything but minor problems. Only the leader had known the truth about my situation.

I'm a Much Smarter Mom Now

My children are now 5, 8, and 9. I no longer see Jim and Char, but I know they're just a phone call away if I feel myself slipping. Fortunately, that doesn't happen often. I think I'm a much smarter mom now.

The other day I was watching my children from the kitchen window. Suddenly I saw Julie raise her hand in a gesture that is totally unacceptable in my book. I ran outside and asked what she was doing. Her explanation told me that she thought she was calling her sister a bad name in sign language. "That's not what God gave you hands for," I said. "He wants you to use your hands for nice things." She looked embarrassed, then gave me a hug and went back to play.

My husband, who had seen Julie's gesture, asked me what I'd said. When I told him, he said, "I never would have thought of explaining it that way. Good work." Those last two words were like music. I suspected then that my kids are going to turn out just fine.

A Doctor's Encounter with Child Abuse

Pamela Grim

One of the most difficult aspects of treating abused children is making the diagnosis, writes Pamela Grim, an emergency room physician and frequent contributor to *Discover* magazine. The diagnosis is all the more difficult in the emergency room, Grim explains, because doctors only have a few minutes of observation on which to base their opinion. However, she explains, one primary clue is when the parent of an injured child wants to leave the hospital quickly. In the following essay, Grim recalls her encounter with such a parent—the angry mother of a child Grim suspected was being abused. When Grim tried to prevent the woman from leaving the emergency room, an altercation ensued and security had to be called. A physical examination of the child revealed injuries and bruises indicative of child abuse, the author states, and the police began an investigation of the boy's father. Grim describes her struggle to determine whether or not her decision to pursue her suspicion of abuse—which would probably lead to the breakup of the child's family—was the right thing to do.

"Medical clearance?" I asked as I paused at the door of Room 7. Inside, a social worker from Child Protective Services (CPS) was watching over two small children. The boy wore only a man's plaid shirt; the girl was dressed in a filthy white jumper. Someone must have reported these children for suspected child endangerment. They were here in the emergency room for a brief physical exam.

"Is it for neglect or abuse?" I asked.

"Neglect, we think," the social worker replied. "Mom left them at a bus stop. Said she'd come back, but she never did." The worker reached out toward the girl. "Now, here is Tonya. She's four. And this is Raymond. He's two."

Raymond stood gazing up at me, one hand gripping the social worker's pants. He looked as if he would never let go. I pulled his shirt open and examined his chest and back, looking for marks. In the last child abuse case I'd seen, a little girl had come in with circular first- and second-degree burns scattered across her back. Cigarette burns. This kid looked okay, though, just dirty.

I knelt down to look at his sister. "How are you doing, little squirt?" She was a beautiful little girl, open and animated.

"I'm four," she said and showed me three fingers.

"Well, that's very big," I said, smiling, "and for big kids we have a big treat. We have ginger ale. Would you like some?"

She nodded, eyes wide.

"What do you say?" the social worker prompted—an instinctual mother.

The little girl smiled even more and ducked her head in shyness. "Shut up," she said. "Shut up, shut up, shut up."

I looked up at the social worker, my jaw slack with surprise.

"You wouldn't believe some of the stuff that comes out of these kids' mouths," she said.

The little girl turned to her brother and gave him a shove. "Shut up, you stupid whore," she said. "Get me a beer."

Diagnosing Abuse Can Be Difficult

Child abuse, child neglect. For a doctor one of the most difficult parts of treating abused children is simply making the diagnosis. In the emergency room (ER) this can be even more difficult because a diagnosis must often be made after only a minute or two of observation. One rule of thumb, I've learned, is to be suspicious of any parent who arrives in an ER with an injured child and wants to leave too quickly.

One hot summer night it happened just that way. A mother had her son by the arm—he was about five—and she dragged him up to me.

"How much longer is it going to be?" she demanded.

It should have been obvious that we were all working as fast as we could. I had just intubated someone who had taken an overdose of antidepressants, and was rushing off to see a woman with heart failure. From where I was standing I could see into the room where the woman lay on her bed struggling to breathe while a burly-looking man sat next to her, holding her hand.

"Ma'am," I said, "It's going to be a little while."

"Well, I don't have a little while. My son is hurt." Something in her tone made me pause for a moment and look at her.

"Dear," I said, "everyone here is very sick tonight."

"Don't you 'dear' me. I'm going to another ER. I've waited over two hours. I want some service."

Ed, the charge nurse, came hustling over. "I put you in that room exactly ten minutes ago." He pointed emphatically at his watch. "So don't tell her you've been waiting for hours." He stopped next to me and whispered in my ear, "I'm worried about this kid."

I knelt down to look at the whimpering child. He had obviously broken his forearm—the radius. There was swelling at the midshaft of the radius, and the arm beyond canted away at an angle. This was odd. When people fall, they generally fracture the forearm near the wrist. A fracture in the middle of the bone is much rarer and usually occurs from a direct blow. They're called nightstick fractures because people have gotten them from defending themselves against blows from a police officer's nightstick. This kid had such a fracture.

"How did this happen?" I asked the boy.

He looked up at his mother and then at me and silently drew away.

"I'm leaving," the mother said, giving the child's other arm a tug. He just stood there, rooted to the floor.

"Wait," I said. "I need to know."

"Don't you 'wait' me. I'm taking my son and I'm leaving." I looked at her. I had seen a thousand women who were fine mothers and who looked just like her, but looks mean nothing. As I gazed up at her from where I knelt, I was sure—well, pretty sure—that she had hurt her child.

"The Kid Stays Here"

I squatted there a moment, debating this. After all, what proof did I have? Besides, she was going to another ER. She said so. But I was angry. I was angry at her for yanking her child around and for being so damn unreasonable.

"I'm sorry," I said, standing up. I was conscious that I was standing between this woman and the exit. "You can't go anywhere with that child."

She glared at me. "What do you mean?"

"You can't leave," I said. Any parent, child abuser or saint, would be angry with this order, but this wasn't the time for second thoughts. I had taken my stand.

"You mean I can't leave?"

"You can, but the child can't."

"You're crazy." She shook her finger in my face and yanked the boy's arm.

I got angrier, much angrier—it was as if the scene was lit up by firecrackers.

"The kid stays here," I said.

"You," she repeated emphatically, "are crazy." She yanked again at her son's arm, but this time he pulled away from her, looking with terror at both of us.

"You can't go," I said loudly. "Not until we know what's going on here."

She tried to pass me.

"Call security," I said, turning to Ed. I hadn't noticed he'd left to take care of a drunk with a head wound dripping blood. I was alone in the hall without backup—very poor planning. If I headed for the desk, she would be out the door before I could get help.

"Maggy," I shouted at the desk clerk, "get security."

"This is my boy," the woman shouted. "I can do what I want with him."

The boy was wailing and trying to back away from her. She yanked at his arm again.

"I'm telling you." It took me a moment to realize that I was the one shouting. "I'm telling you, you can't do anything you want. You can't hurt a child, and you can't leave until I know what's going on. If you do, I'm going to have the police after you."

"Police!" she shouted. "You have no idea. So don't you dare threaten me."

She struck out at me and I ducked. At that moment, the firecrackers went out. I was willing to make a scene, but I was not prepared to be attacked. I stepped away, but she came after me, swinging with her free hand and trying to grab my clothes. She kicked me, just catching the side of my knee. As I went down, all I could see were her feet kicking near my face. When I looked up, I saw the burly man who had been sitting with his mother pin the woman to the wall. I got up and began to unpry her fingers from the boy's forearm. As I pulled him free, security, like the Texas Rangers, came tearing down the hall.

All I could think was that the child would never forget this, me pulling him away from his mother.

"She's got my baby," the woman screamed. "That bitch has my baby."

"She needs to leave," I shouted at the security guards. "She can't stay here."

"Let's go," said Lenny, one of the guards. "That 'bitch' is the doctor, and what she says goes. You gotta leave."

The woman stood, arms crossed, staring at me. Ed had come running back down the hall—he was a big guy and hard to ignore.

"The doctor says you need to leave," he said, looming over her. "I'm escorting you out to the waiting room, and we will talk about what you need to do next."

She allowed Ed to take her by the arm, but then glanced back at me and said, "I'm going to hunt you down, bitch. I'm going to get you for this."

Signs of Abuse

The doors closed. It was a large ER, filled with patients and their families. Everyone stood in stunned silence. After a beat, though, the boy began to wail and the room broke into chatter.

Lenny carried the child back to a cubicle. My ankle was hurt, and I limped after them.

"Are you okay?" Lenny asked me.

"Yeah, fine, fine," I said, but my ankle hurt like hell.

Lenny set the child down on the examining table. He was still wailing.

"Let's get this shirt off him," I said. I thought I had seen marks when I was fighting with the mother.

I had. There were two bruises on the boy's face and bruises on both arms, oval bruises the size of thumbprints. And on his back were dozens of slender, elliptical marks—some were scars, but some were fresh and bright red. They were cord marks, abrasions from being hit on the naked back and buttocks with a loop of electrical cord. Unmistakable signs of abuse.

I traced the scars with my fingers, feeling the ridges. The child was just whimpering now. One of the nurses offered him a stuffed doll.

"Sweetie," I said, as I knelt down in front of him. "How did you break your arm?"

He stared at me, unblinking.

"Can you tell me? You don't have to be scared. I promise no one will hurt you."

His chin shook. He looked away and said, "D-d-d-d."

"Who?"

"D-d-d-d. . . ." He gave up and rubbed at his eyes with the wrist of his good arm.

That's all he would say.

The next afternoon the investigating officer, Tiny, dropped by to take a statement from me. Tiny weighs in at a good 350 pounds. I had taken care of his asthma attacks several times.

"What do you think happened?" I asked him.

"I can't comment on an ongoing investigation," he told me. "But between you and me, it may be that the missus has been knocked around a few times by her husband, and I suspect the guy takes more than an occasional swing at the kids, especially this one."

"Why hasn't she filed a domestic violence complaint?"

Tiny shook his head. "He'd lose his job. In fact, he's already been suspended. He's a cop and there's big trouble down at the station. Apparently some people knew about what was going on and never said anything."

"Why is that?"

Tiny frowned. "You protect your own, I guess."

"What's going to happen?"

"If they charge him—and there's a pretty good chance of that—and if he's convicted, he'll lose his job. That leaves the three kids and Momma. . . . I don't know what will happen to them."

I leaned back in the chair and studied the ceiling. What good does it do to save the child and destroy the family? I looked over at Tiny. "How does this happen? Just who does this to children?"

"Well," Tiny said with a shrug, "the kid's dad . . . he's a good man and all. I knew him in high school. But he drinks, and when he drinks, he gets mean." He paused, then shrugged. "There's lots of other reasons people hit kids, but this is a big one. People will behave like any kind of animal when booze is involved."

A History of Abuse

On a hunch, I pulled the medical records for the police officer's wife. Sure enough, there were multiple ER admissions for minor trauma culminating with, about six months before, an admission for multiple facial contusions and a nasal fracture from "a fall down the stairs." Spousal abuse. Clearly. The problem was—though I had no memory of it—I had seen her. I had read the X-rays correctly; I had sewn up her cuts. But I had missed the diagnosis. Nowhere in my notes did I bring up the possibility of domestic violence. If I had made the diagnosis then, perhaps someone could have intervened before the child got hurt. I had my chance long before the scene in the hallway, and I blew it. I had no one to blame but myself.

As the days and then weeks passed, I tried to find out what happened to the child and the family, but I kept meeting dead ends. Tiny wouldn't give me any information. Nobody I talked to knew the family or admitted that they did.

I wondered if the boy had been farmed out to a relative. What would he remember of the struggle and his broken arm? What about his mother? Was she a victim? She certainly was when I saw her after her "fall," but what was she that day I saw her with her son? Victim or accomplice?

And what about me? Was I an unwitting accomplice by missing the diagnosis the first time? And in doing what I thought was right for a little boy that afternoon, did I ultimately make things worse? Did I destroy a family? There had to have been a better way, but what was it?

That day, I had acted. I had done what I thought I had to do. But as is so often the case in emergency medicine, I will never really know if I did the right thing.

CHAPTER 4

PREVENTING
CHILD ABUSE

Contemporary Issues
Companion

RECOGNIZING THE SIGNS OF ABUSE

Allen Douma

In the following selection, Allen Douma describes signs that frequently indicate the presence of child physical, emotional, or sexual abuse. Although there are no universal profiles of abusive parents or abused children, he explains, researchers have identified a number of common characteristics that can serve as red flags. For example, Douma writes, abusive parents will often be excessively critical of their children; they may also exhibit signs of depression and an inability to cope with stress. Douma also lists typical injuries due to physical abuse that can alert investigators or concerned individuals. For instance, he explains, abused children will often exhibit bruises and welts in the shape of the object that was used to beat them, such as belt buckles and electrical cords. He advises that investigators should also become wary when children sustain suspicious injuries or if discrepancies exist between the child's and the parent's explanation for the injury. Douma is a physician who writes a syndicated column pertaining to health issues.

Most of us, at one time or another, have been outraged by newspaper or TV reports about children who have been abandoned, neglected or abused.

Unable to comprehend such shocking events, we find ourselves hoping that the incidents are isolated and rare. Unfortunately, they aren't. Each year, over 1 million children in North America are abused or neglected, and over 1,000 children die each year at the hands of caretakers. . . .

The Signs of an Abusive Parent

Child abuse, neglect and maltreatment can occur in any family and in any neighborhood. And it can affect children of all ages. Although there is no single profile that fits every case, researchers have identified some factors that are generally characteristic of an abusive parent:
- Is depressed and unable to cope with stress.
- Has experienced violence firsthand.

- Comes from and is part of emotionally isolated family.
- Was abused as a child.
- Has money problems.
- Abuses drugs or alcohol.
- Is very critical of his/her child.
- Is very rigid in disciplining child.

There are four major types of child maltreatment: physical abuse, child neglect, sexual abuse and emotional abuse.

Physical abuse of children includes any non-accidental physical injury caused by the child's caretaker. Although the injury is not an accident, the adult may not have intended to hurt the child.

The injury might have resulted from overdiscipline or physical punishment inappropriate to the child's age. This usually happens when an adult is frustrated or angry and strikes, shakes or throws a child.

Occasionally, physical abuse is intentional. For example, it is highly likely that the injury is intentional when a caretaker burns, bites, pokes, cuts or twists limbs.

Signs of Physical Abuse in Children

Young children frequently fall down and bump into things, resulting in injuries to their elbows, chins, noses, foreheads and other bony areas. But bruises and marks on the soft tissue of the face, back, neck, buttocks, upper arms, thighs, backs of legs or genitals are more likely a sign of physical abuse.

Injuries to the abdomen or the head often go undetected until there are internal injuries. Injuries to the abdomen can cause swelling, tenderness and vomiting. Injuries to the head may cause swelling, dizziness, blackouts, retinal detachment and even death. In particular, bilateral black eyes could be an indication of bleeding in the brain.

Additional signs of possible physical abuse include:

- The injury is in the shape of an object (belt buckle, electric cord, etc.).
- A child too young to walk or climb has broken bones or other very unlikely injury.
- There's a discrepancy between the child's and parent's explanation of the injury.
- The parent has an unreasonable explanation for the injury.
- There's obvious evidence of neglect.
- Fearful behavior by child and parent is evident.

Child neglect can be physical, educational or emotional. Physical neglect includes delay in seeking health care, expulsion from the home and inadequate supervision. Educational neglect includes the allowance of chronic truancy or failure to enroll a child in school without a home program.

Signs of Emotional and Sexual Abuse

Emotional neglect includes marked inattention to the child's needs for affection, failure to provide needed psychological care, spouse abuse in the child's presence, and permission for drug or alcohol use by the child. Sexual abuse includes fondling a child's genitals, intercourse, rape, sodomy, exhibitionism and commercial sexual exploitation. Many experts believe that sexual abuse is the most underreported form of child maltreatment because of the secrecy or "conspiracy of silence."

Sexual abuse may have occurred if the child:

- Tells you he/she was sexually mistreated.
- Has difficulty walking or sitting; genital or rectal pain; genital itching; swelling, redness, or discharge.
- Has difficulty eating or sleeping; soils or wets pants after being potty trained; acts like a much younger child; exhibits excessive crying or sadness; withdraws from activities.
- Talks about or acts out sexual acts beyond normal sex play for his/her age.

Emotional abuse includes acts or omissions that cause serious behavioral, cognitive, emotional or mental disorders. For example, the parents or caregivers may use extreme or bizarre forms of punishment, such as confinement in a dark closet. Less severe acts, such as habitual scapegoating, belittling or rejection, are often difficult to identify, much less prove.

The signs of emotional abuse include aggressive or withdrawn behavior, shying away from physical contact with parents or adults, and being afraid to go home.

Nurseries for Parents on the Edge

Stephanie Simon

In the following selection, Stephanie Simon examines the growing popularity of crisis nurseries, facilities where exasperated parents can leave their children when they feel they are on the brink of physically harming them. Sometimes parents need a few hours or days to collect their wits, Simon writes, and crisis nurseries provide them with the time and space to cool down. However, she notes, crisis nurseries do have some key limitations: They provide a quick fix during stressful situations but do not offer the long-term intervention that some at-risk parents need. Regardless of the limitations of crisis nurseries, Simon explains, they still provide a necessary service. Simon is a staff writer for the *Los Angeles Times*.

You love her so much. But she's whining.

And you can't stand it anymore.

She's pulling on your legs, wailing, her cheeks blotched red, snot gobbed on her nose, whining and wanting, this daughter of yours. She whines, whines, whines and you'll never get peace and she whines, whines, wails and her big brother howls and the baby wakes up in the other room screeching and you'll never, never, never have a moment to yourself.

She whines and he howls and the baby screeches and you could just smack them all.

You could. Just smack them. You could. Next time, you might.

And it frightens you.

"I just felt in tears," said Ellen Jackson-Cato, one mother who has been there. "I felt like I was going to lose control."

She didn't. Her three children are fine. And so is she, thanks in part to the Greater Minneapolis Crisis Nursery, an unusual program designed to head off child abuse by giving on-the-brink parents a break.

Providing a Respite

The nursery's brochure says it all: "Sometimes a few days apart from your kids is the best way to keep your family together." This is not about the county hustling children from dangerous homes. Not about a judge taking custody from bad parents. It's about moms and dads deciding, on their own, that they need some time off before they explode. The nursery gives them that respite.

"We give them space," director Kathy Schaaf said.

Dozens of crisis nurseries around the nation boast similar goals. But most, including Para Los Ninos in Los Angeles, are open only during the day. The Minneapolis program is one of just a few to care for kids around the clock. Parents can drop off children, newborns to age 7, for up to three days at a time. It's free. And anyone in the county can use it. Each year, about 720 families do.

There are bubble baths for the toddlers who lost their mother—and their home—in a fire. Tuna melts for the twins whose mom couldn't stand one more day of dragging her family to shelters. There are puzzles and bikes and *Cinderella* videos for kids whose mothers are fleeing abusive boyfriends or adjusting to new antidepressants.

The nursery cared for Jackson-Cato's three children when she needed some time alone with her husband to talk through the aggravations fraying their marriage. It took in Heather Houge's three kids—redhead Josh, ever-revved-up Jesse and Chelsea, the sturdy toddler—when she felt she couldn't go on without a full night's sleep. And when her grandma died and she couldn't stop crying. And when she suffered an epileptic seizure and had to stay in the hospital overnight.

"There's every reason you can think of, and 100 more, why people use us," Schaaf said.

Or, as Houge put it: "This is a good place for if you're going to fall apart. . . . For the safety of your children and for your own health, you really, really need it."

Yet even their biggest advocates point out that crisis nurseries have a key limitation: They're geared more toward quick fixes than lasting interventions. After all, few parents in crisis—homeless, unemployed, addicted, unstable—can solve their problems in three days.

That's why some experts worry that parents may come to use crisis nurseries as a crutch, forestalling an immediate blowup but never dealing with the stresses that pushed them to the edge in the first place. "If it's used as an excuse for not dealing with the substantive issues that threaten a family, then that can be a problem in itself," said Kevin Kirkpatrick, a spokesman for the advocacy group Prevent Child Abuse America.

To prod parents to confront those deeper problems, social workers at the Greater Minneapolis Crisis Nursery ask them to list three goals they'll work on during their respite. Those goals might be as ambitious as kicking a drug habit or as basic as taking a long, hot bath so they won't be as edgy when their little one whines.

The Staff Stays Attuned to Pleas for Help

If parents aren't willing to cooperate with social workers—if it seems they're using the nursery as a free baby-sitting service, not as a chance to deal with a crisis—administrators will ask them not to return. But such cases are rare. And staff members are cautioned not to dismiss pleas for help just because a parent's problems seem trivial. If a mom feels she's in crisis, she is—and her kids will be too, unless she gets a break.

"We see suburban middle-class moms from intact families, with husbands, in here with a toddler because they're totally stressed out and need help with parenting skills," said Lynn Lewis, who's in charge of the nursery's social workers. "And we see homeless moms not wanting their kids to sleep in the car."

In an initiative that started in 1998, counselors try to nudge those clients with overwhelming problems toward signing "contracts" to work with the nursery beyond three days. If a parent agrees to meet regularly with social workers and allow home visits, nursery staff will prep them for job interviews, guide them through the welfare system, hook them up with food pantries—whatever it takes to stabilize the family so parenting doesn't seem so overwhelming.

One family counselor, a nurse, gave an HIV test to a mom who had been raped and couldn't focus on her kids for fear she had AIDS. Another drove a mother from apartment to apartment to help her find decent, affordable housing.

Even with such help, about a quarter of the nursery's clients return month after month after month, pushing the limit of 30 days of care per child per year. Because so many of their clients are homeless or transient and are hard to track, the nursery has not compiled data on how many parents overcome their problems and how many slide into deeper crisis or even end up abusing their kids. Social workers can point to some cheering success stories. But they also see some children coming into the nursery looking hungrier and more ragged each month.

"We are making progress," Schaaf said. "But it's going to be slow. And it'll never be enough."

While there's no central database to track cases nationwide, several crisis nurseries report swelling demand, due in part to welfare reforms that pile stress on struggling families by cutting off benefits if parents don't move toward work.

To handle the demand, the Minneapolis nursery, founded in 1981, expanded in June, 1999, opening a second facility, bright with Winnie the Pooh murals and Minnie Mouse mobiles. Between them, the two buildings can now serve 35 children a night. Even so, the nursery turns parents away several times a week, sometimes because all beds are full and sometimes because there are not enough care providers to maintain the state-mandated ratio of one staffer for every three children.

Nurseries Seek Different Approaches

In California too, an overnight crisis nursery run by the Sacramento Children's Home has found "we turn away as many kids as we take in," director Sue Bonk said. The center will soon add four beds to its current six. The Bay Area Crisis Nursery in Concord, meanwhile, is opening a facility to serve children ages 6 to 10 after nearly two decades of growing demand.

Other crisis nurseries are experimenting with different approaches, such as sending a baby-sitter to a family's home to take care of the kids while the parents take care of themselves.

The catch, as always, is money.

There are no federal funds set aside for this kind of crisis care, so most nurseries rely on state and local grants—and lots of private contributions.

In Minneapolis, about 600 volunteers pitch in to cook lunches, read bedtime stories and wash off the squirmy 11-month-old who decides mashed potatoes make a nifty hair gel. The nursery also counts on donations to stretch its $1.6-million annual budget by keeping its closets stocked with clothes, baby food, diapers and teddy bears.

Although the nursery is open to anyone, regardless of income, three-quarters of the clients earn less than $10,000 a year. Nearly all are women. And 86% are single. Most say they can't count on any close friends for support. And 38% are homeless. The stresses in their lives loom huge.

By definition, however, they're not bad parents. If they were, they wouldn't realize they need help. "The ones who call us know what it takes to be a good mom," Schaaf said. And they know when they're in danger of falling way short.

Yes, there are times when the nursery staff is wary about returning a child to his parents; they do their best to follow up with home visits. When they suspect a child already has been abused—it happens a couple times a month—they turn the case over to the county.

But for the most part, "you feel good telling the kids, 'Your mommy loves you so much, and that's why you're here,' because you know it's true," nursery volunteer Jennifer Sagawa said. "Their families care enough to try to do something."

It took Angie Rades some time to accept that premise.

The Need for a Break Takes Priority

A college graduate and stay-at-home mom, married with two healthy, bubbly daughters, Rades thought, "God, I'm a failure," the first time she was tempted to use the crisis nursery. She thought she should be able to handle motherhood on her own. Yet there are times, she has found, when she absolutely has to have a break, when her girls need more than she has in her to give.

Those are the times when she feels like slamming 15-month-old Alexis down in her crib and commanding: "Stay in there!" The times when 3-year-old Kiersten requests one more hug and she feels like screaming: "Get away from me! Don't touch me! Can't you just leave me the hell alone!"

Rades says she's never come close to hitting her daughters, not even in these most despairing of moments. But she doesn't want to yell hateful thoughts at them, either. She can't stand the thought that she might lose control and hurt Kiersten with her words, that she might make Alexis feel unloved or unwanted. "I'm afraid," she said. "I'm just afraid."

So when she absolutely cannot cope for a minute longer—"when things," she says, "are just as bad as they can get"—Rades brings Kiersten and Alexis to the nursery, usually just for a 10-hour day, but twice now for overnight stays.

Used to the nursery, which she calls "play group," after several visits over the last few months, Kiersten padded out of her room in borrowed purple pajamas one recent morning, blond hair mussed, bright face peppy, looking for someone to chat with. Her sister was guzzling a bottle from a stranger. Another stranger was guiding a sleepy boy to the bathroom. Unfazed by all the new faces around her, Kiersten sized up her options and went straight for the one empty lap in the room.

"Hi," she said, snuggling up to caretaker Carly Schumacher. "What's your favorite color?"

Hugs, it's clear, are much in demand, even for kids as cheery as Kiersten. For despite the enticing toys in every room, despite the comfy beds made up with cartoon sheets, a stay in the nursery can be disorienting. Home for these kids might be a car, a shelter, or an apartment crowded with three other families, but it's still home, in a way the nursery can never be. Likewise, Mom is still Mom, no matter how frazzled she gets. And it's hard to adjust to three nights without her.

The Joy Gives Way to a Need for Mommy

On this day, for instance, a 2-year-old boy with chubby red cheeks jumps out of bed exuberant, racing around the hallways and grabbing other toddlers in huge, sloppy hugs. But by breakfast, the joy of exploration has faded. Lonely and scared, he whimpers.

"I need my mommy," he says. "Want mommy."

Schumacher tells him his mommy loves him. His mommy, she assures him, will be back soon. He clings to her, unconvinced. "Mommy," he keeps saying. "Want mommy."

At 10 A.M., his mother calls to check on him. Schumacher hands him the phone and he stands there, motionless, listening to mommy, tears rolling down his chubby cheeks. He's too overcome to say a word. When Schumacher finally, gently, hangs up the phone, he jumps in her lap.

For the rest of the morning, he stays there.

FIXING THE FLAWED CHILD WELFARE SYSTEM

David Stoesz and Howard Jacob Karger

Child welfare agencies across the United States are in a state of collapse, write David Stoesz and Howard Jacob Karger, and vulnerable children are falling through the cracks. According to the authors, high staff turnover and a chronic shortage of funds have resulted in child protective agencies that are completely overwhelmed by the rising tide of child abuse and neglect. The child welfare system would benefit from a number of reforms, they maintain, such as the reduction of bureaucratic wastefulness, the reclassification of child abuse as a public safety problem, and the elimination of the family reunification policy. However, the authors explain, the most pressing need is adequate funding, the lack of which has made it impossible for child welfare workers to do their jobs properly. David Stoesz is the Samuel Wurtzel Chair in social work at Virginia Commonwealth University. Howard Jacob Karger is professor and director of doctoral education at the Graduate School of Social Work at the University of Houston. They are coauthors of *The Politics of Child Abuse in America*.

Wearing suits and solemn expressions, New York Mayor Rudolph Giuliani and the city's commissioner of the Administration of Children's Services held a press conference in the spring of 1996 to announce the suspension, for 30 days without pay, of the caseworker and supervisor who had mishandled the Elisa Izquierdo case. Elisa was the six-year-old Bronx girl whose grotesque life and death prompted outraged headlines in November 1995. She had been forced to eat her own feces; she had been sexually abused with a hairbrush; her mother had used her head as a floor mop.

Most maddening of all, city officials had repeatedly been warned by neighbors and school officials that Elisa was in danger, yet they had allowed monitoring of the household to lapse. "It's about time that people be held accountable for their actions, their negligence, and probably even worse than that," the mayor said. "It's the only way you're going to build accountability into the system."

No Accountability

Giuliani had it right. Despite more than 24 deaths of children whose cases were supposedly being monitored, no child welfare employee had ever been dismissed or even suspended by the city. In the wake of Elisa's death, the Child Welfare Administration (CWA) refused to answer questions about the services it had—or had not—provided the Izquierdo family. When journalists and city officials finally penetrated the wall of confidentiality, they found that the agency mandated to protect children from abuse was incapable of doing so.

On average, two children died from abuse and neglect in New York each week. A review of child fatalities by the city's public advocate concluded that "in one third of the cases CWA's own neglect either allowed or contributed to the tragedy." A subsequent state audit found more bad news: In one of five cases child protection workers failed to interview all children in an allegedly abusive family; in two of five cases, workers didn't examine previous reports of child abuse. Nearly a fifth of cases were closed prematurely despite the of risk of future abuse.

The need for accountability is obvious. But at the same time, in pinning the blame on individual employees, we may be missing the forest for the trees. Yes, caseworkers are often poorly trained or underqualified; considering the job description—low pay and daily exposure to profound cruelty—that's not surprising. But most child welfare workers aren't uncaring or indifferent, and they aren't necessarily incompetent. They're simply overwhelmed. The problem is less individual misfeasance than institutional breakdown.

And it's not just the Bronx. In virtually every metropolitan area, services to abused children are in the process of collapse. By early 1996, the public services to care for children had so deteriorated that child welfare agencies in 21 states and the District of Columbia were under court supervision. (Washington, D.C., got its court-appointed receiver when child welfare workers were unable to locate one in four children in foster care.)

A System in Disarray

In 1995, the U.S. Advisory Commission on Child Abuse and Neglect placed the number of child deaths attributable to abuse and neglect at 2,000 per year; of those, most are under the age of four. Together, battering and neglect by parents are a leading cause of death for young children in this country. The Department of Health and Human Services estimates that the number of children abused or neglected annually has more than doubled in the 1990s—from 1.4 million to 2.9 million.

No government function is more crucial than protecting those who cannot protect themselves; no members of our society are more vulnerable than children. Yet few government services are in as much disarray, and as starved for resources, as child welfare services.

Some of the problems, such as archaic and overlapping bureaucracies and a shortage of good applicants, are all too common to city governments in the '90s. But piecemeal policymaking at the federal level has also saddled the system with too many cases—and too few funds. Child welfare efforts have been further distorted by political pressures that have elevated preserving the family above protecting the child.

The result is an overloaded system in which too many children are consigned indefinitely to the purgatory of foster care—or are returned to potentially dangerous homes with insufficient supervision. The real outrage is that, as with Elisa Izquierdo, fatal cases of child abuse are rarely isolated incidents. Rather, a series of incidents over time eventually culminate in a casualty. But that's also a cause for hope: If, as a society, we make the effort, at least some of these deaths are preventable.

Cruel Caps

Reports of child neglect and abuse have skyrocketed since the early '70s, but public funding has stagnated. Therein lies much of the problem. Most federal funding for child protection comes through Title XX, a social services appropriation that was capped in 1974 at $2.5 billion. As of 1996, Title XX is funded at only $4 billion. If it had been indexed for inflation between 1977 and 1992, appropriations would have been $36 billion.

Had funds been calibrated to service demand, they would have increased even more. The same year that Title XX was capped, the Child Abuse Prevention and Treatment Act (CAPTA) was passed. It mandated that a range of children's service providers—teachers, physicians, and counselors, among others—report instances of alleged child maltreatment to public officials. Through CAPTA, child maltreatment was broadly defined to include physical abuse, sexual abuse, and neglect. The result was a dramatic increase in the number of cases reported—but no concurrent increase in funding to process them.

Yet more burdens were piled on child welfare workers in 1980, with the passage of Jimmy Carter's last significant piece of social legislation, the 1980 Adoption Assistance and Child Welfare Act (AACWA). The act had the noblest of intentions: Since the '60s, foster care, designed as a temporary arrangement, had instead become a long-term experience for abused and neglected youngsters, who comprised half of those in foster care. Not only were children left with foster families for years, but many also were bounced willy-nilly from one foster family to another. One study indicated that 34 percent of children in foster care had been there for four years or more. In order to stabilize the lives of foster children, AACWA required "permanency planning" for all children in foster care and, if at all possible, reunification with their biological families.

Title XX funding increased slightly under Carter. But when Ronald Reagan reduced spending by 25 percent and transformed the program into a block grant, AACWA became just one more underfunded mandate for child welfare workers to juggle. By the early '90s, reports of child abuse and neglect had eclipsed 3 million. And by the end of 1992, the number of children in foster care was nearing 500,000. Many children faced a revolving door of foster care, one that in some cases was virtually spinning. A New York boy was placed in 37 different homes during a two-month period; another had lived with 17 different families in 25 days. Compared to children who were never removed from abusive parents, those kids were the lucky ones. In many cases child welfare workers evaded "permanency planning" by avoiding removing children from abusive homes altogether.

Care Rationing

Pressed between static revenues and increasing demand for service, child welfare professionals began to ration care, a tactic that was to prove disastrous over time. One of the authors of this piece worked in San Diego in the '80s and saw the results of care rationing firsthand. Caseloads swelled. Callers to child protective services were put on hold for 20 minutes. There were fewer phone calls and visits to families desperately in need of monitoring. Staff turnover exceeded 50 percent; student interns were catapulted into the position of senior worker; and cases slipped into a black hole. A family could have three or four social workers in a year. One memo instructed case workers not to investigate any abuse complaints involving children of 14 years or older; the presumption, apparently, was that they were at least old enough to run away from home.

It's not hard to understand why staff burned out and left so quickly. They knew—and one suspects were tormented by—what happened to the children in their case files. A case could seem stable enough to set aside for a while. Then suddenly, one day, the child could be hospitalized or dead.

The Child Welfare League of America recommends that a case worker handle a maximum of 15 cases. But in many cities, workers now have 50 to 70 cases apiece. In Milwaukee, when workers leave the agency, their cases are placed in an unstaffed "vacant zone," meaning children are assured of no care whatsoever. Child protection in Illinois has deteriorated to the point that state officials are increasingly the target of legal action. Since 1989, Illinois has paid $7.9 million to a private legal firm to defend state child welfare officials, enough to hire 200 child protection workers each year.

Family Values

With child welfare stretched to the breaking point, a new program known as family preservation came on the scene. The family preservation movement aimed to prevent the removal of abused and neglected children from their homes. It began with a model, known as Homebuilders, developed in Tacoma, Washington, in the mid '70s. Rather than remove mistreated children from their homes, Homebuilders proposed to aid troubled families through 24-hour intensive services provided over several weeks by caseworkers who would manage no more than a half-dozen families at one time. When Homebuilders reported keeping more than 90 percent of at-risk families intact, child welfare administrators began to pay close attention, especially since by avoiding more expensive institutional care, Homebuilders claimed savings of $2,331 per case.

Family preservation not only promised to stretch diminishing public funds, it also placated the increasing public outrage at the impunity with which some child welfare workers removed children from their parents. Ire at overzealous child welfare workers culminated in 1989, when an 8-year-old girl named Alicia Wade was raped in San Diego. With her father, a retired Naval officer, suspected—and later implicated by Alicia after months of prompting—Alicia was isolated from her family for three years. Fortunately, at the time of trial, a court officer arranged DNA testing of the semen from Alicia's underclothes. The test exonerated her father and implicated a pedophile who worked as a mechanic in the community. The Wade family eventually won $3.7 million in damages from San Diego County.

Alicia Wade became a symbol for mainly middle-class parents up in arms about what they saw as child welfare workers overstepping their bounds. By the early '90s, Victims Of Child Abuse Laws (VOCAL), an organization dedicated to restraining child welfare officials and reinforcing parental rights, had become a potent force in several states. VOCAL critics of child welfare workers and their invasive practices argued that because all families could be labeled abusive due to vague laws, professionals had free rein to intrude in family life. For beleaguered child welfare professionals, "family preservation" was an increasingly appealing option.

The Plight of Abused Black Children

Meanwhile, child welfare officials were also being criticized by African Americans who blasted predominantly white welfare workers for placing black children in white homes. The National Association of Black Social Workers formally charged child welfare officials with "cultural genocide."

Kowtowing to these pressures, child welfare workers ignored data showing that poor black children suffered higher rates of abuse and that African American children were more likely than white or Hispanic children to die of abuse or neglect. Long-term research on black children adopted by white parents indicates that they suffer no harm; indeed, most prosper. Conversely, long-term foster care of children in general has been found to be detrimental. Yet child welfare professionals, fearful of the backlash from trans-racial adoption, unnecessarily put many black children in foster care. Even worse, despite evidence of abuse, child welfare professionals would sometimes opt for the path of least resistance—keeping a child at home.

Family preservation allowed child welfare professionals to defuse three controversies: diminishing public revenues, VOCAL's vitriolic rhetoric, and an African American community up in arms. But all the while a growing body of research was questioning the value of family preservation. A series of experimental studies found that family preservation was no better than traditional services on a number of counts—including the likelihood of a child being removed from home. Illinois child welfare officials commissioned child welfare researchers from the University of Chicago to do a three-year assessment of its Family First program; they reached similar conclusions. Despite the fact that the "family preservation" families received 10 times the family support service that the control group did, this strategy yielded no significant improvement in family welfare. In fact, it appeared that Illinois was spending $20 million in family preservation to save $2 million in foster care expenses. But Illinois officials insisted on pursuing family preservation, even if it meant that children stayed in dangerous conditions at home.

National child welfare policy demonstrated the same disregard for the evidence. The Family Preservation and Support Program of the Children's Initiative, featured prominently in the 1993 Clinton budget, earmarked $930 million over five years for family preservation, leaving child protection as an inconvenient footnote. As Mayor Giuliani noted after Elisa Izquierdo's death, "The philosophy of child welfare has been too rigidly focused on only holding families together, sometimes at the cost of protecting children."

Neglectful Policies

Cutting back on family preservation is just the beginning. Here is what else must be done to protect vulnerable children:

• Redefine child abuse as a public safety problem. In many American communities, domestic violence has been reclassified as assault. That means the police must press charges even if the victim is reluctant to do so. The message is clear: Beat a woman and go to jail. Why not institute a similar practice for abused children? "Child abuse is, first and foremost, a criminal act," writes UCLA's Duncan Lindsey, "requiring decisive coercive control, and is therefore a police matter." It is not purely a "treatment" and social service issue. Assigning these investigations to the police would allow child welfare professionals to do what they do best: provide a variety of supportive services to troubled families.

Equally important, it could serve as a powerful deterrent. The threat of stiff criminal penalties might cause a raging parent to think twice. The *Washington Post* recently reported on the sentencing of a man who had beaten his girlfriend's child to death. The boy's injuries were so severe that they resembled those caused by a fall from a tall building; his chest was so badly crushed that rescue workers were unable to perform CPR. The killer got 5 to 15 years—the maximum—and will be eligible for parole in less than four years. What kind of message does that send?

• Tighten the definition of child abuse and neglect in order to cut down the number of unfounded cases. Estimates place the number of unfounded reports of abuse and neglect at upwards of 65 percent in some communities. The reason is the overly broad definition of abuse passed in 1974. The National Committee for the Prevention of Child Abuse includes the following as possible indicators of child sexual abuse: clinginess, a reversion to bed-wetting or thumb-sucking, a display of sexual knowledge beyond the child's years. Although these could come from sexual abuse, they could come from many other factors as well.

But the media hype on sexual abuse, especially among the middle class, has encouraged parents to imagine the worst. Regrettably, President Clinton has failed to fund a Presidential Commission on Child and Youth Deaths, authorized by former President Reagan, which could clear up much of the confusion surrounding data on child abuse, neglect, and fatalities.

• Encourage adoption over indefinite foster care and family preservation. In 1995, *LA Weekly* reported on the death of a child named "Lance": He had been happily living with his aunt, who was willing to adopt him. Instead, in the name of "family reunification," Los Angeles's Dependency Court returned him to his father, despite a history of heroin addiction and abuse in the family. Eleven weeks after his return home, Lance was beaten to death by his father's girlfriend; his body had been used as a virtual punching bag.

The same court had given a pedophile father, who repeatedly raped his retarded daughters, unmonitored reunification visits for 60-day periods. The subsequent abuse was so heinous that the father ended up in prison for six years. Another child, born with fetal alcohol syndrome from her mother's alcoholism, was reunified with her mother—who a short time later killed her daughter by beating her and forcing her to ingest large quantities of rubbing alcohol. If we're going to sanctify the notion of family, we ought to be encouraging safe, stable families—the kind children won't find in foster care or abusive homes. Adoption—by a person of any race or religion—should be encouraged. To his credit, President Clinton has proposed loosening restrictions on transracial adoption.

- End arbitrary confidentiality rules. Social welfare departments, under assault for poor performance, have developed the organizational equivalent of paranoia, using agency procedures to thwart public scrutiny. Two reporters, Marjie Lundstrom and Rochelle Sharpe, won a Pulitzer Prize in 1990 for their work on the failures of child protection. Notable among their findings: There were no reliable numbers on fatalities nationwide because many states simply didn't keep track. Some social workers were actually forbidden by confidentiality laws to confirm that a child had been killed.

Cases in which children are killed by abuse should be opened to the public, and child death review teams should be established to determine the cause of agency failure. The use of confidentiality to cover lapses in the protection of children is untenable for publicly funded agencies functioning in the public interest.

- Consolidate existing services for children into a local Children's Authority. The elaborate bureaucracies inherited from the industrial era—Departments of Social Services, Public Health, and Juvenile Services coexist in most cities—are unacceptably wasteful. It's one thing when a bad public program means your mail is late. But the need for good government takes on considerably more urgency when children are being beaten or killed.

The Need for Real Financial Support

Fixing the system won't be cheap. But is child protection really where we want to look for budget cuts, as we've done in the past? We need to give child welfare workers enough support to do their job—with the specific goal of reducing the number of cases each worker carries. Then we can truly hold them accountable. This won't be cheap; and increasing funding is no guarantee of efficiency. But in the absence of any real financial support, the child protection system has atrophied. In response, caseworkers stint on care and look for easy solutions.

The easiest solution of all, unfortunately, is to leave a child in a dangerous situation. Just seven months after Elisa Izquierdo's death, a foul odor drew police to a Bronx apartment. Outside, stuffed in a garbage bag, they found the rotting body of two-year-old Rayvon Evans. Again, fingers were pointed at child welfare workers: Abandoned by his mother as a newborn at the hospital, he had been returned to his parents from foster care just seven months before his death. Despite the ballyhooed reforms Giuliani announced in the wake of Elisa's death, little seems to have changed in child protection. The agency's record-keeping is still only partially computerized. The Bronx has an estimated 80 unfilled caseworker positions. And an agency official cited state law to avoid discussing details of the case. As Mark Green, the city's Public Advocate, said, "The crisis is accelerating . . . faster than the reforms are coming."

CONFRONTING CHILD SEXUAL ABUSE

Iris Beckwith, interviewed by Ken Adelman

In the following selection, excerpted from an interview conducted by *Washingtonian* national editor Ken Adelman, Iris Beckwith describes the destructive effect that sexual abuse has on children and how it can be prevented. A survivor of childhood sexual abuse herself, Beckwith discusses her work with Childhelp USA, a national organization dedicated to the prevention and treatment of child abuse. Through her Good Touch/Bad Touch program, Beckwith teaches schoolchildren to recognize abusive behavior when it occurs and encourages them to report abusive behavior to trusted adults. Parents have an integral role in preventing abuse as well, Beckwith explains. Mothers and fathers should investigate any suspicious injuries or comments made by their children, she advises, and they should be wary of anyone who shows a greater-than-usual interest in their children.

At the Virginia Office of Childhelp USA, a national nonprofit group that works to prevent and treat child abuse, Iris Beckwith seeks to spare kids the effects of sexual abuse she suffered.

Beckwith heals herself and helps others by teaching Good Touch/Bad Touch in area schools. For the littlest kids, she uses dolls, stories, and videos to explain abuse.

She joined Childhelp, which has programs in 53 area schools, in 1996. Childhelp also runs the Alice C. Tyler Village near Culpeper, Virginia. The village cares for abused kids ages 2 to 12. On 250 acres, including ponds, a swimming pool, and plenty of horses, some 100 staff members work with more than 50 kids.

Beckwith lives in Arlington, Virginia, with her husband, Ed, a tax lawyer at Baker & Hostetler. They have three children: a daughter in her third year of college and a daughter and son in high school.

Beckwith has been active in local community organizations. She is also a founding member of the Arlington Alliance for Parents and Teens, dealing with drug and alcohol abuse. In 1993 she was nominated Arlington Outstanding Citizen.

Reprinted from "Terrible Secret," by Iris Beckwith, interviewed by Ken Adelman, *Washingtonian*, January 1999. Reprinted by permission of Ken Adelman.

Before she again headed out to teach, we discussed what she's learned.

Ken Adelman: How does childhood abuse affect a person's life?

Iris Beckwith: It impacts kids differently depending on the severity of the abuse, the child's age, and the context in which it happened. Generally, it damages self-esteem and interrupts normal development.

Kids naturally want to succeed. When abused, a child's energy is focused on emotional and physical survival. It's hard to concentrate on learning or developing potential—especially when the child wonders when the next beating may come or the next intruder will enter the bedroom at night.

Low self-esteem often continues into adulthood. Abused children later may perpetuate violence, sexual abuse, alcoholism, or drug addiction. That's what they know, what they've lived.

Abuse is extremely damaging if it occurs before the child becomes verbal. Without words, that child can't express or process what's happening. These kids later act out great anger and confusion. Such behavior can be mistakenly diagnosed as a learning disability. It's often not. They simply can't cope with what's happening in their lives.

Studies have shown that 70 percent of teen pregnancy is a direct or indirect result of sexual abuse. Some girls are impregnated during the abusive relationship. Others use promiscuity to take control of their bodies.

Many kids self-mutilate. They turn their anger inward to try to feel something. That self-inflicted pain is under their control.

At the village, some kids try hurting someone or something else. They smash windows or plates. Their actions say, "I'm so bad that you're going to reject me. I'll show you that you'll reject me." There's so much anger inside they're ready to explode.

Abuse Can Happen in Any Family

How can adults do this to kids?

Many were abused themselves and didn't get help. They have low self-esteem themselves. Abusing others takes back some control they lost as a child. They often feel remorse but lack coping or parenting skills.

Abuse can happen in any family. Abuse transcends economic, religious, and racial categories. Remember Marilyn Van Derbur, former Miss America, who described very severe sexual abuse in her prosperous, prestigious family? People ask me, "Does it happen here?" I tell them, "It sure does!"

How did you get interested in this?

I was abused as a child. It happened right in my own family—Jewish and fairly well off. For most of my adult life, no one talked about child abuse. I went through years of shame and painful secrecy.

I had to find my own way of coping. I dove into community activities, feeling I could escape my childhood experiences. But you can't escape them until you deal with them. There was a lot of denial of what happened.

What worked for you?

Confronting the perpetrator, who was my father. Developing a large support network of friends and some family. Reading about it, though ten years ago there was little information out there. Finding a trusted therapist to help me process it all.

Once I faced the shame and secrecy, I was determined not to let it win in my life. I needed to turn the trauma into something healing.

I'd studied psychology in college, so that became a natural fit. I first taught parenting classes at our local elementary school and mentioned sexual abuse. That was healing for me and helpful to others. After so many years in secrecy, it was cathartic to finally say, "Wait a minute. I didn't do anything wrong. I wasn't the one who caused this to happen."

When did you confront your father?

About ten years ago, when I was about 38. It took me that long to confront him. I wrote him a letter, which is what many people do. I'd been in therapy for a long while by then.

I first talked about my abuse with a close friend, after she confided her own by her stepfather. Even after hearing this, it took me four months to confide in her.

I began noticing more about abuse on television, talk shows, and the news. I'd sit alone or watch them on videotape. I had to watch alone since I was overwhelmed by everything I saw and shame was still a big factor.

A major eruption came when I first heard my friend's experience. It took another year to tell Ed, after many years of marriage. He hadn't known or suspected a thing.

What did you say in your letter?

I asked my father why he did it. I told him I knew he had done it. I told him how it had made me feel. I told him the impact it had on my life. That I wasn't sure I could forgive him. How angry I felt. How it had changed my family forever. I was most curious to know what happened in his life that caused him to do this to me.

Fortunately for me, he admitted it. He was relieved it was finally out. He'd been carrying the secret, too. We spent a lot of time talking about it, both face to face and on the phone. And after I confronted him, he spent a long time working on his own issues.

How did your kids handle it?

It's been awfully hard on my kids. They're left without grandparents on my side. Fortunately they have wonderful grandparents on Ed's side.

Each of our kids had to face the issue and deal with it. I didn't tell them when they were little. I needed to work through it on my own then. I told them at different times when I thought they were ready. It was very hard to do.

They were devastated. They had sensed problems in our immediate family. My parents, who had been around a lot, weren't around anymore. Our family was in turmoil. The kids didn't say much, as they weren't sure what was happening. By the time I told them, they knew there was some big issue.

No one outside our family would have imagined it. Fortunately, with good therapy, family, and friends, I have healed.

Confronting the Problem

What was your healing process?

First and foremost, confronting it head on. I've always been the kind of person who takes a problem, faces it, and tackles it. This issue was so much tougher.

I confided in and depended on a few close friends. Having a supportive husband was critical. Hypnosis helped get to some pieces I couldn't reach. Vital to my healing was accepting I'd never have all of the pieces. Yet I had to accept that it wasn't my fault.

What can parents do to prevent your situation from happening to their kid?

One in three girls and one in seven boys is molested before the age of 18, so you need to pay attention and listen to your kids.

Participate in your children's activities. Get to know their friends. Teach them the difference between "good touches," "bad touches," and "confusing touches," which can feel good or bad on the body but can hurt the child's feelings. Pay attention to anyone who shows a greater-than-normal interest in your child, especially if he wants to spend time alone with the child.

Look out for signs of abuse. If kids wear long sleeves all the time or have unexplained marks, bruises, broken bones, welts, burns, then something's wrong. Ask questions. Take action.

Take heed if your children say they don't want to be with someone when you have to leave them—whether it's a favorite uncle or a babysitter next door. Ask why. That kind of comment could be an alarm bell.

One woman told me of a neighborhood boy who was babysitting her kids. Once as she was rushing out the door, her child asked her, "Is this boy going to play the 'show me' game again?"

That question kept playing over in the mother's head. So she returned home and asked her child about it. It turned out the boy had been sodomizing her children for six months while he was babysitting.

So listen to what your kids say. Kids rarely concoct stories of abuse. That's too embarrassing to the child. With babysitters, ask for references and call other parents. Have the potential babysitter spend time with your child when you're home. Ask lots of questions.

Good Touches and Bad Touches

What do you tell children in school?

I teach them the five safety rules of Good Touch/Bad Touch.

Number one, that it's their body. That's simple, but kids don't realize they can control touches and decide what feels good.

Good touches make them feel like smiling—hugs, kisses, pats on the back, shaking hands, high fives. Bad touches are hitting, pulling hair, scratching, pushing someone down. Confusing touches start out feeling good on your body but can change when the child doesn't understand why that person's touching private body parts, or in an uncomfortable way. Private body parts are those covered by bathing suits.

We talk about "uh oh" feelings. With little kids, it's like a little friend inside warning when something's happening they're worried about. For older kids, we teach how that signals something uncomfortable or wrong. It warns of a problem.

We teach them what to do with that feeling—talk to a grownup they trust.

The child should tell until someone believes him or her. Since 85 percent of sexual abuse comes from someone the child knows, often within the family, other adults may not want to believe it. We tell kids that if an adult doesn't believe you, it doesn't mean they don't love you. It means they've made a mistake.

Do most perpetrators stop?

Perpetrators don't want to get caught. If they believe the child will tell, it may interrupt the behavior. But sexual abuse is a repetitive and often addictive behavior.

That's why perpetrators act like bullies or tell the child, "This is our secret."

How do you help an abused child?

Kids who come to the Alice C. Tyler Village of Childhelp in Culpeper have experienced serious abuse and neglect. They've been removed from their homes by the courts. When they reach us, they've been through many cycles of failure and rejection. These kids expect another rejection.

We don't let that happen. We provide whatever the child needs, from medical treatment to educational plans to counseling. We search for that child's strengths and then set goals so they can experience success.

We use art and animal therapy to provide children with ways to express pain and loss. We had one speechless child whose first words at the village were "I love you," spoken to a village horse. And we offer spiritual guidance in the child's religion.

We match village children with foster families well in advance of a child's release, which helps our success. We show a child, through our actions, that his life is of value.

To further awareness and prevention, we offer help through our 800-4-A-CHILD National Child Abuse Hotline. By lifting the secrecy from sexual abuse, we encourage more kids to talk about their experiences.

Breaking the Cycle of Violence

What's your success rate?

I'd say around 95 percent. We get children at the village to realize that what had happened to them wasn't their fault. We give them love. We give them coping skills. They stay in our village until they can be returned home or placed in foster care. Some need further residential treatment.

What have you learned from it all?

That speaking publicly of my own abuse is vital to educate people about child abuse, to help break the cycle of violence.

I learned how to help others by way of my own experience. If I prevent one case, or reach one child who's been abused, I change that family and life forever. That makes my work cathartic and rewarding.

What have you learned about life?

That bad things can happen to good people. That when bad things happen, it doesn't make that person bad. Bad things don't have to destroy your life.

It is possible to use your own experiences to better your life and others' lives. If you let the negative experiences prevail, you lose. But save one child and you may change the world.

The Intervention Dilemma

Bella English

In the following selection, freelance writer Bella English relates an incident in which she observed a mother abusing her child in a restaurant and recalls the difficulty of trying to decide whether or not to intervene. According to English, even childcare professionals concede that there is not an easy answer to the question of when, how, and whether to intervene when witnessing public displays of child abuse. Child-care workers advise that serious incidents of abuse should be immediately reported to the police, she writes, but some experts believe that intervention in intermediate cases may only serve to aggravate an already volatile situation and put the child at risk for retaliation from an enraged parent. For those who choose to intervene, English stresses that it must be done in a nonconfrontational, nonjudgmental manner.

I had picked up my daughter from two weeks away at camp, and, as she was starving from the effects of "gross" (read: healthy) camp food, I took her straight to lunch at a T.G.I. Friday's restaurant in Framingham, Massachusetts. While we waited for her chicken fingers and fries, we witnessed a chilling scene at the table next to us: a mother abusing her child.

Maybe she thought no one saw her. Or maybe she didn't care. Her blond son, who looked very much like her, couldn't have been more than 18 months old. Like most toddlers, he had a limited attention span. He had finished his food and wanted out. He would emit occasional little shrieks, as impatient, pre-verbal children will do.

First, the mother put her hand over his mouth and nose and told him to stop. (Stop what, breathing?) Naturally, as soon as she removed her hand, he wailed. So she whacked him across the face. You could hear the slap and see the imprint.

At his next shriek, she slapped him again and told him to shut up. The third slap, I got up and went over to the table. I wanted to put my hand over her mouth and nose. I wanted to whack her three times across her face and tell her to shut up. I wanted to tell her to pick on someone her own size.

The truth is, I didn't know what to do. And I'm hardly alone.

A Difficult Question

We've all seen them. The harried supermarket moms screaming obscenities at their crestfallen kids, the abusive dads in playgrounds, the uncomfortable scenes in the restaurant. But what are we supposed to do about it? Hillary Clinton says it takes a village to raise a child. As members of that village, what is our role? Do we butt in or out? Do we risk aggravating a volatile situation? Or can we in some way help defuse things?

"Many people ask, and it's a question for which there is no good answer," says Robert Reece, a child abuse specialist who teaches pediatrics at Tufts Medical School and runs a clinic for kids at Floating Hospital for Children at the New England Medical Center. In addition, he is the director of the Institute for Professional Education at the Massachusetts Society for the Prevention of Cruelty to Children (MSPCC). There, he trains doctors, judges, lawyers, social workers, and other professionals about child abuse.

Still, he is stumped by the issue of public displays of abuse. He's seen them himself: the woman sitting behind him on the bus who screamed at and then smacked her 2-year-old. "I decided I would do nothing," he said. "I knew if I turned around and did anything the reaction would not be positive toward me or the child."

In egregious cases, Reece believes the police should be called immediately. Get a license number if you can. In the intermediate cases, such as the scene I witnessed, there are two possible reactions: sympathy or anger, either offering the harried parent help, or screaming at him. There have been no studies to show if the former approach works, he said. And as for anger, you risk retaliation toward yourself or the child.

Mothering the Mother

Loretta Kowal, a clinical social worker who has 30 years of experience with neglect and abuse cases, has witnessed numerous public displays of child abuse, at airports, restaurants, grocery, and department stores. She once saw a nun slap a child across the face on the Boston Common. "I walked right over and told her that was no way to teach anyone anything," Kowal recalled. "She was stunned. Hopefully, she behaved a little better after that."

Kowal, who has two grown sons, understands the stresses of parenting young children. Most of the time, she believes, parents "lose it" temporarily without doing any lasting damage. She favors the "mothering the mother" approach.

"You don't want to make the parent feel worse because they will take it out on the child," she said. "You could go over and say, 'What a beautiful baby! Isn't he adorable? I remember when my kids were little and it could be so frustrating. Can I help you here?' Acknowledge how hard it is, don't pass judgment. Offer to hold the child, or hold the door."

However, if it appears the child is in serious danger, don't hesitate to call the Department of Social Services (DSS), she said. You can make an anonymous report; the state agency can track a license plate and make a home visit. Most of all, DSS can offer home services to support an overwhelmed family, such as respite care and therapy. Kowal, who is on the professional advisory committee to DSS, stresses that the agency only removes children from a family as a last resort. "The best plan is to fix the family," she said.

Kowal firmly believes in some intervention if you see a child being abused. "Parents today, especially single parents, are under a lot of stress. When my kids were little, you could get a baby sitter for a dollar an hour. Now, people can't afford sitters. They're with their kids a lot and there's a lot of stress. Sometimes, we don't get the help we need and others have to step in."

Child Abuse Is Everybody's Business

Joe McElroy, general counsel for the MSPCC, agrees it's a knotty issue. "Our culture is such that we're accustomed not to intervene and stick our nose in other people's business," he said. "But clearly, child abuse is everybody's business." At the least, speaking with the abuser should stop the behavior for the moment. "The problem is, adults don't know their own strength and don't realize how much physical damage they can inflict," said McElroy.

At Friday's, I didn't have a clue what I was going to say when I got to the abuser's table. I saw the red right cheek of the baby, and tried to smile at the mother (it probably came out a hideous grimace). I mumbled something like, "Our food hasn't come yet. My daughter and I would love to hold the baby while you finish your meal. I know it's tough. I have two kids."

This Mother of the Year gathered her things up and said they were finished and leaving. As our food came, she was walking her son out to the parking lot. I wish I'd followed and gotten a license plate number. That woman—and that child—need help.

Preventing Child Stalking on the Internet

Stephen R. Wiley

In the following selection, which was originally presented as testimony before the House Committee on the Judiciary, Stephen R. Wiley addresses the issue of sexual predators on the Internet. Creating public awareness of the problem and educating children about the dangers they face in cyberspace are important elements in the effort to reduce their vulnerability to sexual assault, argues Wiley. Parents can take positive steps to protect their children, he points out, such as monitoring their Internet use and restricting access to adult-oriented websites. However, the most crucial element in the fight against online child sexual abuse is the pooling of resources by federal, state, and local law enforcement agencies into a coordinated attack on online child pornographers and pedophiles, he explains. Wiley is the chief of the Violent Crimes Major Offenders section of the Federal Bureau of Investigation (FBI).

Good morning, Mr. Chairman and Members of the Subcommittee. I appreciate this opportunity to discuss the serious problem of crimes against children facilitated by the Internet. Our children are our nation's most valued resource and they are the most vulnerable members of our society. There is no greater outrage in our society than when we hear of a child who has been mistreated, sexually abused, or murdered. It is paramount that, as a society, we protect our nation's children and keep them from becoming victims of crime.

Advances in computer and telecommunications technology have allowed our children to broaden their horizons, thus increasing their knowledge and cultural experiences. This technology, however, has also allowed our nation's children to become vulnerable to exploitation and harm by pedophiles and other sexual predators.

Safeguarding Children on the Internet

Commercial on-line services and the Internet provide the opportunity for pedophiles and other sexual predators to meet and converse with

Testimony given by Stephen R. Wiley before the House Committee on the Judiciary Subcommittee on Crime, November 7, 1997, Washington, DC.

children. Our investigative efforts have shown that pedophiles often utilize "chat rooms" to contact children. These "chat rooms" offer users the advantage of instant communication throughout the United States and abroad, and they provide the pedophile an anonymous means of identifying and recruiting children into sexually illicit relationships. Through the use of "chat rooms," children can "chat" for hours with unknown individuals, often without the knowledge or approval of their parents. A child does not know if he/she is "chatting" with a 14-year-old or a 40-year-old. The FBI has investigated more than 70 cases involving pedophiles traveling interstate to meet undercover agents or officers posing as juveniles for the purpose of engaging in an illicit sexual relationship.

The advancement and availability of computer telecommunications also demands that all of us—public officials, law enforcement, parents, educators, commerce and industry leaders—be more vigilant and responsible by teaching our children how to avoid becoming victims of sexual predators. Parents must talk to their children about the potential dangers they may encounter through the Internet and on-line services. Several groups, to include the National Center for Missing and Exploited Children (NCMEC), have issued guidelines for parents on safeguarding children who use computers linked to the information highway. . . . I urge parents to review these guidelines and discuss them with their children. Schools that offer computer classes and access to the Internet should include appropriate discussion of this problem in their curriculum. Creating awareness of the problem is a first step toward reducing a child's vulnerability to sexual predators.

Blocking mechanisms for Internet access are available for parents to restrict access to sexually-oriented Internet and on-line bulletin boards, chat rooms and web sites. These mechanisms can help reduce, but will not totally eliminate, the vulnerability of children. It is possible that children, such as teenagers, may be able to circumvent the restrictions of the blocking mechanism or that pedophiles will still be able to meet children through what may at first appear to be innocent non-interactive activity, such as responding to a newsgroup or web site posting.

Building Legal Precedent

The FBI and other law enforcement agencies must continue to develop innovative investigative strategies for dealing with crimes committed in cyberspace and build strong legal precedent to support these investigations and prosecutions.

The FBI is attacking the proliferation of child pornography on the Internet and on-line services and the problem of pedophiles establishing sexually illicit relationships with minors through use of the Internet through a comprehensive initiative focusing on crimes against children. This initiative encompasses several major crime problems, including the sexual exploitation of children, child abductions, child abuse on government and Indian reservations, and parental/family non-custodial kidnapings. In May 1997, each of the FBI's 56 field offices designated two special agents as Crimes Against Children coordinators. These coordinators have been tasked with developing multi-agency teams of law enforcement, prosecutive and social service professionals capable of effectively investigating and prosecuting child victim crimes that cross legal and geographical jurisdictional boundaries and which enhance the interagency sharing of intelligence and information. The FBI has and will continue to aggressively address all crimes against children facilitated by the Internet.

One facet of the FBI's Crimes Against Children Program is the "Innocent Images" initiative which was initiated based upon information developed during a child abduction investigation.

In May 1993, the disappearance of ten-year-old George Stanley Burdynski, Jr., led Prince George's County, Maryland, police detectives and FBI agents to two suspects who had sexually exploited numerous juvenile males over a 25-year period. Investigation into the activities of these two suspects determined that adults were routinely utilizing computers to transmit images of minors showing frontal nudity or sexually explicit conduct, as well as to luring minors into illicit sexual activity. It was through this investigation that the FBI recognized that the utilization of computer telecommunications was rapidly becoming one of the most prevalent techniques by which pedophiles and other sexual predators shared sexually explicit photographic images of minors, and identified and recruited children for sexually illicit relationships. The illicit activities being investigated by the FBI are conducted by users of both commercial and private on-line services, as well as the Internet.

The FBI's national initiative on child pornography focuses on those who indicate a willingness to travel for the purpose of engaging in sexual activity with a child, those who produce and/or distribute child pornography and those who post illegal images onto the on-line services and the Internet. Through this initiative, FBI agents and task force officers go on-line, in an undercover capacity, to identify and investigate those individuals who are victimizing children through the Internet and on-line service providers. There are currently 55 field offices assisting and conducting investigations as a result of the "Innocent Images" initiative.

The "Innocent Images" national initiative is coordinated through the Baltimore Division of the FBI. This initiative provides for a coordinated FBI response to a nationwide problem by collating and analyzing information and images obtained from numerous sources to avoid duplication of effort by all FBI field offices.

The Need for Coordinated Law Enforcement

The Baltimore Division's investigative operation involves the commitment and dedication of federal, state and local law enforcement agencies, working together in a task force environment. The FBI believes that law enforcement agencies should work together, in a coordinated effort, to address crimes against children facilitated by the Internet. It is this sharing of manpower and resources that will ultimately provide the most effective tool in combating this crime problem.

Although the "Innocent Images" initiative is coordinated through the FBI field office at Baltimore, this operation has been franchised to include the Los Angeles field office. The Los Angeles Division also works in a task force environment and is a part of the Southern California Sexual Assault and Exploitation Felony Enforcement Team (the SAFE team).

The FBI has taken the necessary steps to ensure that the "Innocent Images" national initiative remains viable and productive. These efforts include the use of new technology and sophisticated investigative techniques and coordination of this national investigative effort with other federal agencies that have statutory investigative authority, including the United States Customs Service, the United States Postal Inspection Service, the Department of Justice's Child Exploitation and Obscenity Section (part of the Criminal Division), the NCMEC, and numerous commercial and independent on-line service providers.

The FBI also conducts an outreach program to inform the public and local law enforcement agencies about this national initiative. The FBI has addressed a number of civic, judicial, prosecutive and law enforcement organizations concerning this initiative and the assistance the FBI can provide in investigating crimes against children facilitated by the Internet. The FBI is currently in the process of assigning a Supervisory Special Agent, on a full-time basis, to the NCMEC. The FBI strongly believes that it must work closely with the NCMEC, a national resource center for child protection, to locate and recover missing children and raise the public awareness about ways to prevent child abduction, molestation and sexual exploitation. I believe that the assignment of this FBI agent will enhance coordination between the two organizations and benefit the nation in our fight to combat crimes against children.

As I mentioned earlier, the FBI has investigated more than 70 cases involving pedophiles traveling interstate to meet minors for the purpose of engaging in illicit sexual relationships. In one case investigated by the FBI in Maryland and Florida, in conjunction with the Clearwater, Florida, police department, a subject was arrested in November 1995, after traveling from his home in Minneapolis, Minnesota, to Tampa, Florida, for purposes of having sex with what he thought was a 13-year-old girl whom he had met through an on-line chat room. In reality, the "victim" in this case was an undercover FBI agent. This subject, who was married and the parent of three children, was convicted in federal court.

Another example of a traveler case involved a resident of Rockville, Maryland, who pled guilty to two counts of interstate travel to engage in sexual activity with a minor (Title 18, USC, Section 2423). Through investigation, this individual was found to have traveled from his Maryland home to the Springfield, Virginia, public library for the purpose of meeting a 12-year-old female in order to have sex. After this subject's arrest, a review of his Internet e-mail messages revealed that the subject had been posing as a 16-year-old and had communicated with a number of other girls, between the ages of 10–15, attempting to meet them for sex.

Crimes against children are among the most emotional and demanding cases that investigators and prosecutors must face. The FBI will continue to work closely with other law enforcement agencies, NCMEC and the Department of Justice's CEOS to investigate, arrest and convict those individuals who prey upon our nation's children.

ORGANIZATIONS TO CONTACT

The editors have compiled the following list of organizations concerned with the issues presented in this book. The descriptions are derived from materials provided by the organizations. All have publications or information available for interested readers. The list was compiled on the date of publication of the present volume; the information provided here may change. Be aware that many organizations take several weeks or longer to respond to inquiries, so allow as much time as possible.

ACT for Kids
7 S. Howard, Suite 200, Spokane, WA 99201-3816
(509) 747-8224 • fax: (509) 747-0609
e-mail: info@actforkids.org • website: www.actforkids.org

ACT for Kids is a nonprofit organization that provides resources, consultation, research, and training for the prevention and treatment of child abuse and sexual violence. The organization's publications include workbooks, manuals, and the books *My Very Own Book About Me* and *How to Survive the Sexual Abuse of Your Child*.

American Academy of Child and Adolescent Psychiatry (AACAP)
3615 Wisconsin Ave. NW, Washington, DC 20016-3007
(202) 966-7300 • fax: (202) 966-2891
website: www.aacap.org

AACAP supports and advances child and adolescent psychiatry through research and the distribution of information. The academy's goal is to provide information that will ensure proper treatment for children who suffer from mental or behavioral disorders due to child abuse, molestation, or other factors. AACAP publishes fact sheets on a variety of issues concerning disorders that may affect children and adolescents.

American Professional Society on the Abuse of Children (APSAC)
407 S. Dearborn, Suite 1300, Chicago, IL 60605
(312) 554-0166 • fax: (312) 554-0919
e-mail: APSACMems@aol.com • website: www.apsac.org

APSAC is dedicated to improving the coordination of services in the fields of child abuse prevention, treatment, and research. It publishes a quarterly newsletter, the *Advisor*, and the *Journal of Interpersonal Violence*.

False Memory Syndrome Foundation
3401 Market St., Suite 130, Philadelphia, PA 19104-3315
(215) 387-1865 • (800) 568-8882 • fax: (215) 387-1917
website: www.fmsfonline.org

The foundation believes that many "delayed memories" of sexual abuse are the result of false memory syndrome (FMS). In FMS, patients in therapy "recall" childhood abuse that never occurred. The foundation seeks to discover reasons for the spread of FMS, works for the prevention of new cases, and aids FMS victims, including those falsely accused of abuse. The foundation publishes a newsletter and various papers and distributes articles and information on FMS.

National Center for Missing & Exploited Children (NCMEC)
699 Prince St., Alexandria, VA 22314-3175
(703) 274-3900/274-2220 • fax: (703) 22314-3175
hot line: (800) THE-LOST (843-5678)
website: www.missingkids.org

NCMEC serves as a clearinghouse of information on missing and exploited children and coordinates child protection efforts with the private sector. A number of publications on these issues are available, including guidelines for parents whose children are testifying in court, help for abused children, and booklets such as *Children Traumatized in Sex Rings* and *Child Molesters: A Behavioral Analysis*.

National Clearinghouse on Child Abuse and Neglect Information
330 C St. SW, Washington, DC 20447
(703) 385-7565 • (800) 394-3366 • fax: (703) 385-3206
e-mail: nccanch@calib.com • website: www.calib.com/nccanch

This national clearinghouse collects, catalogs, and disseminates information on all aspects of child maltreatment, including identification, prevention, treatment, public awareness, training, and education. The clearinghouse offers various reports, fact sheets, and bulletins concerning child abuse and neglect.

National Coalition Against Domestic Violence (NCADV)
Child Advocacy Task Force
PO Box 18749, Denver, CO 80218-0749
(303) 839-1852 • fax: (303) 831-9251
website: www.ncadv.org

NCADV represents organizations and individuals that assist battered women and their children. The Child Advocacy Task Force deals with issues affecting children who witness violence at home or are themselves abused. It publishes the *Bulletin*, a quarterly newsletter.

National Criminal Justice Reference Service (NCJRS)
U.S. Department of Justice
PO Box 6000, Rockville, MD 20849-6000
(301) 519-5500 • (800) 851-3420
e-mail: askncjrs@ncjrs.org • website: www.ncjrs.org

A research and development agency of the U.S. Department of Justice, NCJRS was established to prevent and reduce crime and to improve the criminal justice system. Among its publications are *Resource Guidelines: Improving Court Practice in Child Abuse and Neglect Cases* and *Recognizing When a Child's Injury or Illness Is Caused by Abuse*.

Prevent Child Abuse America (PCAA)
200 S. Michigan Ave., 17th Fl., Chicago, IL 60604-2404
(312) 663-3520 • fax: (312) 939-8962
e-mail: mailbox@preventchildabuse.org
website: www.preventchildabuse.org

PCAA's mission is to prevent all forms of child abuse. It distributes and publishes materials on a variety of topics, including child abuse and child abuse prevention. *Talking About Child Sexual Abuse* and *Basic Facts About Child Sexual Abuse* are among the various pamphlets PCAA offers.

The Safer Society Foundation

PO Box 340, Brandon, VT 05733-0340
(802) 247-3132 • fax: (802) 247-4233
e-mail: ray@usa-ads.net • website: www.safersociety.org

The Safer Society Foundation is a national research, advocacy, and referral center for the prevention of sexual abuse of children and adults. The Safer Society Press publishes research, studies, and books on treatment for sexual victims and offenders and on the prevention of sexual abuse.

Survivor Connections

52 Lyndon Rd., Cranston, RI 02905-1121
(401) 941-2548 • fax: (401) 941-2335
e-mail: scsitereturn@hotmail.com
website: www.angelfire.com/ri/survivorconnections/

Survivor Connections is an activist center for survivors of incest, rape, sexual assault, and child molestation. It publishes the newsletter *Survivor Activist*.

United Fathers of America (UFA)

6360 Van Nuys Blvd., Suite 8, Van Nuys, CA 91401
(818) 785-1440 • fax: (818) 995-0743
e-mail: info@unitedfathers.com
website: www.fathersunited.com
website: www.fathersforever.com (a branch of UFA)

UFA helps fathers fight for the right to remain actively involved in their children's upbringing after divorce or separation. UFA believes that children should not be subject to the emotional and psychological trauma caused when vindictive parents falsely charge ex-spouses with sexually abusing their children. Primarily a support group, UFA answers specific questions and suggests articles and studies that illustrate its position.

VOCAL/National Association of State VOCAL Organizations (NASVO)

7485 E. Kenyon Ave., Denver, CO 80237
hot line: (303) 233-5321
e-mail: vocal@vocal.org • website: www.nasvo.org

VOCAL (Victims of Child Abuse Laws) provides information, research data, referrals, and emotional support for those who have been falsely accused of child abuse. NASVO maintains a library of research on child abuse and neglect issues, focusing on legal, mental health, social, and medical issues, and will provide photocopies of articles for a fee. It publishes the bimonthly newsletter *NASVO News*.

BIBLIOGRAPHY

Books

Elizabeth Bartholet
Nobody's Children: Abuse and Neglect, Foster Drift, and the Adoption Alternative. Boston: Beacon, 2000.

John Briere, Lucy Berliner, and Josephine A. Bulkley, eds.
The APSAC Handbook on Child Maltreatment. Newbury Park, CA: Sage, 2000.

Carol Lowery Delaney
Abraham on Trial: The Social Legacy of Biblical Myth. Princeton, NJ: Princeton University Press, 1998.

Byrgen Finkelman
Child Abuse: A Multidisciplinary Survey: Physical and Emotional Abuse and Neglect. New York: Garland, 1995.

Jennifer J. Freyd
Betrayal Trauma: The Logic of Forgetting Child Abuse. Cambridge, MA: Harvard University Press, 1998.

Richard B. Gartner
Betrayed as Boys: Psychodynamic Treatment of Sexually Abused Men. New York: Guilford, 1999.

Mary Edna Helfer, Ruth S. Kempe, and Richard D. Krugman, eds.
The Battered Child. Chicago: University of Chicago Press, 1999.

Sandra K. Hewitt
Assessing Allegations of Sexual Abuse in Preschool Children: Understanding Small Voices. Newbury Park, CA: Sage, 2000.

Anna J. Michener
Becoming Anna: The Autobiography of a Sixteen-Year-Old. Chicago: University of Chicago Press, 1998.

Ronald T. Potter-Efron and Patricia S. Potter-Efron, eds.
Aggression, Family Violence, and Chemical Dependency. Binghamton, NY: Haworth, 1996.

Andren Schoen and Brian Prats
Beyond the Big Easy: One Man's Triumph over Abuse. Tempe, AZ: New Falcon, 2000.

Sue William Silverman
Because I Remember Terror, Father, I Remember You. Athens: University of Georgia Press, 1999.

Jane Waldfogel
The Future of Child Protection: How to Break the Cycle of Abuse and Neglect. Cambridge, MA: Harvard University Press, 1998.

Periodicals

Arthur Allen
"She Catches Child Abusers," *Redbook*, March 1999.

Douglas S. Barasch
"Would You Hurt This Baby?" *Redbook*, December 1998.

Nina Bernstein
"Old Pattern Cited in Missed Signs of Child Abuse," *New York Times*, July 22, 1999.

Rosemary Chalk and
Patricia King
"Facing Up to Family Violence," *Issues in Science and Technology,* Winter 1998/1999.

Jennifer Couzin
"Missing the Signals: Doctors Misdiagnose Child-Abuse Injuries," *U.S. News & World Report,* March 1, 1999.

Thomas Fields-Meyer
"Bad Medicine," *People Weekly,* October 25, 1999.

Skip Hollandsworth
"No One Knows What Could Be Happening to Those Kids," *Texas Monthly,* April 1999.

Rael Jean Isaac
"Abusive Justice," *National Review,* June 30, 1997.

David Laskin
"Childproofing the Internet," *Parents,* January 1999.

Stephanie Mansfield
"The Avengers Online," *Good Housekeeping,* June 1999.

Joyce Milton
"Suffer Little Children?" *National Review,* February 26, 1996.

William Nack and
Don Yaeger
"Every Parent's Nightmare," *Sports Illustrated,* September 13, 1999.

Marjorie Preston
"The Molester Next Door," *Ladies' Home Journal,* July 1998.

Carla Rivera
"U.S. Child Abuse at Crisis Levels, Panel Says," *Los Angeles Times,* April 26, 1995.

Rachel L. Swarns
"In a Policy Shift, More Parents Are Arrested for Child Neglect," *New York Times,* October 25, 1997.

Anastasia Toufexis
"Why Jennifer Got Sick," *Time,* April 29, 1996.

Gayle White
"Pain Relief," *Christianity Today,* July 12, 1999.

INDEX

foreword

Love has always been humanity's favorite subject. But work is an excellent candidate for second place.

Voltaire, for example, wryly characterized work as a type of guardian. It spares us, he said, "from three great evils: boredom, vice and need."

Others, such as Longfellow, have viewed work with cynicism. "One half of the world must sweat and groan," he lamented, "that the other half may dream."

And the introspective Mark Twain once pointed out that those of us who claim not to care about careers, promotions, raises and bonuses are denying human nature. "I'm opposed to millionaires," Twain quipped, "but it would be dangerous to offer me the position."

With *Work in the 21st Century* we add significantly to this vast store of commentary and observation on the perennially popular subject of work. The writings that follow were created by some of the top thinkers, writers, researchers, leaders and executives of the late 20th century. Each has addressed a specific facet of work about which they are particularly expert. And each has employed the insight that comes only with time and relentless intellectual pursuit to relate their respective area of comment to the whole.

This collection, first published as a special issue of *Personnel Adminstrator* magazine, was created to celebrate the 35th Anniversary of the founding of the American Society for Personnel Administration (ASPA). But it also commemorates the beginning in earnest of America's transition

1

from the economy created by the Industrial Revolution to that of the Information Age.

This is a transition that prudent people cannot ignore. As long as the basic elements of an economic system—finite goods and services, and virtually infinite wants and needs—exist, civilization must have a way to apportion wealth. Although many of us never view it this way, the job we hold is merely the scale used to measure out the portion of economy's output to which we, as individuals, are entitled.

As managers of America's human resources, ASPA's members have as their underlying goal the constant improvement of the methods by which human energy is applied to creation of goods and services. Better systems of motivation, communication, innovation, organization and the like deliver to our economy more from each unit of work expended. And more, as Mr. Twain reminded us, is something that we can never get enough of.

We hope that *Work in the 21st Century* will inspire those who read it to join us in this goal. We also hope that it will equip us all with the foresight we'll need to cope with the rapid and dramatic changes that already have confused and bewildered some segments of the American work force.

As the authors herein agree, tomorrow's world of work will be one of great opportunity, freedom and excitement. But it will almost certainly be one in which the brain, and not the bicep, reigns supreme.

Ronald C. Pilenzo, APD
President
The American Society for Personnel Administration

Change will prove beneficial only if tomorrow's leadership can ameliorate the tensions.

Zaleznik

ABRAHAM
ZALEZNIK, DCS,
*is the Konosuke
Matshushita Professor
of Leadership at the
Harvard Business
School. He is a prac-
ticing psychoanalyst
and has written exten-
sively on problems of
power and leadership
in organizations.*

Hippocrates, the first physician-scientist, formulated a principle of medicine that has broad application to the problem of change. He stated: "All other things being equal, sick people tend to get well."

When an organism is disturbed, countervailing forces appear that tend to restore the state that existed before the onset of the disturbance. If one goes to Hiroshima, for example, one will find evidence in historic monuments that a nuclear explosion occurred there in 1945. But more apparent will be the evidence of a bustling, modern city filled with the noise and excitement of people engaged in commerce.

Hippocrates' equilibrium hypothesis, when applied to change at the level of society, suggests that the forces toward change encounter the forces toward stability. The new equilibrium contains both the enduring structures of the past with the currents of what is new and changing. The lesson of history is both continuity and change.

The chapters that follow emphasize, for the most part, the changes society faces in preparing for work in the 21st century. While recognizing the powerful effects of information technology and the space age on the nature of work, the authors are up-beat about the capacity of society to absorb these changes and to improve the quality of life.

3

Industry will relocate and require shifts in population; the demands of new technologies will require a better-educated work force; the concept of work will change with the continuing shift from fabrication to service, and from following routines to exercising judgment. Work will not be limited to specific time blocks within the four walls of factory or office.

All of these changes in work will require new practices in human resource management. Above all, the demands of technological and competitive change are for cooperation rather than conflict, and collaborative means of solving problems rather than an adversary relationship between the institutions of management and labor.

Especially impressive in the views of the future presented herein is a concept that explains why the authors are so optimistic about change and its impact on work in the next century. The authors, sometimes explicitly but also implicitly, argue that the generators of change will become the instruments for adaptation. In the Industrial Revolution, the instruments of change in the form of factories and mechanized equipment could not guide the forms necessary to adapt to these changes. This deficiency amplified human conflict and led, in part at least, to the disastrous state of mistrust between corporate authority and its employees. We are still dealing with this legacy of mistrust, but the authors identify a number of factors that will enable society to weather the changes in a constructive fashion.

Above all, the demands of technological and competitive change are for cooperation rather than conflict.

As I have indicated, the strongest basis for optimism is the expectation that what is bringing about the changes will also be useful in implementing them and in helping society to adapt.

For example, the computer will continue to alter job content and the concept of work. But it will also be useful in educating the young and in re-educating the old to enable them to master new technologies and work activities. The new technologies will not appear as the massive threat characteristic of technological change in the 18th and 19th centuries. Power-driven looms did not contain the means of adaptation. They were simply the monoliths to which one had to adapt by giving up skills that took generations to form, and that were acquired

Abraham Zaleznik

In the Industrial Revolution, the instruments of change in the form of factories and mechanized equipment could not guide the forms necessary to adapt to these changes.

by building identifications and social ties.

In addition to providing the means for adaptation, the 21st century forces of change will contain clear rewards for all participants, in the form of higher incomes, more leisure, improved health and a longer life. Above all, the authors visualize a subtle change in power relations, largely through the perfection of participatory methods of the work place instead of the methods of confrontation historically employed by the erstwhile antagonists, corporations and unions. All in all, they describe an optimistic vision of the future, where drudgery and work will no longer be synonymous; neither personal growth reserved only for the intelligentsia, nor leisure only for the economically privileged.

It is a useful exercise in reading the projections of futurists to adopt the position of various critics trained in the disciplines of the human sciences, ranging from biology to political science and history. The aim would not necessarily be to temper the enthusiasm of the futurists, but to extend the argument and to identify the critical variables underlying the predictions.

The biologist, operating in league with the ethologist and the psychoanalyst, would suggest that the critical variable in predicting the predominance of participation and cooperation in human resource management is man's aggression and his capacity to control its uses. I am considering, in the role of the biologist, not just the potential for destructive warfare among nations, which could undermine any prediction. There are other considerations, such as the capacity for relinquishing self-interest in favor of broader goals of longer-term significance for a society.

In fact, we may have so thoroughly removed the threat of massive warfare through the nuclear stand-off as to make the smaller scale conflicts even more destructive, particularly when world leaders no longer have the luxury of maintaining internal cohesion by finding external enemies as the targets of aggression.

Aggression is an innate drive in human beings, as it is in animals. It is necessary for survival, but it can be directed for both constructive and destructive ends. Self-interest, defined to include the interests of kin and group, appears also to be innate.

In combination, these two innate qualities of people mean that when changes occur that are perceived to diminish the interests of the individual and kindred others, aggression will heighten and be directed at some objects for the purposes of securing a favorable balance between what one has and what one wants. When the Detroit automobile worker smashes a Japanese-made car, he is venting aggression at the object that most closely represents what diminishes his self-interest.

When his union, the United Auto Workers, fights the establishment of a joint venture in California between General Motors and Toyota that threatens to reduce the employment of unionized workers, this too represents a mobilization of aggression. The aggression may be controlled and directed, as in the case of formal negotiations and bargaining, or it may be irrationally directed in the form of outright violence or more subtle means of sabotaging the intent of a work contract.

The history of participative methods of governing enterprise does not lead to optimism about the ease with which these methods can be employed or, indeed, their value in overcoming the conflict of interests, real or perceived, between individuals and groups with unequal power. Participatory methods are so fundamentally rational as to make one wonder why they have not been universally accepted.

Participatory methods are so fundamentally rational as to make one wonder why they have not been universally accepted.

Elton Mayo wrote about participation in the 1920s and 1930s. Kurt Lewin urged their adoption during the 1940s when he wrote about his experiments with autocratic, democratic and laissez-faire styles of leadership. Douglas MacGregor also advocated participation during the 1950s when he discussed Theory X and Theory Y types of management as psychological prototypes. Abraham Maslow, Rensis Likert, Robert Blake, Chris Argyris and many others writing in the 1960s and 1970s also presented the case for more expressive, democratic and participatory methods in authority relations.

And for the 1980s, it appears that a new rationalism will prevail, as a justification for sharing power in industry utilizing the examples of Japan, Sweden, West

6

Germany and other industrialized nations to support new modes of distributing decision-making throughout organizational hierarchies.

But given the now more than a half century of advocacy of an idea, why has it not genuinely taken hold? It has not taken hold, except in form, in all industrialized nations, not just the United States. When the historian examines the case of Japan, for example, the easy conclusions we have been fed about the causes of success of Japanese industry will not withstand close examination.

The Japanese are masterful in regulating form while maintaining continuity in substance, as revealed in the history of the Japanese response to the American occupation. There is a powerful respect for authority in Japan and a cohesion that comes from limited alternatives, racial homogeneity and clarity of goals that go hand-in-hand with the dangers imposed by living on a tight island with limited natural resources.

Aggression within a society can be regulated when the power of self-interest, broadly defined here to include the interests of kindred groups, demands that aggression be contained and targeted as a matter of survival. Under these socio-economic conditions, participation becomes a ritual that expresses the attachment of power figures and their immediate constituents to goals held in common.

At this juncture, we may ask the anthropologist for help in clarifying why western nations, particularly the United States, have great difficulty in establishing common interests and goals and, thereby, eliciting willing cooperation. Our question to the anthropologist becomes even more pointed, given the possibility that participatory methods and the democratization of work can take hold only under conditions of cohesion and mutual identification of interests.

In the United States during the last half century, for example, we experienced this mutuality in our national psyche only during World War II. Witness what our society accomplished during this national and world crisis. Productivity astonished friend and foe alike. Morale reached a pinnacle, especially in light of the sacrifice of lives entailed in sending sons to war. It does not seem probable that such conditions can be replicated in the face of the gradual changes that will take place in our society over the next 50 years. While we can easily dramatize the changes affecting work, they should not be exaggerated, especially if we take into account the effects of Hippocrates' equilibrium hypothesis.

Turning more directly to our anthropologist, she would probably point to the secularization of society and human relations as a basic factor to account for the difficulties in establishing cohesion and purpose in our society. The text through which societies express their internal condition is the collection of rituals that elaborate and reinforce those values that bind people to one another.

The fact that rituals are absent in corporate relations and in the conduct of work suggests, on the surface at least, that there is a paucity of values attached to being a member of a corporation. Ritual exists only where the values are deeply established. To create ritual in the hope of inculcating values, as is the case with much of modern-day practice in corporations, misunderstands cause and effect.

To create ritual in the hope of inculcating values, as is the case with much of modern-day practice in corporations, misunderstands cause and effect.

What, in the view of the futurist, will lead to internal cohesion in corporate society? While this book's authors are not precise in their predictions, it appears as though they rely on a common culture arising out of the equalization of power. The shared values will develop around expressiveness, the elaboration of lifestyle which, in turn, will be supported by a better-educated population and economic security.

This optimistic forecast, in answer to the anthropologist's concern about the relationship between values and ritual, would not necessarily satisfy the political economist or the historian. Both of these disciplines lean toward conservative outlooks and eschew utopianism.

The political economist would, in all probability, suggest that the new technologies may lead to new work content and even higher productivity, but would leave untouched the problem of the distribution of wealth. This problem causes conflict in labor relations as it does in international relations, particularly between the Third World and the industrialized societies. The economist would also suggest that optimism must be tempered by the risks associated with the isolation of large segments of the urban population from the work force. Insofar as those who are isolated are also in the racial minorities, unstable and even explosive possibilities exist for the expression of discontent and the counter moves toward a repressive society.

In weighing the alternative views of work and society in the 21st century, it might be useful to draw some lessons from history. What seems to make a difference in the course a society takes? The authors agree with the historical view that technological change is one of the major forces that transform society, and they properly identify the unique characteristics of the present day forms as compared to technological changes of an earlier period.

If work in the 21st century turns into a dismal experience...the cause may well be a failure in leadership.

The historian, in fact, would probably add to the dimensions of change under way by pointing to the probable impact of the knowledge being generated in the biological sciences. To some futurists, progress in biology and genetics may make the information and computer revolutions diminish in importance as engines of change in society.

Some historians would stress the role of leadership in determining whether the new technologies will, in the end, spell progress for humanity. Here, the question is less the appearance of charismatic leaders and more the diffusion of leadership talent throughout the many institutions in society and at all levels in the hierarchy. If work in the 21st century turns into a dismal experience, fraught with conflict and drifting toward alienation and divisiveness in society, the cause may well be a failure in leadership.

One of the first steps that must be taken to encourage the development of leadership is to place less reliance on what structures can do and more on the education of individuals to apply their talents to the aims of productivity and human satisfaction. For social, economic and political change to spell progress, the individual and leadership must once again ameliorate the tension between stability and change. □

The emergence of expressivism will revolutionize the contract between workers and employers.

Yankelovich & immerwahr

DANIEL YANKELOVICH *is president and co-founder of the Public Agenda Foundation and chairman of Yankelovich, Skelly and White. He is the author of* New Rules, Ego and Instinct *(with William Barrett) and* Work, Productivity and Job Satisfaction *(with Raymond Katzell).*

JOHN IMMERWAHR *is professor of philosophy at Villanova University and a senior project consultant for the Public Agenda Foundation. He is the author of* The Speaker and the Listener, *and of numerous articles on philosophy and public policy.*

There is a growing recognition that the productiveness of an organization, or the vitality of the economy as a whole, results from the interaction of at least two sets of factors. On the one hand, hard factors such as technology, investment capital and a favorable trade environment, play a tremendous role. But soft factors such as the values, attitudes and expectations of the work force also have an important role in determining the success of an industry.

America's growth as a world economic leader, for example, was not solely due to technology and an abundance of natural resources. America's industrial might was also the result of a happy marriage of these factors with the needs, hopes and values of America's work force.

The technology of the industrial revolution called for a large and relatively unskilled labor force, willing to work hard at jobs that were difficult and offered little intrinsic reward. But millions of immigrants welcomed these jobs as an opportunity to participate in the American dream— a chance for steady work, good wages, a car, a home and the possibility of a better life for their children.

It is also arguable that the phenomenal power of the Japanese economy in the last 10 years has been fueled by a similar marriage of hard and soft factors. So far,

Japan has been more successful than any of its competitors at integrating the cultural values of its work force with the technology of the 1970s and 1980s. Japanese production techniques, such as the "zero defect" approach to quality control, combine both sophisticated use of automation and the availability of a work force committed to teamwork and quality workmanship. This combination has helped make Japan, with virtually no natural resources, an industrial giant—occupying the pace-setting position that was long the prerogative of the United States.

In looking ahead to the work place of the 21st century, then, it is important to look at the evolving relationship between the values and expectations that people will bring to their jobs, and the qualities that the jobs will demand from the work force. Our thesis is that the economic health of the nation (and of specific organizations) will be a function of how well these factors can be integrated.

We foresee the growth of two trends. The first concerns the increase in the amount of control or discretion that jobholders have over their work; the second concerns the emergence of a new set of work place values which we call the philosophy of expressivism. These trends already have transformed the American work place and can be expected to have an even more significant impact as we enter the 21st century.

The task of integrating these two trends will be one of the central tasks of managers and administrators. Many of our conclusions are based on research conducted by the Public Agenda Foundation as part of *Jobs in the 1980s and 1990s*, a three-year international project focusing on jobs and the economy in the United States, Germany, Israel, Japan, Sweden and the United Kingdom.

The beginning of the 20th century witnessed a remarkable shift from the farm to the factory as the place where most Americans worked. Even today, our vision of the American jobholder is still sometimes similar to Charlie Chaplin's portrayal of the assembly line worker, endlessly repeating the same simple task. But the work place is now involved in a second major transformation, from the factory to the office as the major place of work, and from industrial technologies to the new computer

Daniel Yankelovich

If the number of white-collar jobs continues to grow, then we can project a corresponding growth in the amount of discretion in the work place.

and information technologies.

By the time we reach the 21st century, the American work place will be as different from the industrial world caricatured by Chaplin as that industrial world was from the rural America of the 19th century.

One of the most dramatic changes has to do with the growth in the amount of discretion or control people have over how they do their jobs. It is obvious that there are vast differences in the amount of freedom people now have in their jobs. Some workers (fast food restaurant employees, for example) have such narrowly defined and closely supervised jobs that they have relatively little control over the quantity and quality of their output. Other jobholders (tenured college professors, for example) have tremendous latitude in how they do their jobs; some do little more than show up for (most of) their scheduled classes, while others engage in incredibly ambitious programs of scholarship, teaching and counseling.

Although there has always been a significant number of jobs with high discretion, our research shows that the total amount of discretion in the work place has increased dramatically and will, no doubt, continue to increase. This growth in the amount of discretion is related to two major changes in the American work place:

- *Changes in the nature of jobs*—One of the most important changes is a shift in the kinds of jobs that Americans hold. As Figure 1 shows, there has been impressive growth in the number of white-collar and service-sector jobs, and a corresponding drop in the number of blue-collar and manufacturing jobs. Today, managers and professionals outnumber unskilled laborers five to one, and public school teachers outnumber all of the production workers in the chemical, oil, rubber, plastic, paper and steel industries combined. This trend can be expected to continue into the future. Peter Drucker projects that by the beginning of the 21st century, blue-collar/manufacturing jobs will follow the pattern of agricultural jobs and shrink to an extremely small percentage of the work force, perhaps as low as seven percent.

This shift has also created rapid growth in the amount of discretion in the work place. Common sense suggests that professional, technical and managerial jobholders have much more control over how to do their work than do factory workers on assembly lines. Our research bears this out by showing that white-collar and service-sector jobs typically involve a great deal more freedom or discretion than blue-collar and manufacturing jobs. Close to half of all white-collar jobholders (49 percent) say they have a great deal of freedom over how to perform their jobs, as compared to only a third (33 percent) of blue-collar workers. If the number of white-collar jobs continues to grow, then we can project a corresponding growth in the amount of discretion in the work place.

● *New technologies*—The work place is also being transformed by a technological revolution that is, in many ways, more far-reaching than the first industrial revolution. One of the most interesting effects is the way in which

...nearly half of all jobholders say they do not put much effort into their jobs over and above what is required.

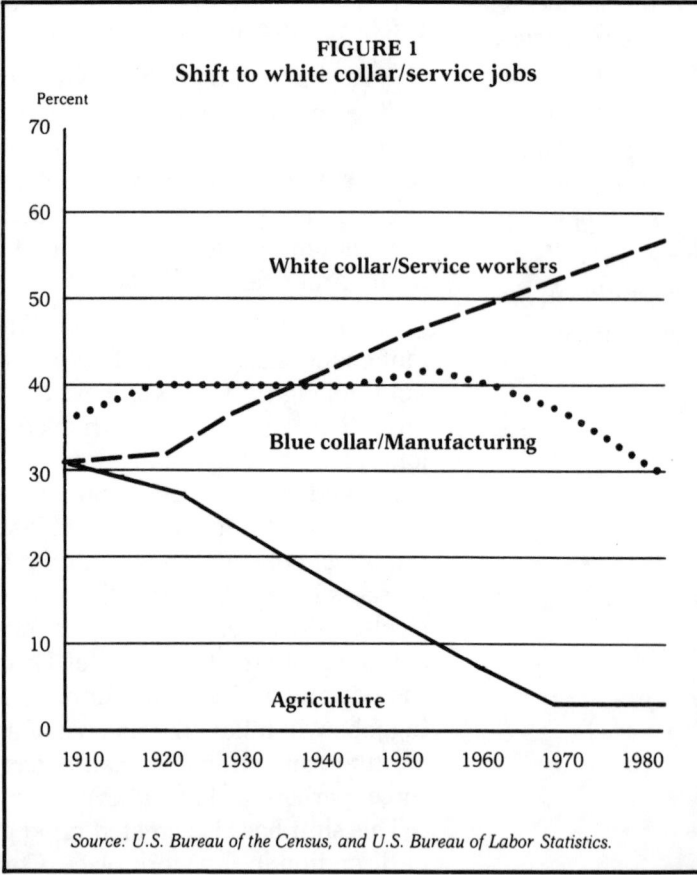

FIGURE 1
Shift to white collar/service jobs

Percent

Source: U.S. Bureau of the Census, and U.S. Bureau of Labor Statistics.

John Immerwahr

Rather than making jobs more trivial, monotonous and uncreative, the new technology usually gives jobholders more discretion.

new technology also increases discretion. In this respect, the second industrial revolution has an opposite effect from the first. The steam engine and the assembly line made it possible for complex products to be built by an uneducated and unskilled labor force. By simplifying and dividing tasks, the technology of the first industrial revolution made the individual worker less important.

The new technology has the opposite effect. The jobs created in a high-technology, knowledge-intensive economy are geared to skilled and educated employees. Rather than making jobs more trivial, monotonous and uncreative, the new technology usually gives jobholders more discretion. The computers and the robots can do the routine tasks, leaving people to do the thinking and the work that requires skill and discretion.

The impact of automated teller machines (ATMs) in many banks is typical of the effect of much of the new technology. One bank teller we interviewed put it this way: "Now that we have the ATM, many of the routine transactions are handled by the machine. I spend a great deal more of my time on the judgment calls. We've had a lot of stolen payroll checks in this area, and when someone who doesn't have an account here walks in with a large payroll check, I'm the one who has to decide whether or not to cash it. A much larger proportion of my work is now taken up by this kind of transaction, and it has definitely made my job more challenging."

Our data show that this reaction to the new technology is widespread. Approximately 44 percent of the American work force say that they have already experienced significant technological change in their jobs, and most of these jobholders also report that technology has increased their degree of control. Just under three-quarters (74 percent) say that the changes have made their work more interesting, and more than half (55 percent) say that technological changes have given them more independence.

So far, however, we have only seen the tip of the iceberg. The new technologies are destined to transform virtually every aspect of the American work place—even further increasing the amount of discretion in the work place.

Growth of discretion in the work place is also being accompanied by a major change in the values that jobholders bring to their work. A new set of meanings and values, which we call expressivism, already has made a significant impact and can be expected to continue to grow in importance.

After experiencing two world wars and world-wide depression in the '30s, the advanced industrial democracies such as the United States, Sweden and Germany have enjoyed more than a generation of prosperity and peace. To some extent, the people who grew up in this postwar period took for granted the quest for security and affluence that was so important to their parents, and have come to place great emphasis on what we call the values of expressivism.

Although these values grow out of the affluence of the '50s and '60s, they have proved to be remarkably durable in the environment of economic slowdowns in recent years. Observers have given a variety of different names to the values— e.g. "reproductive" (Zetterberg), "post materialist" (Inglehart), "third wave" (Toffler), and "inner directed" (Mitchell)—but whatever they are called there is overwhelming evidence that new cultural values have come to play a major role in the United States and in the other advanced industrial countries.

These values are familiar to all students of the "baby-boom" generation. One of the most important components of the new values is a focus on a new meaning of success. Rather than defining success in terms of externals—large homes in good neighborhoods, expensive cars and clothing— expressive success focuses on inner intangibles, valuing personal self-expression and fulfilling one's potential as an individual. Those who adhere to the values of expressivism place great emphasis on autonomy and freedom of choice, reacting uneasily to most forms of rigid hierarchy and to lack of involvement with decision-making that affects their lives. Expressivism is also associated with a desire to live in closer harmony with nature, and with a need for closer bonds of community with others.

To chart the impact of expressivism in the work place, the Public Agenda research explored the fundamental question of what people see as their primary motivation for

Rather than defining success in terms of externals...expressive success focuses on inner intangibles...

16

working—what might be called the "core relationship" to work.

Specifically, we presented three possibilities: The first level sees work primarily as a means of survival; at this level the motive for working is the desire to feed, clothe and shelter one's self and one's dependents in order to stay alive. A second level of motivation places a heavy demand on improving one's standard of living. These two stages do not measure expressivism. The new expressive values are measured by a third level, which takes both survival and standard of living for granted and focuses on personal growth and self development as the primary motives for working.

A jobholder who identifies self development as the main reason for working holds an extremely strong version of expressivism. The jobholders we studied were asked to

Those who adhere to the values of expressivism place great emphasis on autonomy and freedom of choice, reacting uneasily to most forms of rigid hierarchy...

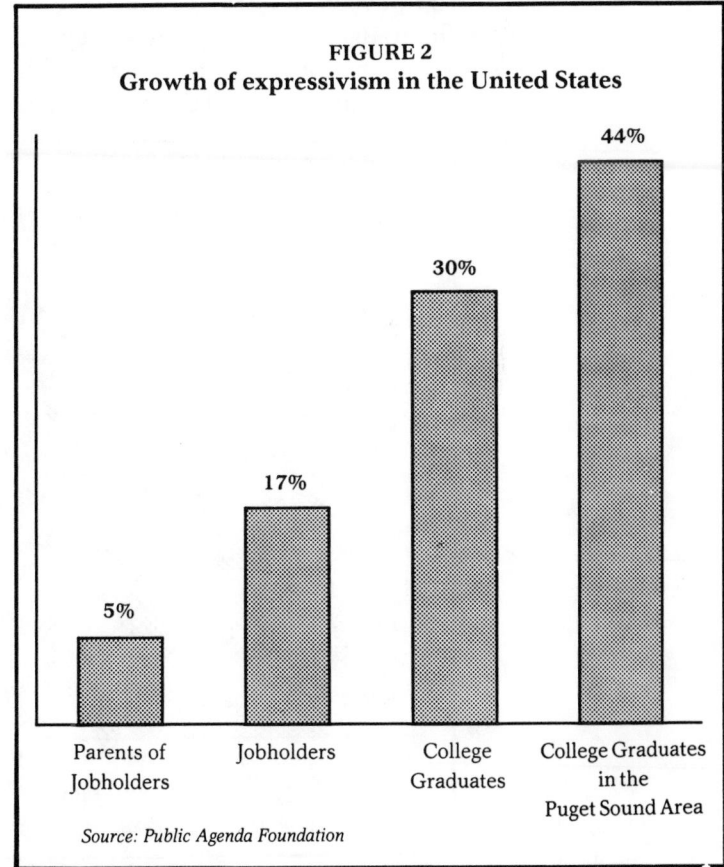

FIGURE 2
Growth of expressivism in the United States

Source: Public Agenda Foundation

describe their parents' core relationship to work, as well as their own.

We found an impressive shift in the core relationship to work, from work as a means of survival to work as a means of self expression. Half of the work force say their parents worked primarily to survive, while only a small fraction (five percent) feel that their parents worked primarily for self-development. When jobholders describe themselves, however, there is a significant decrease in the number who work for survival (from 50 percent to 38 percent) and the number who work primarily for self-development (from five percent to 17 percent) more than triples.

College-educated jobholders are much more likely to say that they work for self-development...

What is even more significant is the relationship between self-development and education. College-educated jobholders are much more likely to say that they work for self-development, and college-educated jobholders in affluent high-technology areas such as the Puget Sound area are even more likely to adhere to this strong form of expressivism (Figure 2). Since education levels have been ris-

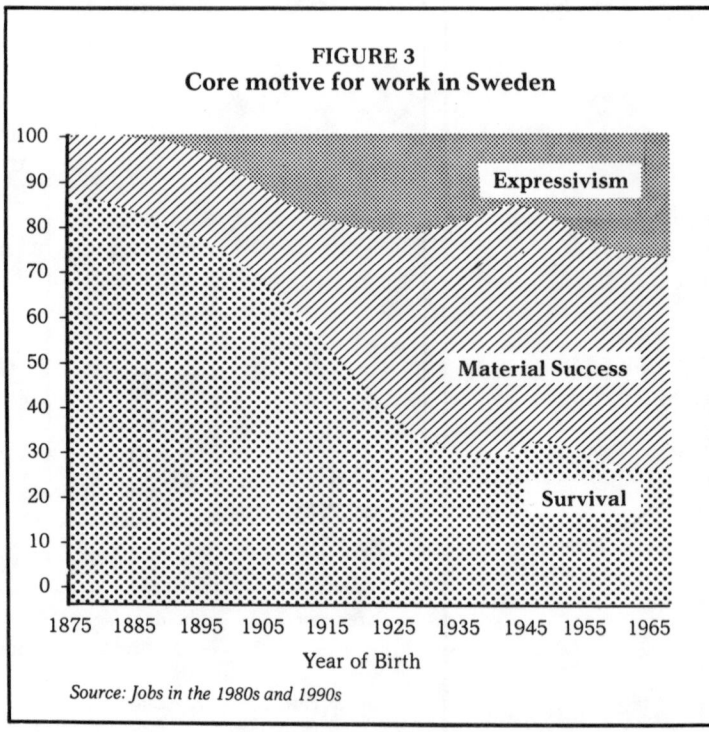

FIGURE 3
Core motive for work in Sweden

Expressivism

Material Success

Survival

Year of Birth

Source: Jobs in the 1980s and 1990s

ing significantly in America and the other industrialized democracies, this suggests that expressivism may also be on the increase.

The Swedish research team used another method to document the growth of expressivism. By including both teenagers and retirees in their sample, they were able to show the relationship between expressivism and age in Sweden (Figure 3). Since other areas of comparison show considerable similarity between Swedish and U.S. values, this finding may apply to the U.S. as well.

These findings suggest that the philosophy of expressivism has made a steady increase and can be expected to increase even further in the decades ahead.

If these two trends—the growth of discretion and the growth of expressivism—continue for the next 20 years in the same way that they have in the past 20, they will have a significant impact on the work place as we enter the 21st century.

The work place will be primarily characterized by high-discretion jobs, where individual jobholders have a great deal of latitude over how they perform their work, and where control of work lies largely in the hands of individual jobholders, rather than in the hands of their employers or managers. But the jobholders themselves will also be different—a much larger proportion of them will see themselves as primarily working to fulfill their expressive needs, rather than their needs for survival or for material success.

...the philosophy of expressivism has made a steady increase and can be expected to increase even further in the decades ahead.

What implications does this possibility have for the future viability of the American work place? Rather than attempting to make any prediction on this point, we will sketch out two scenarios—a best case and a worst case. The success of either will depend on the ability of American managers to respond to the new conditions.

It is painfully easy to anticipate the worst case. There are many ways that expressivism can find outlets. In the '60s, many young Americans who held expressivist attitudes sought their fulfillment outside of the work place— through nature, alternative lifestyles and drugs.

Expressivism has changed its focus in the tougher economic times of the late 1970s and early 1980s. Today, rather than "dropping out" of the world of work altogether, many jobholders are holding back effort on the job. They are working a full day in terms of hours, but giving less than they could give. We found that fewer than one in four working Americans (22 percent) say that they are currently working at their full potential, and nearly half of all jobholders (44 percent) say they do not put much effort into their jobs over and above what is required. Researchers at the University of Michigan found that the amount of time spent actually working dropped by 10 percent from 1965 to 1975. If this trend continues, it is possible that the expressive jobholders of the year 2000 will see their primary focus outside of the work place—and will see their jobs as making only a limited demand on their energies and intelligence.

This potential lack of commitment might not be a serious problem, if it were not also accompanied by a growth of discretion. In a low-discretion work place, the presence or absence of commitment is not necessarily an important factor. If jobholders have little discretion, acceptable levels of effort will be guaranteed by the supervision built into the nature of the work itself. But in a high-discretion work place, such as the one we have anticipated, the presence or absence of commitment makes a great deal of difference.

A jobholder who has a great deal of freedom can use that freedom in different ways. They may use it primarily to "goof off", socializing with co-workers, talking to friends on the telephone, or planning leisure activities for after work. The worst-case scenario, then, envisions a high-discretion/low-commitment model, where large numbers of jobholders take advantage of the fact that there is little control over their output.

They may put in the required number of hours, but use high discretion as an opportunity to hold back from their jobs, so that they can invest their energy in meeting their expressive needs outside of the work place. If we couple this scenario with a continued growth in the competitiveness of the world economic marketplace, we would expect to see the United States falling into a secondary economic position, with a stagnating standard of living.

High-expressive jobholders do not have to find the outlet for their expressiveness outside of productive work. There is considerable evidence that expressive jobholders can find an arena for the expressivism within the work place. In *The Soul of a New Machine*, journalist Tracy Kidder gives us a portrait of high-discretion jobholders/high-expressivist jobholders giving a virtually total commitment to the design of a new computer. The engineers themselves had a phrase for the kind of commitment that transcended a routine investment in the job:

> The term the old hands used...was "signing up". By signing up for the project you agreed to do whatever was necessary for success. You agreed to forsake, if necessary, family, hobbies and friends—if you had any of these left (and you might not if you had signed up too many times before).

In its research on the attitudes of job holders, the Public Agenda Foundation documented the degree to which high-expressivist jobholders are ready and willing to "sign-up" if the conditions are correct. In our research we measured respondents' commitment to the work ethic. Significantly, a majority of American jobholders (52 percent) endorsed a strong form of the work ethic, saying that they "felt an inner need to do the best job possible." What is even more important, however, is that the extreme expressivist jobholders have an even broader level of support for the work ethic. We found that more than seven in 10 (72 percent) of these expressivist jobholders say they have an inner need to do the best job possible.

Our survey showed that expressivist jobholders do make different demands on their work than non-expressive jobholders. They are much more likely to want freedom about how to do their work, and they are much more concerned with creativity. They are also less concerned with economic security. But these differences do not mean that they are incapable of high levels of commitment.

Our research suggests that expressive jobholders are willing to give a great deal to their jobs—if their expressive needs can be met in the work place. In the best-case scenario, then, expressivist jobholders use the high discretion of the work place to give reign to their creativity and entrepreneurship, and see the work place as an appropriate arena to seek self development.

We believe that, barring major catastrophes such as nuclear war, there is a strong probability that a high-discretion/high-expressivism work place will emerge as we move towards the 21st century. But it is much more difficult to predict how the American economy will respond to these conditions, and where, on the continuum between the best case and the worst case described above, the bulk of American industry will fall. The determination of whether the country is able to forge a successful integration of this new combination of hard and soft factors will largely be in the hands of managers and administrators.

The most important variable may well be the status of what might be called the unwritten work contract. In addition to the formal work contract governing hours and salary, there is an implied contract governing the psychic rewards and necessities of a job. The emergence of a high-discretion/high-expressivism work place will require a new unwritten contract that will be responsive to these conditions. What we mean by a new contract can best be explained by contrasting it with the contract that was dominant for much of the post-war period.

Until fairly recently, the primary unwritten contract in the American workplace offered material well-being and the status of being a breadwinner in exchange for a limited commitment to jobs that were often dull and unrewarding. But it is clear that this kind of contract will not be adequate for a high-discretion/high-expressivism work place.

In addition to the formal work contract governing hours and salary, there is an implied contract governing the psychic rewards and necessities of a job.

Jobholders with expressivist values demand more than the external rewards of material well being and status, and high-discretion jobs require more that a limited commitment. The engineers that Tracy Kidder described did not spend 18-hour days writing micro code in a windowless basement because of a desire for money or external status. What drove them on was that their expressive needs were also being met; the work place had engaged their need for creativity, autonomy and involvement.

What is needed is a contract that will offer rewards that appeal to the new values of expressivism, in exchange for the greater dedication and commitment that will be required of jobholders in a high-discretion work place.

Specifically, managers and administrators must find

ways of structuring work so that it appeals to the needs of expressivist jobholders for autonomy, creativity, community and entrepreneurship. The specific details of this new contract will vary widely from one organization to another—but it is clear that many elements of the American work place will need to be re-thought. Managers will need to re-evaluate the rigid hierarchies and sharp status differences that characterized the low-discretion work place.

High-discretion workers respond poorly to these structures, and sharp status division undercut the sense of teamwork and community that can engage the effort of expressivist jobholders. Unions and managers will have to re-evaluate their adversary relationship and accept the thesis that non-monetary rewards are as important and valuable as monetary ones. And industrial engineers need to design systems that take advantage of and reward people's needs for self-fulfillment on the job, rather than attempting to develop technology that bypasses the human element.

The task is to develop reward systems that make the work place of the 21st century as well suited to the needs of the 21st century jobholders as the work place of industrial America was suited for the needs of an earlier American work force. □

Creativity will dominate our time after the concepts of work and fun have been blurred by technology.

Asimov

ISAAC ASIMOV *is a professor of biochemistry at Boston University School of Medicine, but he doesn't work at it. What he works at is his writing. He has published 280 books, fiction and non-fiction, for children and adults.*

Periodically in history, there come periods of great transition in which work changes its meaning. There was a time, perhaps 10,000 years ago, when human beings stopped feeding themselves by hunting game and gathering plants, and increasingly turned to agriculture. In a way, that represented the invention of "work," the hard daily labor designed to ensure food and the wherewithal of life.

"In the sweat of thy face shalt thou eat bread," says God to Adam as the first man is expelled from the garden, and the transition from food-gathering to agriculture is symbolized.

Then, in the latter decades of the 18th century, as the Industrial Revolution began in Great Britain, there was another transition in which the symbols of work were no longer the hoe and the plow; they were replaced by the mill and the assembly line. The aristocrat no longer cultivated a pale skin as his mark that he did not have to go out into the fields to labor; instead, he cultivated a deep tan to show that he did not have to stay indoors to labor.

And now we stand at the brink of a change that will be the greatest of all, for work in its old sense will disappear altogether. To most people, work has always been an effortful exercising of mind or body—compelled by the bitter necessity of earning the necessities of life—plus an occasional period of leisure in which to rest or have fun.

People have always tried desperately to foist off work on others: on slaves, serfs or peasants; on hired hands, on animals, on ingenious machines. With the Industrial Revolution, machinery—powered first by steam, then by electricity and internal combustion engines— took over the hard physical tasks, and relieved the strain on human and animal muscles.

There remained, however, the "easier" labor that did not require muscle, and that machines, however ingenious, could not do—the labor that required the human eyes, ears, judgment and mind. If this work did not require huge effort, bulging muscles and sweat, it nevertheless had its miseries, for it tended to be dull, repetitious and boring. Whether one works over a sewing machine, an assembly line or a typewriter, day after day, there is always the sour sense of endlessly doing something unpleasant under compulsion, something that stultifies one's mind and wastes one's life.

And yet, such jobs have been characteristic of the human condition in the first three-quarters of the 20th century. They've made too little demand on the human mind and spirit to keep them fresh and alive, made too much demand for any machine to serve the purpose—until now.

The electronic computer, invented in the 1940s and improved at breakneck speed, was a machine that, for the first time, seemed capable of doing work that had until then been the preserve of the human mind. With the coming of the microchip in the 1970s, computers became compact enough, versatile enough and (most important of all) cheap enough to serve as the brains of affordable machines that could take their place on the assembly line and in the office.

...the dull, the boring, the repetitious, the mind-stultifying work will begin to disappear from the job market—is already beginning to disappear.

This means that the dull, the boring, the repetitious, the mind-stultifying work will begin to disappear from the job market—is *already* beginning to disappear. This of course, will introduce two vital sets of problems—is *already* introducing them.

First, what will happen to the human beings who have been working at these disappearing jobs?

Second, where will we get the human beings to do the new jobs that will appear—jobs that are demanding, in-

26

Isaac Asimov

We are sure to find among the technologically unemployed those who, because of age, temperament or the mental damage done them by the kind of lives they have led or work they have done, are not able to profit from retraining.

teresting and mind-exercising, but that require a high-tech level of thought and education?

Clearly, there will be a painful period of transition, one that is starting already, and one that will be in full swing as the 21st century begins. The first problem, that of technological unemployment, will be temporary, for it will arise out of the fact that there is now a generation of employees who have not been educated to fit the computer age. However (in advanced nations, at least) they will be the last generation to be so lacking, so that with them this problem will disappear— or, at least, diminish to the point of non-crisis proportions.

While the problem exists, the unemployed must, first of all, be re-educated or re-trained to the best of their capacity so that they may be fitted for new jobs of the kind that the computer age will make available. (It is, after all, reasonable to suppose that computers will create far more jobs than they destroy—at least technological advance has always done so in the past. The only difficulty is that the created jobs are widely different from the destroyed ones.)

Consequently, as the 21st century opens, one of the most important jobs available (for those who can fill it) will be that of teaching the use of computers and the myriad skills involved in the design, construction and maintenance of computers and their mobile offspring, the robots. (And, of course, this will for a while further exacerbate the second problem, that of finding all the people necessary to take part in the computer revolution.)

We are sure to find among the technologically unemployed those who, because of age, temperament or the mental damage done them by the kind of lives they have led or work they have done, are not able to profit from re-training. For these, it will be necessary to create jobs they can do, or, in the extreme, to support them — for they are human beings. And this, too, will require much work in the way of administration and thoughtful and creative humanitarianism.

But the second problem — that of developing a large enough number of high-tech minds to run a high-tech world — will prove to be no problem at all, once we adjust our thinking.

In the first place, the computer age will introduce a total revolution in our notions of education, and is beginning to do so now. So far in history, there have been only two fundamental ways of educating the young, individual tutoring and mass education.

Individual tutoring has always been confined to a small minority who can afford a family tutor, and even if everyone could afford one, there would not be enough qualified tutors on the basis of one to a student. Therefore, when it turned out that an industrial society needed general literacy (which a strictly agricultural society does not), there was a move toward mass education.

It will undoubtedly turn out that the "average" child is much more intelligent and creative than we generally suppose.

There are enough teachers (at least of a sort) if each one is saddled with from 30 to 50 students, but the disadvantage is that the students must then learn according to a fixed curriculum with very little account taken of individual differences. As a result, every youngster learns to read and write after a fashion, but almost everyone of them becomes bored, or confused or alienated, depending on whether the teacher is going too slow, too fast or too "sideways" into uninteresting topics.

The coming of the computer means a return to individual tutoring on a new basis. If every home has a computer outlet, and if, through these, youngsters (and oldsters, too) can tune in to a thoroughly computerized library, it will be possible to probe into any field of interest about which one is curious. Schools will not vanish. They will serve to introduce subjects to their students and they will deal particularly with those fields of study that require human interaction. But each student, having grown interested in something (and we, each of us, grow interested in *something*) can follow it up at home in an individual way and at an individual time and speed.

This will make learning fun, and a successfully stimulated mind will learn quickly. It will undoubtedly turn out that the "average" child is much more intelligent and creative than we generally suppose. There was a time, after all, when the ability to read and write was confined to a very small group of "scholars," and almost all of them would have scouted the notion that just about *anyone* could learn the intricacies of literacy. Yet with mass education general literacy came to be a fact.

Right now, creativity seems to be confined to a very few, and it is easy to suppose that that is the way it must be. However, with the proper availability of computerized education, humanity will surprise the elite few once again.

Of course, that means there will be enormous opportunity for computer engineers to organize knowledge properly, to work out teaching programs, to keep them up to date, and to revise them for greater efficiency and interest. They will be the teachers of the future, and will be more important than ever to all of us.

Granted, now, that the problems of unemployment and education will be on the way toward solution, what kind of work will there be aside from what is involved in that solution?

For one thing, much of human effort that is today put into "running the world" will be unnecessary. With computers, robots and automation, a great deal of the daily grind will appear to be running itself. This is nothing startling. It is a trend that has been rapidly on its way ever since World War II. As an example, the telephone industry is now so automated that when hundreds of thousands of employees go out on strike, those who use telephones are hardly aware of any change. The telephone system runs itself.

The result of this trend will be that more and more working people will have more and more leisure. That is also not startling, for we have been witnessing the steady increase in leisure for a long time. This means that more and more "work" will involve the filling of this leisure time. Show business and sports will grow steadily more important. (A comment I once made, which has been frequently quoted, is: "One third of the world will labor to amuse the other two thirds.")

Hobbies of all sorts will grow steadily more important, and so will those industries catering to hobbies. This is not to be deplored; it will be another way of unleashing creativity. The devil may always find mischief for idle hands to do, but the true hobbyist is never idle—in fact no one works as assiduously and with such satisfaction as the hobbyist—and so the hobbyist will never be in mischief.

Right now, creativity seems to be confined to a very few, and it is easy to suppose that that is the way it must be.

And what of the kind of work that is more easily recognized as work in the traditional sense?

There will still be much that is peculiarly human and will not be computerized, except at the fringes. (I use a word processor, which makes the mechanics of my work a bit easier, but the thing steadfastly refuses to write my essays for me. I still have to sit here, thinking.) In other words, those who are involved in literature, music and the arts will be busier than ever in the leisure society, since their audience will grow steadily greater.

There will also be enormous changes. In business, the accent will be on decision-making, on administration. Offices and factories will be "black boxes" in which the routine details will run themselves, but in which men and women will handle the controls.

Nor will this have to be done on the spot. We will be living in an "information society" in which we will not have to transfer mass to transfer information. We won't have to send human beings from A to B in order that their mouth may give directions or their ear may receive directions. We won't even have to send letters back and forth to accomplish that. The information can be transferred at the speed of light, and—thanks to computers that do the remembering, the selecting and the transmitting—more efficiently than ever.

This means that the necessity of commuting will be increasingly a thing of the past. Business travel (as opposed to pleasure travel) will go way down. Oh, it will exist, since personal contact for psychological or social reasons will still be needed in business. But the inconvenient trip taken out of business necessity will be a thing of the past.

With computerization knitting the world into a tight unit, and with the work of directing operations and gathering information easily done from anywhere, the world will begin to decentralize. There will be an increasing tendency for cities to dwindle (this is already a recognized trend, at least in the United States).

It may sound as though the 21st century, with its increasing leisure, its black-box offices and factories, its emphasis on long-distance work from the home, may become the kind of society that will be too secure, too easy.

Not so!

We will also be entering the Space Age with a vengeance, and perhaps the most important type of work facing us as the new century opens will be that which is involved in gaining command of the resources of space.

We will be building solar power stations that will absorb the full range of sunlight in space and turn it into microwaves that will be beamed to Earth. We will be building observatories to study the Universe away from the interference of Earth's atmosphere and of human-made light and radio beams. We will be building laboratories to study the effects and uses of space's unusual properties—high and low temperature, hard radiation, zero gravity.

We will be building factories that will be turning out products making use of these properties, products that could be turned out only with difficulty, if at all, on Earth's surfaces. We will be building mining stations on the Moon to get the material out of which all these structures will be built, and space settlements on which the men and women working on all these projects can live—and on which they can build families and new societies.

...all the future of humanity will be coming to fruition in the emptiness that we will be filling, and there will be incredible excitement and precious little boredom in that.

And for every person in space engaged on these magnificent new goals, there will be a dozen people on Earth supporting the ventures.

In the opening decades of the 21st century, with the aid of computers and robots, all the future of humanity will be coming to fruition in the emptiness we will be filling, and there will be incredible excitement and precious little boredom in that.

In fact, the 21st century, for all its advancement, will be one of the great pioneering periods of human history, as people work under totally new conditions, doing totally new things in totally new ways, taking totally new risks to achieve totally new triumphs.□

Educators must advocate holism to prepare our human resources for the coming decentralization.

Lodge

GEORGE C. LODGE *is a professor of business administration at the Harvard University Graduate School of Business Administration and a former assistant secretary of the U.S. Department of Labor. He is the author of several books, including* The New American Ideology, *and* The American Disease, *to be published early in 1984.*

Looking toward the 21st century from where we stand today, one must predict that American schools will get better. Reports on their deterioration abound. Other nations, such as Japan, are putting U.S. industries out of business, in part because of more effective education and training.

Unemployment and alienation, arising from inadequate education, are contributing to the emergence of an underclass that threatens to unravel our social fabric. Scientific and technological innovation is growing faster than our ability to understand or manage it.

As a consequence, it seems reasonable to assume that business will play a leading role in educational renovation, "adopting" schools, working closely with all kinds of educational institutions to ensure that an industry's particular needs for technicians and experts of one sort or another will be met.

So schools will get better. But what does "better" mean? It could mean more effective preparation of the individual for the occupation of increasingly specialized bureaucratic and hierarchical slots. In such a case we will likely land in a *Brave New World* that will make Huxley's pale. The sequence of events is all too easy to predict: the inexorable, empirical, rational drift; an ever-increasing centralization of power into the hands of a specialized elite capable of manipulating unlimited numbers of people; the people *lodge*

themselves, neatly engineered, pulled together into burgeoning concentrations for surveillance and control.[1]

At issue are two quite different ideological patterns of science and education. The first embraces five powerful theories created by the genius of Copernicus and Newton, developed by their followers, and employed even today as the justification for much of our educational system.

The first of those theories is *specialization,* the inevitable process of fragmentation that accompanies the efficiency of division of labor. This is a necessary and powerful tool for the deep analysis of matter; it has guided our creation of the expert, the person competent to analyze man, society and the world in one particular aspect—say chemistry or anthropology.

The second, related theory is *reductionism,* the belief that the way to understand systems or wholes is to break them apart. If you know enough about the parts, you can put them together and understand the whole; or, to put it another way, if you concentrate on the parts, the whole will take care of itself. Understand Humpty Dumpty's organs, cells, molecules and atoms, and you can put him together again.

In combination, specialization and reductionism have produced the proliferation of "disciplines." Their proliferation is accelerating. Shortly after World War II, there were about 54 specializations in the sciences; 20 years later there were more than 900.[2]

The third theory is the Newtonian belief that knowledge, to be scientific, must be *objective.* That is, it must be quantifiable; what cannot be measured presumably is not worth knowing. Although this idea began and predominated in the physical sciences, it has also become pervasive in the social sciences. Sociologists, for example, busy themselves with counting and quantifying. In their pursuit of what is good, corporations insist that somehow "goodness" must be measured in a "social audit" or something of the kind.

The fourth component of traditional scientific ideology has been *rationalism.* Reason was exalted; the emotions, the intuition, spiritual perceptions were considered unscientific, the domain of mystics.

Finally, the overwhelming emphasis of science has

Shortly after World War II, there were about 54 specializations in the sciences; 20 years later there were more than 900.

George C. Lodge

The whole, we now know, does not take care of itself...

been on physical matter. It has tended to identify reality with matter and thus to sustain *materialism.* As a consequence: "What counts is what I can feel and touch and see. If it feels nice and looks magnificent, so much the better—especially if I own it."

Plainly there has been, and will continue to be, great power and convenience in these old theories. But they have become increasingly suspect. Anachronisms have developed, as have inconsistencies between the concepts and the real world to which they were supposed to relate. The ideas no longer work very well.

The whole, we now know, does not take care of itself; nor is it necessarily understood or cared for through an analysis of the parts. Furthermore, the rigid bureaucracies of specialization, each with its covey of experts rewarded for knowing more and more about less and less, have constrained the outlook of science and limited the variety of frameworks with which it can approach the world and nature.

The eclectic empiricists who, in the best tradition of experimentalism, set forth to find out what is really happening in the world, frequently find themselves put down by the refined and elegant constructs of the specialists.

This is reminiscent of Copernicus' problems with the church in the 16th century, the church today being the economics department or some such hallowed group. As what the Fathers determined then was not to be questioned, so it is with specialists now. Thus, their constructs have come to obscure our vision of reality by imposing on it too segmented and finely divided a filter; the absolutes of reality—which seem to exist and operate, although we may never know them directly—are straining such constructs to the breaking point.

Thus several new ideological components are at hand. In place of specialization, or rather as a counterweight to it, there is holism. This is the recognition that everything must be considered in relation to everything else; that mankind is one; that it lives on a spaceship, Earth; that the resources available to it are limited; that to survive, people must become harmonious with each other and with all of nature.

Complementing reductionism, there is a new appreciation of synthetic thought, a kind of synodism among the sciences. It stems from the awareness that wholes cannot necessarily be understood solely by the analysis of their parts and subsystems.

Complicating objectivity, there is the recognition that all observation, all measurement, all experience is necessarily subjective. Neither the measurer, the measure, nor the measured are absolute.

Complementing the purity of rationalism, there is an awareness that the power and scope of objective reason are slighter than we had supposed. The subjective and the irrational have been granted status as real, and it follows that an understanding of reality cannot rely exclusively on the severely logical—one might even say, syllogistic—reasoning processes on which science has prided itself in the past.

Even the understanding of oneself, both in terms of one's internal nature and one's relation to the surrounding whole, depends on varieties of consciousness that are intensely subjective, intuitional and psychic. The concept of self-realization, now taken seriously by science, also obviously depends on such subjective consciousness.

Complementing materialism and, to an extent, replacing it, there is a new tenderness for the value of the human being and humanity.

Let us assume that this new paradigm will gel with the older one into a new guidance system for science. What will it mean for the educational system?

Education in America...is increasingly deficient in providing young people with what they need to cope with in a changing environment.

Education in America is rooted firmly in the old paradigm. As such, it is increasingly deficient in providing young people with what they need to cope within a changing environment. Children are taught about a series of matters which, for the most part, are unrelated to one another and to the world as they find it. They are not provided with any sort of framework within which to order or derive meaning from the information they get. They are not helped to understand the great integral transition in the midst of which they must live and die.

Together with the idea of scientific specialization, this lack of structure has produced an educational system unable to train minds to understand the relationships between things, to grasp the whole.

As Alfred North Whitehead remarked: "It... 'produces' minds in a groove. Each profession makes progress, but it is progress in its own groove." We have replaced the celibacy of the medieval learned class with:

> ...a celibacy of the intellect which is divorced from the concrete contemplation of the complete facts... Consequently, the specialized functions of the community are performed better and more progressively, but the generalized direction lacks vision. The progressiveness in detail only adds to the danger produced by the feebleness of coordination.

In an attempt to become more concrete, education has directed itself increasingly toward the real world, but its focus is piecemeal, governed by the old abstractions and disciplinary divisions. Furthermore, in the name of rationalism, education has been guilty of a form of irrationalism.

By limiting itself to what is considered rational, education halts at a particular set of abstractions, which may greatly curtail learning. Thus, we are apt to miss what is important. Again, as Whitehead put it: "When you understand all about the sun and all about the atmosphere and all about the rotation of the earth, you may still miss the radiance of the sunset."[3]

One can see Whitehead's point by taking a brief look at the modern American college. There was a time, in the more medieval past, when the college told the incoming freshman: "We know what an educated man or woman needs to know. We will give it to you, and once you have it, you can go forth and cope." Today it says instead, "We don't know what you need to know. We assume that you do. Here is a thick catalogue. Take your choice."

... lack of structure has produced an educational system unable to train minds to understand the relationships between things, to grasp the whole.

The college is a series of long, dark tunnels. Each represents a specialty, a field of expert knowledge that has been carefully dug over the years. The best person in each tunnel is at the end, digging a little groove in the darkness. If persistent, the student may find that individual, and if the student is lucky, the expert may look up and mumble.

Students wonder whether this is what is needed. They ask themselves: "Do I not need to know what ties these tun-

lodge

nels together? What are the implications for politics and economics of genetics and microbiology, for example? "Who will help them to integrate the available information to make it useful in explaining the world around them?"

It is hard to say. Maybe some maverick, some wandering guru, some amateur on the fringes of things. But respectable professionals don't get their brownie points that way. They must go to the end of the tunnels; once having made that trip, it is hard for them to come back.

Holism will be a long time coming to education, but a start has been made at some universities with the establishment of a variety of centers to which specialists come for the integrated study of problems...

The prescribed remedy for disturbed students is to go into the world, take a year off, and through experience build their own integrative model of what is happening out there. Practical as this may be, it is an institutional cop-out, a chancy and expensive way of doing the school's work.

The situation is reminiscent of the one faced by John Locke at Oxford in the 17th century. We can be quite sure that the philosophy department had little use for this marginal chemist, with his amateurish insights; they didn't even let his books into the library until he had been dead 70 years. And the person today who attempts a radical synthesis between the revelations of science and the changing real world will find the university environment a chilly one. There is a double danger here: first, that the vital task will be delayed; and, second, that it will be left to the untrained hands of irresponsible amateurs.

The vitality of traditional academic bureaucracies does not suggest that the old structures of education will dissolve easily or quickly. Holism will be a long time coming to education, but a start has been made at some universities with the establishment of a variety of centers to which specialists come for the integrated study of problems: urban growth, pollution, world order, and so on. Out of these problem-oriented studies hopefully will come new integral curricula and forms of knowledge.

At the Harvard Business School, for example, pioneering work has been done in preparing teaching material that relates economics, politics, sociology, ideology and other environmental factors for the integrative study of comparative national strategies.

Taking the nation as the unit of analysis, the student is provided with a way to perceive the critical relationships among public and private policies and institutions, and thus to understand the particular evolution of different countries, such as Canada, Japan, Germany, France, Brazil, Mexico and the United States. The holistic study of different patterns of national development has the added value of helping students understand their own country far better than if they looked only at it.

So much for colleges and universities. The problem of the school in society at the elementary level is perhaps, even more serious. In his book *The Micro-Society School: A Real World in Miniature*, George Richmond describes his experiences as a fifth-grade teacher in Brooklyn:

> Mass society has generated the kind of alienation that allows neighbors to live side by side without knowing each other. It has produced a human experience that is fragmented, often ideologically and aesthetically bankrupt, an impersonal world that may be over-industrialized and over-mechanized. Together these components of modern life sum to a condition of self-alienation and estrangement from society...If the student is lucky, he will graduate from school with a piecemeal understanding of how the major institutions of society operate. He will have obtained fractions of experience without having been exposed to the ideological networks that order that experience and make it coherent. He will look at the "great society" he enters as a large, unmanageable, chaotic series of stimuli that will atrophy every response he makes to them.[4]

Schools too often are disconnected from society, teaching separate packages of knowledge which students firmly believe will make no difference whatsoever in their relationship to what they find around them. If parents and children are convinced that they could cause change—that participation, power and influence would be theirs if they had the skills—education would follow.

If primary and secondary education are to gain any kind of integral value by the time we reach the 21st century, parents, alumni, neighborhood businesses and political institutions all must be brought into its processes. Students must be allowed to see, in fact, that all of these institutions contribute to life and then students can contribute to the institutions—that the student can make a difference. This cannot be a game; it must be for real.

Schools too often are disconnected from society, teaching separate packages of knowledge which students firmly believe will make no difference whatsoever in their relationship to what they find around them.

In an earlier time, the task was easier—when, for example, the community was integrated around the farm or the factory. In each case, however dismal may have been the children's lot, they felt useful; they were part of a perceptible community. Today they are not. I do not mean to suggest that the school can abandon the basic knowledge that it now tries to impart. This knowledge is critical. The problem is that, increasingly, it is not being imparted, or rather it is not being absorbed.

Special efforts must...be made to trace and demonstrate the relationship between critical areas of knowledge and to connect that knowledge to the real world...

Special efforts must, therefore, be made to trace and demonstrate the relationship between critical areas of knowledge and to connect that knowledge to the real world so that the child can believe that it will be useful. The framework that used to allow the child to take it on faith has gone.

Many means of building bridges between the school and the community come to mind: student involvement in community projects and political activities, summer jobs, student letters or guest columns in the local paper, student task forces to work on solutions to community problems and the like.

I know of one community, for example, in which pollution had closed a beautiful lake to swimming. A resourceful science instructor organized his students to identify the polluting elements as well as their sources. Publicity and community pressure forced the polluters to change their ways, and the following summer the lake was once again swimmable. Those students had learned the value of education.

Finally, there is the crucial task of educating those who will manage our institutions in the 21st century. The skills are in very short supply. They have been gathered by, and largely reside in, a handful of graduate schools of business administration.

Implicit in this fact are the antique assumptions that management is peculiarly a business skill; that it is concerned with the organization of private economic activity—which is separate from political and social relationships—and that it is presumably less pertinent to the conduct of the nation's largest collection of institutional activity, government.

These are dangerous assumptions. They tend to limit

managerial training to those interested in business. They bias such training toward the specialized skills associated with business as it has existed in the past. And they cause many who will be engaged in the management of non-business institutions to be deprived of necessary training.

Further, schools of public administration generally do not train managers, focused as they are on the relatively abstract conceptualization of policy problems and only slightly concerned with the functions of the executive. The merger of business schools and public administration schools would be an excellent thing, in step with the movement to synthesis.

Clearly, the old distinctions between what is private and what is public have less and less meaning; in many areas they are merely artificial remnants of the old ideology, figments of the old notions of property, competition and the limited state.

The management problems of Consolidated Edison, the oil companies, General Electric, IBM, ITT, AT&T, savings and loan associations, and the like are as inseparably involved with public questions of community need as are those, let us say, of the TVA, COMSAT, the Port Authority of New York and New Jersey and HUD. The management of garbage disposal, health systems, land use and welfare is equally complex and in many ways quite similar to the management of the so-called private sector. There may be different measures of efficiency, different sources of capital, different allocations of profit, different problems of incentive, but these differences are closing and they do not detract from the overall similarities.

...consolidation of the business school and the public administration school is hindered by traditional academic bureaucratization and deeply felt loyalties to old specializations.

Yet consolidation of the business school and the public administration school is hindered by traditional academic bureaucratization and deeply felt loyalties to old specializations. In consequence, both sets of schools are in danger of obsolescence.

This attitude will have to go. Managers will increasingly be concerned with the design and direction of whole systems oriented to a variety of community needs. The job of the manager will be to perceive and understand these systems, and to manage them using such administrative skills as marketing, finance, control, accounting and organizational psychology. More than ever, the manager will need to be a generalist, a person uniquely trained to integrate the specialized skills of experts to give purpose and direction to the whole and maintain maximum efficiency.[5]

Managers in the 21st century also will need to be boldly imaginative, sensitive to the changing criteria of the environment. Their task increasingly will be one of transforming old institutions and building new ones. The forum in which many decisions will be made will be profoundly political.

The task of these managers, in whatever sector they find themselves, will be to emphasize this fact, not to obscure or resist it; to assist the political order in gathering the required information and analyzing it; to give government the confidence it requires to plan, respecting its objectivity and its essential independence from any special interest, mindful of its communitarian nature; and then to execute community need as efficiently as possible. The corporate manager's task also includes competing with others to serve that need.

L et us assume that the community decides there shall be no such thing as waste any more, that everything we once called "waste" shall in fact be only part of a circle, a point in a process; and that the whole cyclical process must be managed. It follows that science and technology must be concentrated and organized to invent the means of meeting this need most effectively. Implementation of the new scheme will strike many components of the status quo.

Some institutions may die—the town dump, for example. Costs and benefits must be calculated and a legitimate system designed to do the task. A system of such scope will necessarily impinge upon many other systems in the community, as a whole within a larger whole. The task of the manager here involves perceiving those wholes and recognizing their relationship to the political order and to the social needs and activities of the community.

Peter G. Peterson, speaking as chairman of Lehman Brothers in a speech to the *Pacem in Terris III* meeting in the winter of 1974, described the need for managers of international systems, "a new breed of public official and

Managers in the 21st century also will need to be boldly imaginative, sensitive to the changing criteria of the environment.

corporation executive, one who can relate his own specialty to the larger whole, one who can switch from one area to another, and not be a narrow special-interest pleader...who can at all times see the new interrelatedness of things.''

For the years ahead, managers must see themselves perhaps first and foremost as changers, architects of a smooth transition from the traditional ideology to the new, seeking reconciliation between the status quo and what must come in the nation and the world. In this task, crisis will be an essential tool of management.

When the cities burn and crime is the rule, when the lights go off and the radiator grows cold, when the air is foul and the rivers run dry, when bankruptcy is imminent—then we know something is wrong, and we are prepared to change. But we seem as a nation to be very poor at anticipating crisis. All the components of the energy crisis, for example, were in place at least four years prior to the fall of 1973, but few people calculated their significance.

The fragmented nature of management, both political and economic; the ideological insistence that government's role does not embrace effective planning; the momentum of great bureaucratic interests—all precluded a proper anticipation of what was at stake.

The usefulness of crisis as a stimulant to efficient change is unquestionably enhanced by perceiving crisis sooner rather than later, and in real rather than mythical terms. There is a premium, therefore, on managers comprehending the precise nature of crisis without illusion or scapegoating. Early perception requires holistic vision.

Often we perceive crisis only when an expert tells us it is at hand—which is already too late. Even in 1969, the oil companies firmly believed that prices of oil would remain stable, because economists told them so. When political forces in the Arab world in 1970 produced effective organization of the oil-producing countries, crisis followed. A skilled generalist surely could have foreseen Arab unity; a generalist would have been swifter than a specialist in perceiving and defining the crisis.

It is common to blame crises on some familiar foe—the

young, the old, blacks, whites, government, business or labor. Perception is thus blinded and managers lose the utility of a clearly defined crisis as a means to change their institutions. Although all self-respecting managers generally acknowledge the need for change abstractly—for a safe and pure environment, for an end to poverty and racism, for urban renovation, and the like—they are apt to harden when change threatens the structure they manage, and become positively antagonistic when it threatens an idea they have conventionally used to define values.

I rreversible, permanent structural changes that have undermined some cherished ideological assumptions already have occurred in America. In many instances, business itself has spurred them on.

Workers' participation in management, for example, appears to be necessary if workers are going to restrain wage rates and achieve the higher productivity levels necessary for competitiveness. These changes profoundly disturb not only the old adversarial notion of a trade union but also traditional conceptions of management authority. Increasingly, the right to manage is coming from the managed, not from some mythical body of shareholders endowed with property rights.

...the old notion of a legally binding contract connecting employer and employee is giving way to an evolving consensus from which all members of the corporation derive both their rights and their duties.

And the old notion of a legally binding contract connecting employer and employee is giving way to an evolving consensus from which all members of the corporation derive both their rights and their duties. Managers may resist so troubling and radical a change, preferring to maintain the existing order of things—at least until they retire. In their way lies continuing deterioration. Or they may grasp the challenge and seek to be prepared for the radical structural changes that will not only erode their old conception of "prerogatives", but also quite possibly put a number of them out of work.

And when I say "prepared" I don't mean dug in behind the barricades ready to fight. The introduction of change should be a primary order of work, not so much out of any sense of nobility— although this is not unimportant—as out of an awareness of the requirements of survival and justice.

Once managers join the side of change and survival, they will require a clear perception of how an engine of change works. First, as I have noted, its task is a holistic one, addressing the system to be changed as a whole. Next, it must be capable of producing motivation and organization for change. Generally speaking it must begin its activities with agitation; that is, education about a precise need—often born out of crisis—for purposes of motivating and organizing.

Further, a successful engine of change must have five characteristics. First, *authority;* when leaders speak, they must be believed and trusted. It is noteworthy that for this reason religious figures are often involved in the early phases of change. Then, too, leaders must have the *ability to communicate* with—talk the language of—the most remote element they are trying to affect.

We must educate men and women in considerable numbers to become engines of change.

Third, they must have *access to power,* to bring to bear the resources required for change at the appropriate time. Fourth, they must be capable of providing *protection* to the forces of change against the inevitable retaliation of the status quo. And, finally, they must have *competence,* that special ability to integrate the skills of experts conscious of the nature of the whole system in which the change is occurring.[6]

We must educate men and women in considerable numbers to become engines of change. Much is at stake. In the 21st century good management will be measured by the levels of waste and violence in society; by the quality and standard of life in our communities; and by the creativity and self-respect of our people. □

References

1. Portions of this essay are drawn from the author's *New American Ideology,* Alfred A. Knopf, New York, 1975, pp. 329-340.

2. Daniel Bell, *The Coming of Post-Industrial Society: A Venture in Social Forecasting,* New York: Basic Books, Inc., 1973, p. 187.

3. Alfred North Whitehead, *Science and the Modern World,* New York: The Macmillan Co., 1925, pp. 197, 282-3, 286, 289.

4. George Richmond, *The Micro-Society School: A Real World in Miniature,* New York: Harper & Row, 1973, pp. 265, 266.

5. See Chester T. Barnard, *The Functions of the Executive,* Cambridge, Mass.: Harvard University Press, 1938, pp. 136-7.

6. See G. C. Lodge, *Engines of Change,* New York: Alfred A. Knopf, Inc., 1970, Chap. 6.

Corporate pyramids will tumble when horizontal organizations become the new global standard.

Klaus

As scorching flames are engulfing floor after floor of the highest and mightiest building in America, its owner, played by William Holden, maintains stubbornly that nothing could destroy it. *Towering Inferno's* awestruck audiences nevertheless witness the vulnerability of this structure while its unbelievably ignorant management, pointedly isolated on the top floor, eventually are decimated in the fiery holocaust.

Awesome scenarios such as this portend the advent of similar events in nearly all other areas of management. Literally for thousands of years, sacrosanct and complex hierarchies of government, churches and other organizations have been maintained. Even the most modern of managements have felt secure in the belief that a pyramidal structure would best serve the accomplishment of organizational goals.

Anybody who has the unique experience of standing in front of the great pyramids outside Cairo must feel humbled. In an unprecedented display of power, unequaled in history, the pharaohs piled three million huge stones one upon another for each pyramid.

As I climbed dutifully up inside Cheop's structure, I was suddenly overcome by an attack of terrible claustrophobia. It was utterly frightening. My heart pounded at frenetic speed from sheer panic. Being surrounded and practically encased by three million quarried blocks exceeded my

GUNTHER KLAUS *is an internationally recognized business economist and management consultant, and is managing director of the Institute for Advanced Planning in Beverly Hills, CA. He is one of the leading advocates of management by objectives, and has been instrumental in the development of the concepts of team management and horizontal organization.*

human ability to cope. Once outside again, my loud sighs of relief began to scare the camels.

I have encountered similar feelings many times when interviewing members of both giant and small organizations. Their managerial pyramid structures, so carefully engineered by tradition, frighten employees and threaten their need for security more than they provide comfort. People often feel totally deprived of association and, thus, an ability for commitment. Amazingly, many executives cannot understand why the average employee doesn't seem to feel the same sense of urgency as they do. Employees, in turn, have coined such phrases as "ivory tower" and "managerial cuckoo land."

Enter almost any contemporary business in the Western World today, and ask who is in charge. Inevitably, somebody will rush forward to claim the driver's seat. Alexander Haig made this "perfectly clear" when an assassination attempt had put President Reagan temporarily out of commission. "I am in charge," he stated categorically, although he certainly was not.

But if the same question was asked in Japan, the answer would be: "All of us are in charge."

Triggered by events in Japan and elsewhere, the traditional managerial pyramid is being subjected to the wrecker's ball. An almost flat horizontal organization structure is emerging, signaling enormous change for the 21st century—perhaps even for the third millenium.

One cannot miss noticing the excellence of quality in many foreign products and services, their ingenuity of design and their real value compared to price. American and European countries, while plowing ahead with stunning technology and impressive mass organization, have not been able to maintain market position in general.

An almost flat horizontal structure is emerging, signaling enormous change for the 21st century...

The reasons given are manifold. They range from managerial complacency to spoiled unions, and from xenophobic management viewpoints to "profit now" concepts expounded by narrow-minded accountants. While some of these do apply, the picture is far more complex.

While interviewing potential franchisees, the president of a highly successful franchise operation told me, the most frequent answer to his question, "Why do you want

Gunther Klaus

In one of the buildings of a telephone company in Florida, the president's office occupied the entire penthouse suite, fittingly dubbed "Taj Mahal" by bewildered employees...

to buy a franchise?" was, of course, "I want to be my own boss." Add to that the often-expressed notion that really nobody jumps up and down in the joy at having an overseer.

And what has management come up with to answer this demand of human nature? More and more hierarchy. Yet another layer of supervision, and another manual upon another manual. It has ultimately culminated in such excesses as the stuffy executive suite, privileged policy, special living rooms and ridiculous titles such as "Senior Executive Vice President" and "First Honorary Chairman of the Board." In one of the buildings of a telephone company in Florida, the president's office occupied the entire penthouse suite, fittingly dubbed "Taj Mahal" by bewildered employees crammed in small cubicles below deck.

Famous authors of years past have explained to us the principle of maximum span. According to them, no manager can effectively supervise, say, more than seven people. There simply isn't the time otherwise to pay proper attention. Hence, the superstructure of the pyramid, neatly segmenting the whole organization into "manageable" divisions, departments, sections and groups. Needless to ask that, if there are so many supervisors supervising, who does the actual work?

Imagine now, in contrast, an organization where everybody's tasks, goals and objectives are absolutely clear, understood and agreed upon. Imagine, further, that the rewards this organization disperses are tied to only two aspects: the accomplishment of the agreed-upon objectives, and the cooperation between people helping each other to come out ahead together as a group—somewhat as a sports team works or an orchestra plays. No particular hierarchy there, nobody peeking over one's shoulder demanding progress reports in writing, thus indirectly inviting camouflage and mediocrity.

The Greek-Orthodox church has no Pope. It operates its various sections under the principle of "primus inter pares." The respective Metropolitan is clearly only the first among equals. While this principle has been adopted occasionally by Western organizations, particularly by liberal politicians, it was grossly violated because even then some proponents emerged more equal than most.

While addressing an Inter-Asian conference in Singapore, I met the head of one of Japan's dinosaur companies, a jovial and well traveled chap.

"What do you do?" I asked.

"A good question indeed," he chuckled, "for I do *nothing*."

"Wait, that couldn't be. After all, your company is world-wide, does double-digit billions of dollars in sales, with hundreds of thousands of employees in Japan alone."

"Do you really believe, that if I say frog, hundreds of thousands of people jump?" he came back.

"No, that's quite impossible. But you must do *something*. Why then, otherwise, would your position even exist?"

Since I had studied Japanese management culture for some time, his ultimate reply was not too hard to digest. He did only three things, he said:

- The first and second are selection and development of key people, encompassing the tasks of identifying their niche in the organization and then maximizing their latent skills.

"We don't train, we develop human potential. You train a dog..."

"We don't train, we develop the human potential. You train a dog. A human being can think and innovate. That's important to bring out," he said.

Perhaps that explains why the great Walt Disney named his company's training department "University of Disneyland" instead.

- The Japanese executive's third duty is being—in Western terms—the Godfather. This meant he would not engage in short-range organizational detail, but concern himself instead with ensuring his company's long-range future. In addition to these functions he was accessible to *anyone* within his firm.

Many will agree that most organizations are run for the benefit of their executives. The executives personally enjoy the trimmings that come with high office. Their cars are bigger, their planes private, their personal whims catered to, their palaces adorned, their time skillfully managed—and they generally get more money than anybody else. While a point can be made about their shouldering enormous responsibilities, there can be found an astonishing amount of lesser folk whose psychological and emotional involvement runs neck and neck with those of their contemporaries in higher places, without the benefits, such as those who drive a school bus, filled with unruly children, day after day.

Having to assume responsibilities and producing results is, of course, a welcome change from the overrated "just doing my job" syndrome. Most of us believe, and I think rightly so, that people in general are not principally lazy. They do want to do a good job, want to be recognized for having done so, and can soberly relate to rewards based on the relative magnitude of the job accomplished.

Cherished seniority principles, the "right to work," undue job protectionism, featherbedding and other concepts of fostering mediocrity are, by and large, rejected by the majority. The present struggle of the unions for mere survival is ample evidence.

Now the direct result of this renaissance in managerial thinking is not only the dismantling of the pyramid with its readily foreseeable destruction in short order, but also the emergence of the horizontal organization as we move toward the 21st century.

Forerunners of this concept can be recognized in increasing numbers. A few years ago I was invited to speak to an engineering consulting firm in California. Three things struck me. For one, the switchboard operator had abandoned her desk and attended my meeting. The leader of the firm explained that *all* employees were to benefit from my presentation.

"Yes, but what about incoming calls?"

"Well," he said, "there are only two kinds of calls you'll ever get. Important ones and unimportant ones. The important ones will eventually call back. The unimportant ones, well, they don't matter."

Secondly, he explained that there were only two ranks and two payscales in the company: vice presidents making $65,000 and associates making $35,000 per year, plus benefits. So the switchboard operator was indeed an associate, with commensurate pay, as was the lady preparing the meals (most employees preferred to eat at

Cherished seniority principles, the "right to work," undue job protectionism, featherbedding and other concepts of fostering mediocrity are, by and large, rejected by the majority.

the company dining room). He, although acting as president legally, was only a vice president. In fact, the president's office rotated every year. "We need fresh ideas," he said.

Third, in most engineering firms the general drafting room is about as exciting as the credit office in a department store. This company's drafting room, although reasonably large, was a noticeable exception. On two sides were huge glass panels opening to a view of verdant trees growing directly outside. The other two walls were hung with wallpaper showing lifesize color photographs of the inside of a forest. The floor covering was deep green, lusciously thick carpeting, resembling moss. Throughout the room were placed a good quantity of well kept live plants, leased to ensure their everfresh quality.

Also, everybody was on the board of directors, as it turned out, and—needless to say—everybody was happy and thoroughly enjoyed working there.

The assistant to the president, a young woman, had an MBA from UCLA and spoke five languages fluently, among them Arabic. She was already a vice president. Perhaps the most astonishing fact about this company was that their billing income per employee exceeded the national average by 200 percent!

The horizontal organization in the 21st century will be characterized by the absence of a boss.

The horizontal organization of the 21st century will be characterized by the absence of a boss.

The idea of an omnipotent and omniscient boss goes back to the dawn of civilization. Referring once more to the pharaohs, so impressed were they with their divine ancestory that they would only consent to marrying their own sisters. Across the Atlantic in the New World, Inca emperor Atahualpa fell easy prey to Francisco Pizarro on the principle of bossy omnipotence. The 54-year-old Spanish Conquistador had deftly figured out that without the emperor the many thousands of Inca warriors surrounding the handful of Spanish in Caxamalca were unable to function. Thus, the treacherous Pizarro invited the imperial Inca for a meeting, during which time he apprehended the Inca, thus dispatching one of the two magnificent pre-Columbian empires into quick demise.

Judging by frantic efforts of many of *Fortune's* 500 to preserve the sacred pyramid, and some of the musical chairs played involving highly placed executives, one doesn't wonder any longer why foreign competition has managed to elbow its way into our business lives, discarding the old and possibly tired institutions as did the Goth's with the decaying Roman Empire.

The Japanese Ringi system offers an intriguing glimpse at what is to be expected in the future. Naisbitt, in his magnificently presented *Megatrends,* makes little mention of this definitely megatrendish occurence, however.

Management by consensus, as predominant in Ringi, has the unique feature of no witch-hunting. No energy whatsoever is expanded towards "who dunnit". The novel idea being that we've done it *together,* good or bad. In our 20th century corporate world, which is becoming alarmingly more obsolete, we devote excessive resources towards finding the culprits. As everyone knows, however, they are rarely found, if ever. As of this writing, nobody has learned the real name of Watergate's "Deep Throat." Conversely, should something turn out splendidly, just about everybody tries to claim propriety.

As we know, people generally abhor rank above them. Yet, they get turned on considerably by being asked to participate in the decision-making process, particularly with respect to their own areas of concern. Thus a pyramidal structure, by the very nature of its design, must be considered alien.

Productivity, envisioned here to be real output per resource committed, is the true measure of managerial effectiveness. Since Japan has proved to be superior in many areas, but has little material resources to brag about, the organization of its people must be the key.

This offers yet another interesting speculation about the 21st century, if not the third millenium: If the Japanese, after only a half a century of "liberation", have been able to achieve these great breakthroughs, what about their close relations, the Chinese? No way, one may argue; they happen to be under the system of communism, known to all as the cradle of organizational and managerial inefficiency.

Taking one's blinders off, however, one must realize

immediately the tremendous productivity and efficiency realized by predominantly Chinese management under non-communist rule, such as in Hong Kong, Singapore and Taiwan, not to mention others who are akin, such as the South Koreans. With this kind of firepower emerging, the Pacific Basin deserves extraordinary scrutiny and consideration.

Studying these corporate cultures in Asia, one stumbles into multitudes of horizontal organizations. Everyone knowing and agreeing to their specific task, pursuing this task enthusiastically, expecting rewards connected to their accomplishments only, and committing themselves to the winning of the team, not necessarily only to themselves.

The flat horizontal organization, with no rank, no boss, no seniority, is emerging...

Idealistic? Perhaps not, because ample evidence has been gathered that the 5,000-year-old pyramids that management has so carefully constructed are being shattered. The flat horizontal organization, with no rank, no boss, no seniority, is emerging—signaling, hopefully, a greater commitment by each individual to participate in the decision-making process, to perform, to accept responsibility jointly, and to become realistic once more toward what this everchanging world is all about—progress. □

Employers will follow workers south and west, away from cities and toward training programs.

Choate

PAT CHOATE *is senior policy analyst for economics at TRW Inc., and the author of* Retooling the American Work Force: Toward a National Training Strategy. *He is also a co-author of* America in Ruins: The Decaying Infrastructure, *and* Being Number One: Rebuilding the U.S. Economy. *He has an extensive background in government, and holds a PhD in economics from the University of Oklahoma.*

Two irreversible trends seem certain to dominate the geography of work in the United States as we enter the 21st century. First, extensive population and job losses will occur in the Northeast and North Central regions at the same time that extraordinarily high population and job gains are registered in the South and West. Second, the migration of people and jobs out of central cities and the innermost suburbs will persist, generating additional growth and development in suburban fringe areas and sustaining the decade-long resurgence of rural America.

These shifts in the geography of work are driven by irresistible forces, including the rapid and pervasive automation of work, the widespread application of advanced communications systems, the relative development capacities of specific places and the locational desires of the workers themselves. The shifts will have profound economic, political and social implications—not only for the places that are losing population and jobs, but also for the places that are gaining them.

The population of the United States is projected to increase from 226.5 million in 1980 to 267.5 million in the year 2000. This overall increase of 41 million people is impressive, but it masks important differences in the growth rates of the various regions.

For the period 1980-2000, the Bureau of the Census projects a small decline in the population of the northeastern states, while the population of the north central states is expected to remain stable. But in the southern and western states population increases of 31 percent and 44 percent, respectively, are anticipated.[1]

If these projections (which assume a continuation of the migration patterns of the 1970s) are accurate, they represent a profound and unprecedented shift in the nation's demography. And even if they're high or low by one-third, the shifting of humanity—and of business activity—will be such that much of working America's grass roots will have been pulled up and plowed under by the time we step into the 21st century.

The implications of this shift for the geography of work in America come into sharper focus when the aggregate population figures are broken down by age group. An examination of changes in the size of the working-age population—defined broadly as being between the ages of 20 and 64—reveals startling shifts in the potential labor supply in various regions. Indeed, little or no increase in the working-age population is projected for the northeast and north central states, but massive growth in the number of working-age people is projected for the South and West (see Figure 1).

Specifically, the working-age population is expected to increase by 36 percent in the South and by over 48 percent in the West. Expressed in absolute numbers, in the year 2000 the Northeast will have 242,000 fewer potential workers in this age group than it does today; the north central states will gain 1.8 million potential workers; the South will have an additional 15 million people in its potential labor pool, and the West will gain over 12 million potential workers.

The magnitude and direction of population shifts within regions—including both the spectacular resurgence of rural America and the deceleration of urban growth—are as impressive as those between regions.

In a dramatic reversal of long-term demographic trends in the United States, the growth of the nation's rural population matched or exceeded that of its urban population for the first time during the 1970s. More than 2.8 million people moved out of the nonmetropolitan counties during the 1960s, but in the 1970s more than 3.5 million

...the South will have an additional 15 million people in its potential labor pool, and the West will gain more than 12 million potential workers.

Pat Choate

...the number of people available to continue the migration from city to suburb to non-metropolitan and rural communities is large indeed.

moved in. This unprecedented shift was widespread, involving all states except Connecticut and Rhode Island.[2]

This migration of people and jobs from central city to suburb has been under way since the 1950s. As late as 1960, more than 50 percent of the residents of metropolitan areas lived in the central cities; by 1980, only 40 percent did.

During the 1970s, however, the familiar pattern of declining city vs. growing suburb was altered in two important ways. In a detailed analysis of 1980 Census data, Census Bureau demographers Larry Long and Diana DeAre have described the changes under way.[3] First, the geographic area subject to population loss has expanded to include the close-in suburbs of many of the nation's older cities. Because of heavy population losses in both central city and inner suburb, one in six urbanized areas lost population during the 1970s.

Second, the declining city vs. growing suburb phenomenon is no longer confined to the mature cities of the northeast and north central regions. During the 1970s, this pattern was found for the first time to be nationwide, affecting half of all urbanized areas—including a fourth of the cities in the South.

Since nearly 75 percent of the U.S. population still resides in metropolitan areas and over 40 percent of metropolitan area residents still live in central cities, the number of people available to continue the migration from city to suburb to non-metropolitan and rural communities is large indeed.

People move for a variety of reasons, including economic opportunities; quality-of-life considerations such as climate, access to recreation and the outdoors; pursuit of lower living costs; proximity to family and friends; and retirement.[4]

These and other forces often exert their influence for decades, lasting until they exhaust themselves—or until more powerful stimulants emerge. Seven decades of migration off the farm, for example, ended only when the farm population had been reduced to 3.5 percent of the nation's population, down from almost 40 percent in 1900.

The potent forces that have fueled recent shifts in the geography of work also seem likely to sustain them. They include improved technology and communications; the growing appeal of rural areas for both industry and workers; the shifting demography of the work force itself; the relative capacity of various locations to support economic and population growth and the rising influx of immigrants, both legal and illegal, to this country.

Improved technology and communications—These factors have fostered and supported the dispersal of work and people both within and between regions. Office work and service industries, primary sources of employment in most central cities, are automating very rapidly. Word processors, computers and communications networks permit

FIGURE 1

Resident population of regions in the United States by age, 1980 - 2000

(millions)

Population	Northeast	North Central	South	West
19 Years and Under				
1980	14,903	19,214	24,567	13,753
2000	11,654	17,199	27,551	18,377
Absolute Change	-3,249	-2,015	2,984	4,624
Percent Change	-21	-10	12	33
20 to 64 Years				
1980	28,155	32,941	42,292	25,112
2000	27,913	34,747	57,689	37,273
Absolute Change	-242	1,806	15,394	12,161
Percent Change	-1	5	36	48
65 Years and Older				
1980	6,069	6,689	8,482	4,295
2000	6,824	7,760	13,579	6,821
Absolute Change	755	1,071	5,097	2,526
Percent Change	12	6	60	58
TOTAL*				
1980	49,136	58,853	75,349	43,165
2000	46,400	59,714	98,827	62,519
Absolute Change	-2,736	861	23,478	19,354
Percent Change	-5	1	31	44

Source: *Calculated from U.S. Bureau of the Census, Current Population Reports, Series P-25, No. 937, Provisional Projections of the Population of the United States, by Age and Sex: 1980 to 2000, U.S. Government Printing Office, Washington, DC, 1983, p. 12.*

Regional calculations are rounded; totals are the estimates reported by the Bureau of the Census.

the fast, efficient replacement of traditional paperwork. Many types of clerical work, such as data entry, are already being done in locations remote from the computer, including locations outside the nation.

The increasing automation of office work will diminish the need for large centralized office complexes, permitting even wider geographic dispersal of work. Similarly, modern communications and transportation permit the location of manufacturing and other facilities in many places, often far from headquarters.

Growing appeal of rural locations — Improvements in technology, production processes, transportation and communications have been particularly important in making rural sites more attractive for industrial development. Thus, the rampant resurgence of rural areas during the 1970s did not signify a return to traditional rural life, but rather a movement of skilled and professional workers drawn to the new jobs being created there. In a special analysis of employment data by county, Census demographers Long and DeAre found that the rate of job creation during the 1970s was higher in rural counties than in urban areas.[5]

...the rampant resurgence of rural areas during the 1970s did not signify a return to traditional rural life, but rather a movement of skilled and professional workers drawn to the new jobs created there.

Numerous surveys also have documented the desire of people to live in less densely populated areas. Today, it is possible for workers to move to rural areas without sacrificing the amenities once available only in urban locations. After a half century of intensive investment by the public and private sectors, nearly all rural locations have the basics of contemporary life, including electricity, assured water supplies, telephone service, paved roads, good schools and medical service. What's more, the interstate highway system has put many such locales—previously difficult to reach by car— within a one-day drive of big-city cultural and sports events.

Demography of the work force — Now that the post-World War II "baby-boom" generation has matured, the brakes have been applied to the growth rate of the work force. In the 1970s, the work force grew at an annual rate of almost 2.45 percent; in the 1980s, the work force will expand at only half that rate. In the 1990s, it will grow at an even slower pace. Consequently, more than 75 percent of the

59

people who will be working in the year 2000 are adults today—and most are already at work.[6]

Thus, strange as it seems today, massive worker shortages will develop before the year 2000. Ironically, these shortages will emerge at a time when rapid technological advances and intense foreign competition are making human capital an increasingly critical element in the competitive capacities of American companies. As a result, worker shortages may force companies to either create incentives to attract workers from other companies and other places—or go where the workers are more plentiful.

This means that a growing number of companies may be compelled to move to southern or western states to find workers. Others will be forced to leave central-city locations for suburban, nonmetropolitan or rural places to recruit a work force.

Relative development capacities — The relative capacities of places to support economic and population growth represent another key influence on the geography of work. Although many factors determine the development capacities of specific places, two are critical: the condition of the public infrastructure and the capacities of the human capital—the workers.

Obviously, adequate public infrastructure—roads, bridges, water systems, wastewater treatment facilities and ports, for example—are crucial to the location of virtually all firms. Yet today, the basic public facilities that underpin the economic activities of most communities are limited, worn out and obsolete.

Almost 45 percent of all communities have wastewater treatment facilities that are operating at or near full capacity, and another third have water treatment facilities in the same limited condition.[7] These communities cannot support renewed economic growth until they make major investments to modernize and expand these facilities.

When all other public facilities such as deteriorating bridges and inadequate ports are also considered, perhaps two-thirds, and likely three-quarters, of all communities will be unable to support new economic growth until major investments are made in their basic public facilities.

Inadequate public facilities are found in all parts of the nation—urban, suburban, rural, Northeast, North Central,

...strange as it seems today, massive worker shortages will develop before the year 2000...at a time when rapid technological advances and intense foreign competition are making human capital an increasingly critical element in the competitive capacities of American companies.

South and West. Yet some places within each region and state still have the extra infrastructure capacity required for new growth. Thus, the condition of public facilities is likely to have towering influence in determining where growth will occur within regions—whether in the core city, the suburbs, the nonmetropolitan or rural areas.

In the 21st century, the pace of technological change and the intensity of foreign competition will require that workers take booster shots of training. In the tight labor markets ahead, communities that are able to assist firms in this process will be more attractive for investment than places that can not.

Today, the capacities of individual states to provide worker training and retraining vary enormously. The best prepared are the southern states: they have extensive facilities, skilled faculty and more than two decades of experience in operating state-sponsored, customized training programs designed to meet the specific needs of specific employers.

Recently, a number of states in the northeastern and north central regions have recognized the need to modernize their training systems. Ohio and Massachusetts, for example, are creating customized training programs in efforts to attract private investment and create long-term jobs for residents.

Immigration—a significant segment of the nation's population growth during the next two decades will reflect a rising tide of immigration. Based on conservative estimates of immigration levels, the Census Bureau projects that net immigration will account for 22 percent of U.S. population growth between 1980 and 2000.

A tight U.S. labor market in the early years of the 21st century, coupled with vast disparities in wages and incomes between the United States and other nations, will serve as a powerful magnet for foreign workers—both legal and illegal. Irreversible demographic trends and difficult economic circumstances in Mexico, for example, make increasing immigration from that nation a virtual certainty for many decades to come. As a result of high population growth, 730,000 new jobs would have to be created in Mexico each year between now and 2000 just to accommodate the burgeoning young work force, yet

A tight U.S. labor market in the early years of the 21st century, coupled with vast disparities in wages and incomes between the United States and other nations, will serve as a powerful magnet for foreign workers — both legal and illegal.

half of Mexican workers are unemployed or underemployed today.[8] During a 10-month period following the devaluation of the Mexican currency in September 1982, U.S. border authorities in the Southwest apprehended over 840,000 illegal aliens—a 40 percent increase over the same period a year earlier.[9] These inexorable demographic and economic trends are sure to have serious long-term effects on states in the South and West.

The movement of people and jobs over the next two decades will have profound implications for the nation. One of the most obvious will be the reapportionment of Congressional seats on the basis of population. As a result of these population shifts, New York could lose 10 seats and Pennsylvania could lose five, while Florida may gain as many as nine seats and Texas could add seven. Similarly, the nonmetropolitan and rural areas are likely to regain some of the representation they lost when the nation urbanized earlier in this century. The movement of people will also produce major shifts in the allocation of federal funds, since most federal programs distribute monies on some population-based formula.

But political change is only one of many consequences of these changes in the geography of work in America. For the nation's cities, these shifts will be costly indeed. The fiscal condition of many hard-pressed cities is likely to deteriorate precipitously with the continued loss of residents, jobs and federal funds. In their efforts to adjust to a shrinking tax base, many cities will be forced to reduce services; in this process, the quality of urban life is likely to decline still further.

Yet growing areas will also incur substantial costs as a result of the population and job shifts now developing. To accommodate a population increase of over 42 million new residents, the southern and western states will have to invest additional billions to provide basic infrastructure such as water and wastewater treatment, roads and bridges. This will create thousands of construction jobs in those areas, but it will also place heavy new burdens on fiscally strapped state and local governments.

As a result of these population and job shifts, the southern and western states will also face massive

To accommodate a population increase of over 42 million new residents, the southern and western states will have to invest billions to provide basic infrastructure...

demands for additional education and youth-related services. While the population 19 years and under will decline by 21 percent in the Northeast and 10 percent in the north central states, this population segment will increase by more than 12 percent in the South and 33 percent in the West during the next 17 years.

The number of people aged 65 and over will increase in every region. But the greatest increases in the older population will be registered in the South and West, where escalating demands for health care and special facilities for the aged will be reinforced politically by the growing numbers of older voters residing in these states. The northeastern and north central states, which will experience smaller increases in the growth rate of this age group, will nevertheless face enormously expensive investment requirements to satisfy the needs of the elderly. And these states must do so without the economic growth likely to occur in the South and West.

Finally, rising levels of immigration, legal and illegal, will continue to burden many state and local governments in the South and West. In Texas, for example, the number of students enrolled in bilingual education has doubled in the past three years. In the border city of Brownsville, TX, a third of the 30,000 public school students are aliens from Mexico, and nine of every 10 kindergarten children speak little or no English.[10] The influx of new immigrants from Mexico and Latin America clearly threatens to overwhelm the capacity of governments throughout the South and West to provide the social and community services these aliens will require.

...rising levels of immigration, legal and illegal, will continue to burden many state and local governments in the South and West.

While the movement of people and jobs has been one of the constants in American history, it has rarely been a graceful process. It requires difficult adjustments and substantial investments by both growing and declining areas. Today, the fundamental shift of people and jobs between regions is to the South and West; within regions, the movement is away from central cities and to the suburbs, nonmetropolitan and rural areas. These shifts seem to be irreversible. Moreover, there is every indication that they will persist long after the year 2000.

Fortunately, these shifts will not occur immediately or

all at once. The direction and pace of these changes are known today. Thus, we have the knowledge and time needed to minimize the political, social and economic disruptions that are likely to occur. The crucial question now is do we have the foresight—and the will—to take needed actions in time? □

References

1. U.S. Bureau of the Census, Current Population Reports, Series P-25, No. 937, *Provisional Projections of the Population of the United States, by Age and Sex: 1980 to 2000*, U.S. Government Printing Office, Washington, DC, 1983.

2. Calvin L. Beale, "Population change in rural America and implications for economic development", testimony before the Subcommittee on Economic Development, House Committee on Public Works and Transportation, 97th Congress, Nov. 19, 1983.

3. Larry Long and Diana DeAre, "The Slowing of urbanization in the U.S.", *Scientific American* 249, July 1983, pp. 33-41.

4. William P. Butz, Kevin F. McCarthy, Peter A. Morrison, and Mary E. Vaina, "Demographic challenge in America's future", Rand Corp., Santa Monica, CA, May 1982.

5. Larry Long, and Diana DeAre, "The slowing of urbanization", p. 37.

6. Pat Choate, "Retooling the American work force", The Northeast — Midwest Institute, Washington, D.C., July 1982.

7. Pat Choate and Susan Walter, *America in Ruins: The Decaying Infrastructure*, Duke University Press, 1982.

8. Leon F. Bouvier, "Future population of Latin America and the Caribbean," testimony before the Subcommittee on Inter-American Affairs of the Committee on Foreign Affairs, Washington, D.C., September 8, 1982.

9. Jessica Lee, "Illegal alien numbers jump during crisis", *USA Today*, August 15, 1983.

10. Jonathan Dahl, "In Texas, troubles spread northward", *New York Times*, August 21, 1983.

...we have the knowledge and time needed to minimize the political, social and economic disruptions that are likely to occur.

Minority workers of tomorrow must tread a much different path than did today's middle class.

Norton

ELEANOR
HOLMES
NORTON
is professor of law at Georgetown University Law Center, Washington, DC, and is a former chairperson of the Equal Employment Opportunity Commission. She also chairs the National Council on the Future of Women in the Workplace.

Historically, America has been a virtual job machine. A continually expanding economy and need for labor throughout the peak periods of European immigration and assimilation produced unprecedented equality of opportunity and economic success. The result for the descendants of European immigrants has been phenomenal economic and social mobility, the virtual abolition of the permanent peasant and working class status that entrapped their forebearers, and an almost certain place in an overwhelmingly middle class majority.

This is surely a tribute to the hard work and ability of the immigrants and their descendants. But the contrast between the permanent lower-class status of the immigrants in Europe and the near universal economic success of their progeny in America suggests that the central ingredient in their mobility has not been the vagaries of individual talent but the availability of opportunity. Personal failure could be arbitrated by a move to new frontiers or new jobs in a country rich in land and resources and hungry for labor.

But what of those whose opportunity has been retarded by racial discrimination, particularly blacks and Hispanics but including other minorities as well? What of those whose right to equal opportunity is only now emerging and will ripen in the 21st rather than the 20th century?

As minority workers move toward the 21st century they are encountering unique and decidedly contradictory trends.

On one hand, a powerful body of anti-discrimination law that proved necessary to assure them jobs and job mobility is beginning to take hold, and if present patterns persist will show tangible results by the time we enter the 21st century. On the other hand, historic structural changes in the American economy make it far less productive of jobs and more specialized in its need for labor than it was when the European immigrants and their descendants were so successfully absorbed.

Most European immigrants encountered a job-rich economy upon their arrival in America. Their descendants solidified their economic position in the extraordinary post-World War II period of the 1950s and 1960s, when economic growth was the highest in our history, averaging an annual four percent increase in the Gross National Product. In contrast, by the time the civil rights laws began to have their first impact in the 1970s, economic growth had slowed to an average of 2.9 percent per year. Given global economic competition, a return to consistently high economic growth is, at best, problematic.

As minority workers move toward the 21st century, they are encountering unique and decidedly contradictory trends.

Yet in spite of long-term unfavorable economic trends, minority workers, at least those able to acquire skills and education, could find their rightful place in the American labor force by the early 21st century. However, if this is to happen, both minorities and the government will have to be sensitive to the special efforts both must make to overcome economic trends that do not favor rapid advancement. These efforts include sensitivity to demographic changes and the need for upgraded and specialized training and education by minorities, and the necessity for unflinching enforcement of equal employment laws and regulations by government agencies.

The most conspicuous demographic factor that will increase pressure for equal opportunity in the 21st century is the dramatic and persistent growth in the proportion of minorities among Americans. Overall population growth has steadily and substantially diminished, and as a whole increased only 11.4 percent in the 1970s; but the black population increased 17 percent.[1]

Eleanor Holmes Norton

Together, women and minorities are already the majority of today's labor force, and white males will be a considerably smaller minority by the beginning of the 21st century.

Most significantly, Hispanics increased by a phenomenal 61 percent in a single decade, and with that rate of growth, increased their overall proportion in the population by one-third, from 4.5 percent in 1970 to 6.4 percent today.[2] The Hispanic portion of the population, including uncounted undocumented aliens, is almost certain to continue to burgeon in such numbers that some analysts predict that by the 21st century a huge Hispanic market will bring bilingualism to the United States. In the same period, Asians and Pacific Islanders, though much smaller in absolute numbers, nearly doubled as a percentage of the population.[3]

Taken together, minorities are 20.2 percent of the American population.[4] Together, women and minorities are already the majority of today's labor force, and white males will be a considerably smaller minority by the beginning of the 21st century. As these proportions continue to shift, the stake the nation as a whole has in the economic success of minority workers will be enormous.

Just as European immigrants and their children achieved success by going to industrializing and soil-rich parts of the country, minority workers also have much to gain by conforming to regional growth patterns. Actually, regional growth patterns favor the sections of the country where minority workers are most concentrated and are growing—the South, where growth is fastest, and the West. These two regions accounted for 90 percent of population growth in the 1970s.[5] Today, 53 percent of blacks live in the South, where population growth in the '70s was twice the national average.[6] Opportunity in this region increased so rapidly that as many blacks moved into the South as moved out, reversing the historic trek northward.

Blacks found that the racial segregation and lagging economic development that had always meant inferior educational and income levels in the South were disappearing. Southern median income increased from 78 percent to 91 percent of the national average between 1950 and 1980.[7] With the advent of federal equal employment laws covering every state, and robust economic growth in the South, that section ironically could become for blacks in the 21st century what the Northeast and

Midwest were in the 20th.

Hispanics and Asians are even more concentrated in growth areas, especially the West, and are less dispersed to declining regions than are blacks. In 1980, more than 60 percent of Hispanics lived in California, Texas and New York; 50 percent of Asian and Pacific Islanders lived in Hawaii; and 50 percent of American Indians, Eskimos and Aleuts lived in the West.[8] Population growth was even higher in the West than in the South in the 1970s, but the western rate of growth has fallen every decade since the 1950s.[9] This probably will make the West second to the South in economic growth by the early 21st century, but this is not likely to hurt Hispanics, given the substantial growth still likely in the West. In any case, of the 25 fastest

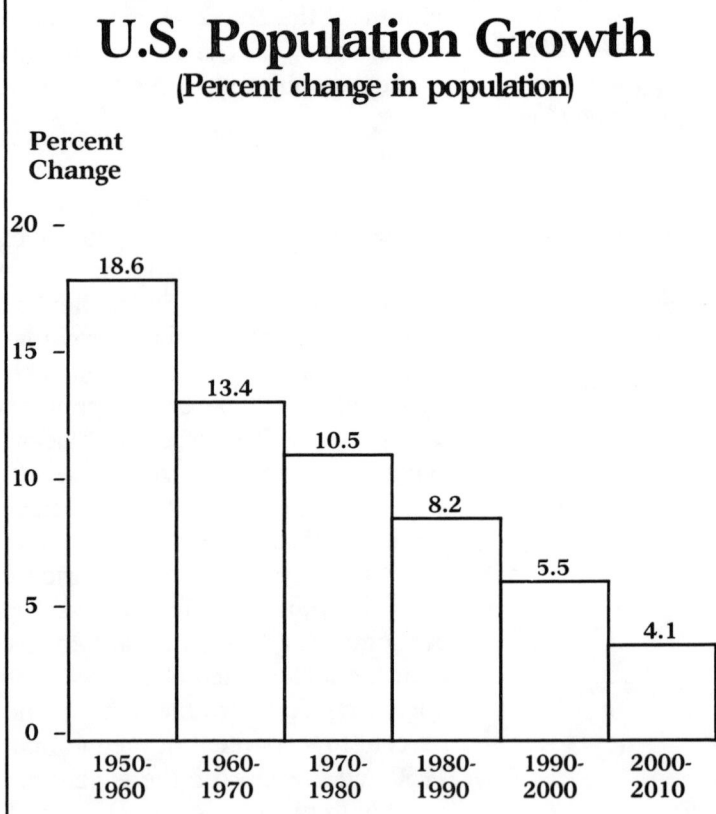

U.S. Population Growth
(Percent change in population)

Source: The Conference Board, 1982

growing metropolitan areas, 10 are in Florida and five are in Texas, states of high Hispanic concentration.[10]

These bright trends all have an important, perhaps critical downside. Growth areas in Southern states of high black concentration often meet their match in job-starved Northern and Midwestern cities, where the black and sometimes the Hispanic poor are increasingly isolated and more concentrated than ever.

In 1980, only 25 percent of whites lived in central

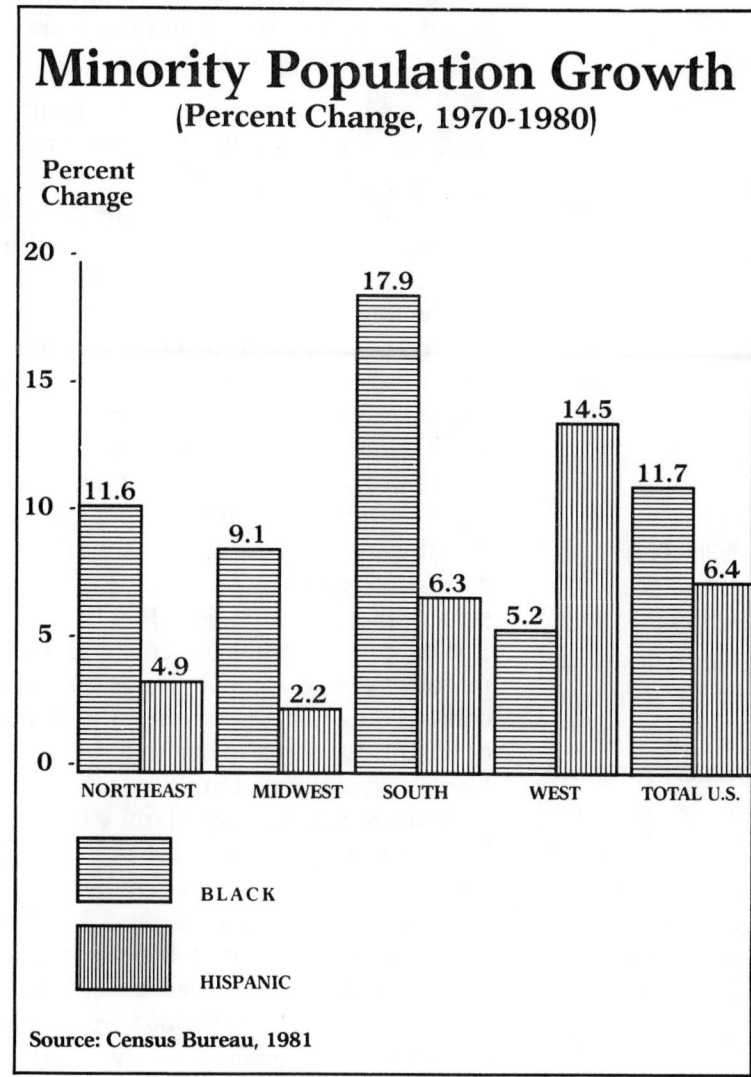

Minority Population Growth
(Percent Change, 1970-1980)

Source: Census Bureau, 1981

cities, while 58 percent of blacks did; and 75 percent of blacks in the Northeast and 65 percent in the North Central region lived in central cities.[11] The forecast for these cities is especially dire, and according to the Joint Economic Committee of Congress, "crisis cannot long be avoided."[12] The lack of jobs, housing and other amenities has caused an exodus of the white and, increasingly, the black middle class from these cities. Those who are left often lack the skills that might encourage them to migrate or business to remain; and with the collapse of federal commitments to the poor, neither the remaining jobs nor tax resources are sufficient to keep minority city populations from becoming increasingly dependent.

Much of the economic advancement that will be achieved by the better trained and educated minority workers of the 21st century is likely to be retracted by the growth of a new underclass whose educational and cultural roots in the deep recesses of ghetto poverty leave them unprepared for the new job market. The outlines of this minority society, outside both the black and white mainstream, are seen most clearly in the rapid growth of poor female-headed households—now at almost 50 percent in the black community—and its corollary, the declining labor force participation of minority males. Already, 12 percent of black males (but only five percent of white males) of working age are outside the labor force, a trend that has been accelerated by the decline of unskilled and semi-skilled manufacturing jobs.[13]

Much of the economic advancement that will be achieved by better trained and educated minority workers of the 21st century is likely to be retracted by the growth of a new underclass...

Whatever the gains of better trained and educated minority workers, bleak trends for the disadvantaged could retract progress for minority groups as a whole. Indeed, this has already begun to happen. In the 1970s, black husband-wife family income grew at a faster rate than white husband-wife family income. However, large increases in the number of black households headed by poor women resulted in a five percent decline in overall black family income; otherwise, black family income would have increased 11.3 percent in the '70s.[14]

Can the decidedly mixed results promised by demography, uneven regional economic growth and cumulative disadvantage be overcome as minority workers prepare for the 21st century? The growing gap between trained and unskilled minorities strongly suggests that access to education and rapid upgrading of educational standards could be the critical determinant.

For example, suburban and central-city blacks had the same median income in 1969, but 10 years later suburban blacks had experienced a 9.1 percent increase in 1979 dollars while the income of central city blacks had declined by almost 14 percent.[15] Suburban blacks, although only 22 percent of the black population, accounted for most of the upward movement among blacks in jobs.[16] Thus, the pattern for the 21st century seems set. Minorities with good education and proximity to those parts of metropolitan areas where there is economic growth may be able to overcome the more competitive economic conditions that seem assured. But to continue to improve their own competitive position, minorities will have to quickly close the remaining education gap.

The importance of training and education is borne out by studies showing that during the recent recession, nine million people would have been unemployed even if every available job had been filled.[17] Many of the unemployed comprise a new group of previously employed but now permanently jobless manufacturing workers, who are disproportionately minority workers from declining industries such as steel and autos. Minorities who enter the 21st century with this level of skill will find that well-paid manufacturing jobs have been replaced by low-paid, dead-end service jobs.

Almost all the job growth in the 1970s was in service jobs, and the range of service jobs showed the largest growth—54 percent at the bottom earnings levels, the next largest growth is 35 percent at the top, and only 11 percent of the growth at middle earnings levels.[18] As might be expected from these figures, the largest growth occupations of the 1990s all are bottom-level service jobs—janitors, nurses' aides and orderlies, sales clerks, cashiers, waiters and waitresses.[19] Without new skills and education, many minorities will find that they dominate such jobs, as they often do today, and that the narrower band of better-paying service jobs are far from reach. A disturbing pattern showing that as manufacturing jobs retrench, black males share

Suburban blacks, although about 22 percent of the black population, accounted for most of the upward movement among blacks in jobs.

very little in better-paying service jobs already is clear. Noyelle and Stanback report that for black male workers the situation is "extremely serious," and that "opportunities for upward mobility appear not only to be shrinking with growth in the service economy but to be largely

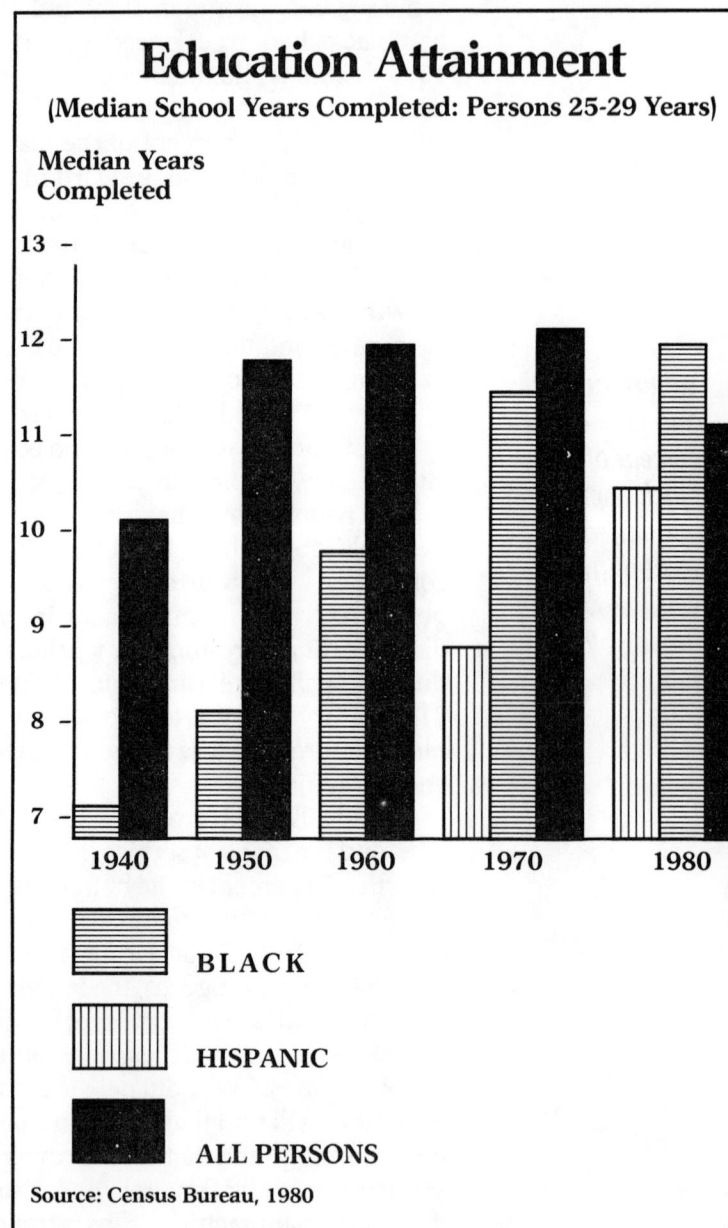

Education Attainment

(Median School Years Completed: Persons 25-29 Years)

Median Years
Completed

BLACK

HISPANIC

ALL PERSONS

Source: Census Bureau, 1980

restricted to white workers.''[20] The combination of skewed proliferation of service jobs at the bottom and scant job growth in the middle, where most workers might be expected to fit, puts an especially high premium on training and education.

Despite a significant remaining education gap, this is a hopeful area for the minority workers of the 21st century. To be sure, today among males, 50 percent of whites are college graduates, but only 18 percent of blacks and 15 percent of Hispanics.[21] Among females, 38 percent of whites have graduated from college, but only 19 percent of blacks and 15 percent of Hispanics.[22] Yet minorities are increasing their enrollment in college at a far faster rate than the general population. Between 1966 and 1978, overall college enrollment grew by an impressive 64 percent, but black enrollment tripled.[23] Hispanics, who start with an even greater educational disadvantage, are four percent of the college population, approaching their percentage in the population.[24]

What is even more encouraging is the rapid penetration by minorities of new fields and their willingness to leave fields whose minority concentrations were often dictated by old discriminatory patterns. In 1966, 40 percent of black students were majoring in education or the social sciences, while 15 percent were majoring in business.[25] By 1978, business was the top major for blacks (22 percent), as it has long been for whites, and 20 percent of Hispanics chose business, while only 10 percent chose education.[26] Moreover, during this same period, the increases in enrollment produced greater selectivity in majors, reflecting market trends in growth areas. For example, dramatic increases among blacks concentrating in business—up from 41,000 to 220,000—were matched by large increases in majors in other growth fields, such as engineering, up from 12,000 to 41,000; and biology, health and medical fields, up from 27,000 to 113,000.[27]

Nevertheless, the essential challenge for minorities with the start of the 21st century will be whether promising new directions in education and income can be maximized while disquieting trends that are already apparent are minimized.

Is the 70 percent increase in the 1970s in blacks living in

With the advent of federal equal employment laws covering every state and robust economic growth in the South, that section ironically could become for blacks in the 21st century what the Northeast and Midwest were in the 20th.

suburbs, close to areas of job growth, the wave of the future?[28] If so, what of forecasts that the number of cities with black majorities—10 in 1980—will be 32 in 1990 and 53 by the year 2000?[29] Will these cities be habitats for the dependent minority poor with a few gentrified areas scattered about and a scarcity of appropriate job opportunities? What can be done to ensure that the 21st century will see the consolidation of a prosperous minority middle class in the American tradition and to avoid the growth of a new permanent low-paid or dependent lower class consisting primarily of minorities who lack skills and job opportunities?

Whatever the complicated requisites, affirmative action efforts are indispensable. The essential task is to hasten entry into the mainstream of the job market—for people who have been artificially barred—before structural changes in the economy make this difficult for the best prepared and impossible for others.

This does not overstate the case. Even if the American economy regains its strength, it will be within a new global context where there will be competition never experienced before for every market, for every job and for every dollar. Few analysts believe our economy will reach the heights it did in the post-war period (1948-1973), when average real wages increased 60 percent.[30] The fact that real wages have fallen eight percent since 1973 is reason enough for cautious forecasts.[31]

The fact is that minorities are getting their first fair chance at jobs in the late 20th century, when the economy that produced the white middle class is in a fitful and by no means satisfactory transformation. Minorities, unlike Americans before them, must overcome not only the old discrimination, but also entirely new economic hurdles at the same time.

...to continue to improve their own competitive position, minorities will have to quickly close the remaining education gap.

If this is to be done—and I believe that it can be—affirmative action will have to be pressed both voluntarily and by government with vigor—a vigor that has diminished markedly in this decade. The quarrel with settled legal principles of affirmative action and anti-discrimination law by the federal government today translates into the kind of impediment that can mean the difference between significant and scant economic progress as minority workers try to prepare themselves for the 21st century. Gains that minorities experienced in the '60s and '70s cannot continue if the government becomes an adversary to affirmative action, as it increasingly has under the leadership of the Reagan Administration, and especially Assistant Attorney General for Civil Rights William Reynolds.

...minorities are increasing their enrollment in college at a far faster rate than the general population.

Not until affirmative action was developed and applied, was there any appreciable occupational mobility for minorities and women. For example, even with the recessions of the 1970s, black professionals and managers doubled, blacks in crafts increased 50 percent, and black technical and sales people each rose by one-third. These increases helped produce the substantial and consistent narrowing of the income gap between blacks and whites. Thus, in constant dollars, 39 percent of blacks earned over $20,000 in 1979, compared with 35.2 percent in 1970 and only 17.3 percent in 1960.[32] While affirmative action alone cannot account for these gains, who can believe that they could have been achieved without it?

The 21st century will be tough for Americans, and especially tough for those still outside the economic mainstream. The United States is no longer an ascendant society, like Japan and some Third World countries just building their industrial and technical base and experiencing large increases in economic growth. It may turn out to be harder to sustain than it was to build the economic power that created the burgeoning job market and high standard of living that has become the hallmark of American life.

For minorities, denied entry on equal terms when the American economy had few competitors, there is special urgency attached to achieving equality and the economic mobility equality brings. For minorities, the 21st century is not just another way to describe the future. □

References

1. *Data User News,* Vol. 16, No. 4, April 1981, pp. 2-3. Where in this chapter I do not refer to data on Hispanics, it is because it was unavailable.
2. *Id.*
3. *Id.*
4. *Id.*

5. *Data User News*, Vol. 16, No. 5, May 1981, p. 3.

6. William P. O'Hare, *Blacks on the Move: A Decade of Demographic Change*, Joint Center for Political Studies, Washington, DC, 1982, pp. 6-10.

7. *Id*. at 14.

8. U. S. Department of Commerce, Bureau of the Census, *1980 Census of Population Supplementary Reports*, PC 80-51-1, May 1981, p. 1.

9. O'Hare, supra, note 6 at 10.

10. *Data User News*, supra, note 5.

11. O'Hare, supra, note 6 at 34, 39.

12. U.S. Congress, 1982, "Emergency interim survey: fiscal condition of 48 large cities," Joint Economic Committee Staff Report, pp. 88-492.

13. William P. O'Hare, *Wealth and Economic Status: A Perspective on Racial Equality*, Joint Center for Political Studies, Washington, DC, 1983, p. 23.

14. Joint Center for Political Studies, *A Policy Framework for Racial Justice*, Washington, DC, 1983, p. 12.

15. O'Hare, supra, note 6 at 44.

16. Diane Nilsen Wescott, "Blacks in the 1970s: Did they scale the job ladder?" *Monthly Labor Review*, June 1982, p. 36.

17. Katherine G. Abraham, "Too few jobs," *The Entrepreneurial Economy*, Corporation for Enterprise Development, Washington, DC, September 1982.

18. Thierry Noyelle and Thomas Stanback Jr., *Cities in Transition*, Conservation of Human Resources Series, Land Mark Studies, Allenheld, Osun, Totowa, NJ, 1982, p. 39.

19. Henry Levin and Russell Rumberger, "The educational implication of high technology," Institute for Research and Educational Finance and Governance, Stanford University, February 1983, pp. 4-5.

20. Noyelle and Stanback, supra, note 18 at 133-134.

21. Yohel Caymayd-Freixas, and Marc Fried, "The Loss of Opportunity: Social Mobility and Minority Group Membership," a paper presented at the 59th Annual Meeting of the American Orthopsychiatric Association, San Francisco, March 1982, p. 10.

22. *Id*.

23. *Major Fields of Study of College Students: October 1978*, Current Population Reports, Population characteristics, Series, P-20, No. 351, May 1980, p. 2.

24. *Id*. at 3.

25. *Id*. at 2.

26. *Id*. at 2-3.

27. *Id*. at 2.

28. O'Hare, supra, note 6, at 49.

29. *Id*. at 34.

30. *Economic Report of the President* 1983, Table B-38, p. 206.

31. *Id*.

32. O'Hare, supra, note 13 at 24.

Basic industries won't die away: technology will strengthen them, despite socio-political problems.

Roderick

As we draw near to the end of a century, and a millenium, it is increasingly fashionable to speak of anything with a history as old and anything with an allure as new.

Some music is described as New Wave. Gourmets refer to the *nouvelle* cuisine. What isn't new is "neo" — the old in a new guise. And if it's really new, it's called post-modern.

If all this preoccupation with newness was only a glossary fad, it would be simple diversion. However, there is an emerging philosophy that accompanies this fear of aging that does not serve society's best interests.

This is especially true in terms of economics. To throw out all systems that have a date of origin before 1980 simply because they predate the '80s is dangerous business. And to consign to the proverbial ash heap of history all industries that were in business prior to this decade is utter nonsense.

Business in the 21st century—if it's good business—will be much like business today. There will be evolutionary gains in understanding and revolutionary gains in techniques, but the good sense of the marketplace and the reliable common sense of the work force will keep futurism from undoing all established commerce in the name of modernism.

DAVID M. RODERICK *is chairman of the United States Steel Corporation, America's largest steel producer.*

Of course, high technology will continue to work its marvels, and basic industry will adapt to it, adopt it and profit from it. But basic industries will remain—though transformed. And while labor-intensive industries such as steel will become less labor intensive, they will not be robotized to the exclusion of a substantial labor force requirement.

Some observers already have characterized our society as post-industrial America. Basic industry has been assigned a passe status.

Well, I don't mean to date myself, and I admit to basic industry perspective, but there's more to be said on the matter.

I remember during the early '50s when audio-visual was a new concept in educational circles. A-V became a code term for those who were "with it." Three divergent schools of thought quickly appeared in reaction to this new development. The first was made up of the enthused adherents who believed that audio-visuals in all their forms and shapes would revolutionize the classroom and reshape the role of the teacher.

The second was a threatened group, quite afraid that audio-visuals would indeed replace the teacher.

But a synthesis group discerned that the teacher was not an endangered species and that audio-visuals, while not a replacement, could prove an enhancement to classroom instruction.

I believe this analogy applies directly to the subject at hand: the status in the 21st century of America's basic industry—those extractive and processing and manufacturing industrial operations that, indeed, are *basic* to our economy.

Steel is but one of the metals industries, and metals are only a part of what are commonly referred to as basic industries or the "smokestack" industries—certainly not an insignificant sector of the economy.

Yet we hear about the post-industrial economy. We are told that the future belongs to high tech, with no room for basic industry in the new order of things.

It's said, oh so smugly, that if the smokestack industries close down, it's because their time has come—*and gone.* High tech will be the victor. Such conclusions are falsely predicated on the notion of a contest—between basic industry and technology. It is the usual bad habit of comparing apples and oranges.

The confirmed role of technology in basic industry affirms a compatible, rather than an adversary, relationship.

David M. Roderick

The U.S. economy can't be a healthy economy if its vision lines are blurred by high-tech myopia.

They simply are not head-to-head competitors, since they compete in different arenas. The confirmed role of technology in basic industry affirms a compatible, rather than an adversary, relationship.

Basic industry is not threatened by high tech—more to the point, basic industry looks to high tech for the tools to secure its own future. Putting high tech to work in improving our industrial base is a number-one priority, and it can be accomplished only if basic and high-tech industries see themselves as partners.

Whether it's a continuous caster in a steel mill, a word processor in a manager's office or a computerized sales order entry system, high tech is making basic industry more productive.

The U.S. economy can't be a healthy economy if its vision lines are blurred by high-tech myopia. Our economy is too complex for any one business to dominate it to the exclusion of others. Our economy is made up of goods *and* services—not goods *or* services.

Basic industry is mature industry; high tech is growth industry. And while there's more glitter with growth, there's not always an equal amount of constancy.

People provide another reason—a very important reason—why basic industry will not become an economic antique.

Even by doubling the output of the less labor-intensive high-tech industries, one could not begin to substitute for the contraction of employment in basic industry.

Basic industry will always be more labor-intensive than its other manufacturing counterparts; however, it will be less and less so. The employment opportunities available over the long term will be in the area of manufacturing labor-saving goods and machinery. Thus, as high tech enters heavy industry and displaces some workers, it will in turn provide employment in its own production. The employment pattern comes full circle—with attrition.

The increased use of microprocessors in industrial machinery and machine tools will sharpen performance, while the use of computer-assisted design/computer-assisted manufacturing techniques will provide optimum sophisticated design at lower cost.

The same will be true in the offices of the corporation, where computer systems will provide instant information storage and retrieval, thus improving productivity.

The growth of high tech will help basic industry survive and grow, and their combined growth will enable the economy to grow in tandem. Only by improving—not by abandoning—our basic industries can we find a way to employ our people. And we cannot dismiss this need as trivial or tangential. One final reason for rejecting a forced rivalry is that an economy as vast and as diversified as ours finds added strength in added diversity.

The Industrial Revolution did not eradicate agriculture. It made it more efficient, improving it and making it into the most productive agricultural system in human history. And while agriculture now has a smaller slice of the total pie, it remains and adds a necessary national self-sufficiency.

Only by improving—not abandoning—our basic industries can we find a way to employ our people.

As the U.S. economy experiences some expansion, and basic industry output rises due to a resurgence in rebuilding the infrastructure, we can expect heavy industry to hold its own in the total Gross National Product. In the post-World War II period, basic industry's share of output has been relatively stable at about 25 percent of total production, and I expect this will continue over the next several decades.

The share of jobs will be reduced, however, by somewhere between 10 and 20 percent of present employment levels.

The loss of basic industry capability would put us in a position of dependency. Could a nation with a world leadership role be a nation without mining or aluminum or steel mills, a nation without refineries or chemical plants or assembly capacity or machine tool building capability? Impossible! That's why the *basic* in basic industry is a meaningful distinction.

We did not characterize our industrial economy as post-agrarian; why then speak of the 21st century as post-industrial?

The industrial, the agrarian, the informational and the service sectors co-exist. The wealth of one sector need not be earned at the expense of another.

Historically, steelmaking is basic industry's

roderick

largest segment. What can be said of its future direction?

The automotive business, already engaged in joint ventures with foreign producers, will continue to rely on steel as the basic material of choice in its manufacture of cars and trucks. However, this amounts to only 15 to 20 percent of the steel market, while 70 to 75 percent of its market is in capital goods. And America's infrastructure rebuilding requirements will be significant as we begin the 21st century.

The steel industry will continue—but the 100 percent fully integrated steel company will go the way of the dinosaur, since financial needs and the cyclical nature of its business will demand that steelmakers either concentrate on a specific product market or be diversified corporations in order to be profitable enterprises.

The growth in heavy industry in the United States will be arithmetic, not geometric, as was the case in the early 19th century. A return to global domination, or even statistical leadership, is not a realistic expectation for America's heavy industry. The new uses of steel, for example, are limited, and population trends in developed nations project a restricted demand—which is to say population trends will determine the range of growth in steelmaking.

The 21st century business leader will have many changed environments, but will still find that good judgment and sound planning are pivotal to the success of the enterprise, particularly in our basic industries.

...the 100 percent fully integrated steel company will go to the way of the dinosaur, since financial needs and the cyclical nature of its business will demand that steelmakers be diversified corporations...

The 21st century manager will be obliged to forego simple textbook solutions, since traditional textbook problems will have been relegated to antiquity. Variable costs, including unstable labor rates, will dictate the need for maximum flexibility in decision making.

Adaptability will be the most necessary requirement for planning and performance.

One thing the 20th century will bequeath to the 21st will be continued labor-management hostility and unfair foreign trade practices. The challenge will be to eliminate the hostility and develop a mutuality of interest in the former; and, in the latter, to enlist the government—at least as monitor and honest broker in trade, and, at best, an ally.

Most problems of basic industry will not be

Most problems of basic industry will not be technical ones, but sociopolitical ones.

technical ones, but socio-political ones. Their solutions, therefore, are less likely to be found in the laboratory than in legislative corridors and union halls.

Labor, management and government must surely discover that conflict is counterproductive in the face of increased international commerical competition, and that increased competition provides good reason to reduce the conflict. If so, an economic pressure will have produced a positive social gain.

I see the 21st century work place as more than an amalgam of tomorrows. And that means not summarily dispatching basics for the latest attractions. The old and the new, and the newer still—side-by-side—will be the order of the day. □

Lobbyists for special interests are employing the bureaucracy to twist tomorrow's job market.

hatch

SENATOR ORRIN
G.HATCH
*is chairman of the
Senate's Labor and
Human Resources
Committee. He was
primary sponsor of the*
Job Training Partner-
ship Act, *and led the
successful opposition
to the* Labor Law
Reform Bill. *He has
been rated by
Washington columnist
Jack Anderson as one
of the 10 most effective
senators.*

A brilliant historian of our time, John Lukacs, several years ago wrote a book marking 1945 as both the beginning and end of our "modern" era. Dr. Peter Drucker, a more familiar name to today's business-minded readers, has already labeled the 1960s the Age of Discontinuity, suggesting first what Dr. Daniel Bell and others would later propose by terming the 1970s and 1980s "post-industrial" decades.

Of course, none of these great men would argue that time is conceptualized in decades. We don't need historians to tell us that time marches to its own drum beat. The fall of the Roman Empire is something that took place gradually over a span of approximately 420 years; during no one decade were any Romans historically conscious that their society was undergoing a complete decline.

Years from now, historians studying the year 1967 will probably cite the Vietnam War, protests, sit-ins, the Great Society and flower children as their chronological yardsticks. Yet most of us who lived through those years recall many other more important events and symbols about the late '60s which better define the time. We *remember* 1967. It was only 16 years ago, and 16 years from now we will be entering the 21st century. We know that, counting all things as being equal, a two-year-old child of today will be voting in the year 2000. What can we expect? What will work be like in the 21st century? Will there be an America, at least as we know it?

Even the most optimistic among us, if set to wonder, can visualize the torch of human freedom, which has flickered during each great crisis in our history, and wonder if it will continue to burn 16 years from today. Like the Romans, however, our question is becoming not whether our society can survive a single catastrophic event such as a stock market crash or nuclear war, but rather whether we can survive the consciousness of individual citizens toward liberty and free enterprise before our two-year-old is ready to vote, and before such rights have been completely eroded.

conomists James Buchanan and Gordon Tullock, in their book *The Calculus of Consent*,[1] develop a theory of economics that draws its roots from the early classical economists Adam Smith, John Stuart Mill and David Ricardo. Its basic premise is the concept of rational "economic man". A rational man will always choose more, rather than less, of any normal good, and will seek to spread the costs of his consumption among as many others as possible. Government will grow larger as additional public benefits and protections, demanded by well-organized groups, are granted by lawmakers seeking to maximize their own chances for votes among the so-called median voters.[2]

The "public choice" theory of political economy has a lot to say about government and public policies toward business today and in the 21st century. Unless the course described by the theory is reversed, we can anticipate the transfer of not only tax resources to government, but also many of today's private-sector prerogatives to government.

It is certainly in organized labor's best interests to pursue legislation that would subsidize the "re-industrialization" of big manufacturing...

A case in point is the current lobbying on behalf of a national industrial policy, including the creation of taxpayer-supported financial institutions. Designed to push back the clock to a time when our smokestack industries were the unchallenged leaders of the industrialized world, organized labor, in particular, has been urging the creation of a 1930s-like National Development Bank to plan investment strategies.

Implicit in any national industrial policy is the assump-

Senator Orrin G. Hatch

Whether an industrial policy becomes a reality will depend on the strength and organization of those who would benefit by it, versus the strength and organization of those who would pay for it.

tion that government can better determine economic priorities than the market, as well as the objective of shifting costs from the private sector to the public sector.

Not surprisingly, labor unions are worried about the future of our nation's large manufacturing companies. The smaller, less-centralized companies that are replacing them are more difficult to organize. It is certainly in organized labor's best interests to pursue legislation that would subsidize the "re-industrialization" of big manufacturing, as well as control the phase-in of new technologies and the benefits accruing to workers who must learn new skills to use them.

It is relevant to the question of whether such an industrial policy and its subsidiary government planning and lending agencies should be part of the U.S. economy in the year 2000 to note that the nation has been through recessions, as well as periods of exponential technological change, before without an industrial policy.

It may be a more interesting question to ask whether our nation could today employ over 100 million people, especially given tremendous population growth and social change enabling women and minorities to participate in the labor force, if our economic growth had been funneled by bureaucractic planners over a period of time instead of allowed to occur at the market rates.

To what extent will our economy be able to accommodate a still larger work force in the 21st century if we stifle the natural economic adjustment process?

Whether an industrial policy becomes a reality will depend on the strength and organization of those who would benefit by it, versus the strength and organization of those who would pay for it. The strength of organized labor, as measured by membership, seems to have been waning since World War II. This trend seems most evident within industries recently deregulated and subject to greater competition, including trucking and the airlines, where new jobs are being created in new non-unionized companies.

While this might be reason enough for this group to fight even harder for the enactment of national policy protecting their largest sanctuaries of activism, it is hard to predict what labor's emphasis will be as we approach the 21st century. Will it concentrate on a single solution, or choose to expend its financial and political capital on a variety of initiatives, such as domestic content laws? Clearly, if it is the former, the prospect of an industrial policy increases.

One distinction must be clear, however. That is the difference between public policies that unite the public and private sectors to *manipulate* the free market, as in an industrial policy, and those which call for public/private partnerships to *adapt* solutions to the market. The new Job Training Partnership Act (JTPA), passed in October 1982 and which took effect in October 1983, is an example of the latter.

The JTPA could become the prototype for public/private efforts to solve a number of community problems if it is successful as an approach to job training. As a replacement of the old Comprehensive Employment and Training Act (CETA), the JTPA endeavors to formulate local programs to the conditions of local labor markets both in terms of occupational supply and demand and employment competencies. Private Industry Councils (PICs) will play a substantive role in determining the training program's components under the new law.

The PIC's ability to forecast changes in a local economic picture and to encourage acceptance of the new program by other members of an area's business community (impractical if not impossible assignments for a governmental entity), coupled with local government's experience in program administration, will make the JTPA, on its merits, a successful innovation in public policy worthy of repetition.

...labor unions may adopt new organizing and bargaining strategies to match the new economic climate, thus enabling them to recapture past membership and lobbying strength.

The recognition that the private sector should participate in job training programs for the economically disadvantaged is of particular significance when viewed against the prevailing thought that "national" problems should always be addressed exclusively by federal intervention into the marketplace.

The 21st century will further dilute the government's monopoly on such problem-solving if the many special interest groups with a stake in job training programs find it easier to deal with local decision-makers under JTPA and find their opportunities for profitable involvement at least as satisfactory as under CETA. The public/private partnership concept can work and be replicated only so long as the interests to which politicians are responsive continue to support it.

Perhaps, however, the truthfulness of the public choice theory expressed by Buchanan and Tullock[3] is no more evident than in the changes in the traditional employer-employee relationship. Since the 1930s, we have watched the list of labor laws and regulations grow longer. The Fair Labor Standards Act, most notably the minimum wage, effectively restricts growth in the supply of labor and therefore keeps wages high, by denying employment to those low-skilled individuals and youths who cannot find jobs paying at least the minimum wage even if an individual was willing to work for less.

Our civil rights statutes and the remedies found in them were based on the presumption that the number of employment opportunities in this country would always grow.

What is next for the employer-employee relationship? A national right-to-work law, or a repeal of Section 14(b) of the Taft-Hartley Act perhaps? To answer that question, we would have to be able to predict the abilities of organized labor and the national right-to-work sympathizers or a defense of the status quo. While neither of these legislative proposals is a serious contender for enactment today, the situation may change during the next 16 years.

Prolonged unemployment or a major restructuring of American industry may lead to a relaxation of current closed-shop rules, particularly as the demand for some occupations decreases. Alternatively, labor unions may adopt new organizing and bargaining strategies to match the new economic climate, thus enabling them to recapture past membership and lobbying strength.

The panoply of federal civil rights statutes has caused a related problem. The promise of fairness and equity has a different meaning today than it did in the 1960s, when several key employment discrimination statutes were passed.

Equal employment opportunity is no longer interpreted literally. In fact, some now claim that the true measure of equity is the provision of actual numbers of jobs, specific amounts of pay. In an effort to rid discrimination from the work place, to move our country away from quotas and segregation, we are mandating quotas. More and more, we attempt to remedy discrimination by discriminating.

Our civil rights statutes and the remedies found in them were based on the presumption that the number of employment opportunities in this country would always grow. It was presumed that to remedy discrimination, we would never have to punish one group or individual in order to reward another. We would simply ensure that victims of discrimination received their fair share of tomorrow's opportunities.

We are now faced with the reality that in some instances where there is a declining demand for labor, we must choose between groups. As a result, we often see employers forced to choose between preserving such basic labor policies as seniority systems and preserving the gains made by minorities and women under affirmative action programs or consent decrees.

Since Congress, as a political body, reacts to public opinion, any new legislation to ease or restrict current laws and regulations will come as a result of demand. Congress itself is a supplier given to the motto that the customer is always right.

Will the bleak picture of progressive bureaucracy and taxation painted by the public choice theory, due to the success of an active, organized minority lobbying for federal favors at the expense of a silent majority, actually be our lot? We will not have to wait long to find out, nor will we have time to waste if we hope to influence the outcome.

It is up to us individually to create the quality of work life we seek for the future and to set the values we require of our government.

America's way of life is most severely threatened by the deadly combination of apathy and mediocrity. These are progressive diseases that could sap our strength as a nation and world peace-keeper. They are not terminal, however, if we can begin thinking as individuals again, rather than as anonymous members of the largest interest groups.

We must understand that the costs of public benefits are directly attributable to those individual taxpayers who are not eligible for benefits.

We must sacrifice dependence and sloth for in-

Unless we can inspire a renaissance of personal honor, initiative and commitment...we will be led like sheep into the 21st century.

dependence and ardor. Our society has been blessed with so many material benefits and conveniences, too many of us view them as givens instead of rewards to be earned. Our society has put such emphasis on speed that we have forgotten there is satisfaction in craftsmanship.

Unless we can inspire a renaissance of personal honor, initiative and commitment—in ourselves as individuals, and in our children—we will be led like sheep into the 21st century.

Government cannot create this renaissance for us. It is up to us individually to create the quality of life we seek for the future and to set the values we require of our government. We *do* have a public choice. It will be up to us, in the next 16 years, to set the stage for the preservation of freedom and the promotion of economic growth. □

References

1. James Buchanan and Gordon Tullock, *The Calculus of Consent*, University of Michigan Press, 1962.

2. Thomas Romer and Howard Rosenthal, "The Elusive Median Voter," *Journal of Public Economics*, Volume 12, 1979, pp. 143-170.

3. While Buchanan and Tullock have pioneered the public choice theory, others have written worthwhile articles and books interested readers may want to peruse. Some of these are William Niskanen, Geoffrey Brennan, Thomas Borcherding and Robert L. Tollison.

Workers will have legal rights to jobs through state courts; affirmative action will expand.

gerson & britt

The business environment of the 21st century will bring a variety of new and challenging legal problems to the employment setting. The economic climate of the 1980s and 1990s, in concert with the evolving demographics of the work force, will be reflected clearly in the legal atmosphere as it relates to the employer-employee relationship in the 21st century.

Although management will be required to adapt to many changes in the work place, the one change likely to have the greatest overall impact on the employer is the decline of the long-recognized employment-at-will doctrine. Conversely, it is likely that an implied "right" to employment will be an accepted principle, either through state-imposed "just cause" requirements for employment decisions or through implied employment contracts.

HERBERT E. GERSON and LOUIS P. BRITT III *are attorneys engaged exclusively in the practice of labor relations and employment discrimination law, representing management. They are with the Labor Section of the Memphis law firm of Wildman, Harrold, Allen, Dixon & McDonnell and are frequent contributors to the* Legal Trends *column of* Personnel Administrator *magazine.*

The human resource managers of the 21st century are likely to spend as much time preparing for hearings before a "Just Cause Termination Board" as their predecessors did in preparing for fact-finding conferences before the Equal Employment Opportunity Commission.

During the 1980s, a number of state courts will reject or severely restrict the traditional employment-at-will concepts, while others will reaffirm the viability of the theory. Partly in response to such state court decisions and to the demand of the electorate for increased employer accountability, state legislatures may enact legislation requiring just cause, or other similar standards, for employee terminations.

To oversee the newly imposed responsibility upon private employers, and to lessen the burden upon the legislatures may also establish state administrative boards with jurisdiction over complaints of terminated employees. For convenience, many of these boards may be established in conjunction with the states' departments of employment security, thereby allowing a combined hearing to determine if an employee's termination was for just cause or if the employee is entitled to unemployment compensation benefits.

In this setting, the state board will have the power to order the employer to reinstate unjustly terminated employees with back pay, thereby eliminating the need for unemployment compensation.

As a result of just-cause requirements, employers not covered by collective bargaining agreements will be forced to establish internal grievance procedures to defend their employment decisions. These procedures may include an internal appeal process, possibly culminating in hearings conducted by management and employee representatives.

...state legislature may enact legislation requiring just cause, or similar standards, for employee terminations.

Thus, early investigation and close evaluation of employment decisions prior to implementation will become a standard operating procedure. One positive outgrowth of such a mandatory grievance procedure will be the ability of the employer to determine quickly if reconsideration of the decision is warranted, and, if so, the employer will have the opportunity to attempt to resolve the dispute before large back pay liability accrues.

The traditionally unrepresented service sectors of the economy will probably constitute an ever-increasing percentage of the work force in the 21st century. In response to the shift in the work force, the National Labor Relations Board (NLRB) will afford more quickly to unrepresented employees certain rights that had previously been considered to attach only in a unionized setting.

This is evidenced by the NLRB's recently announced rule that unrepresented employees, as well as represented

Herbert E. Gerson

...the National Labor Relations Board will afford more quickly to unrepresented employees certain rights that had previously been considered to attach only in a unionized setting.

employees, have the right to have a co-employee present during an investigation that may result in discipline or discharge. In fact, the NLRB has indicated that unrepresented employees may be in greater need of co-employee assistance because they do not have union representation available to protect their interests.

Due to the increased protection for unrepresented employees, many companies will find it necessary to establish internal grievance procedures for all employees to ensure compliance with NLRB standards, as well as state-imposed just cause requirements.

This change in employment practices should benefit those employers facing union organizing campaigns. Such an employer should be able to rely upon the internal grievance procedure to counteract a union's claim concerning job security and favoritism.

Further, a properly implemented and maintained grievance procedure will be of particular appeal to employers engaged in high-tech and information-based industries, whose employees typically will be more educated and better informed than their forerunners. However, in such an employment environment, an employer should expect that its practices will face close scrutiny by its employees, necessitating constant monitoring of procedures.

Along with the need to establish internal grievance procedures, corporations also will be faced with the task of establishing and implementing uniform personnel policies and practices. This task may become more difficult as companies continue to move from large, centralized facilities to schedules based purely on the marketplace in order to meet the "gender-free" compensation systems required by the EEOC.

As a result of the expected creation of a body of law recognizing a right to employment (either through implied or actual contractual relationships), much of the litigation arising out of the employment setting will probably take place in state courts, under state statutes and case law. This will create an added burden for companies, since, unlike a just-cause hearing, disgruntled employees may seek relief in state courts before juries in an effort to recover actual and

Louis P. Britt, III

...employers will be required to meet certain affirmative action employment goals to even qualify to bid on local governmental projects.

punitive damages.

Employees will increasingly rely on theories of breach of employment contract, tortious interference with the employment relationship, libel, slander, defamation, mental distress, fraud and similar claims. Accordingly, the 21st century employer will be required to develop accurate performance appraisals and documentation procedures, and to implement impartial investigation procedures in anticipation of defending or explaining its employment decisions to a judge and jury.

The 1980s and 1990s also will see a growth in city and county affirmative action requirements. So as we begin the 21st century, cities and counties in urban areas are likely to expand the concept of affirmative action requirements of U.S. government contractors to include employers and contractors who deal with city, county and state governments.

Thus, employers will be required to meet certain affirmative action employment goals to even qualify to bid on local governmental projects. Additionally, due to the fiscal crisis that will plague many local and state governments, those governments will become more involved in the selection of contractors and employees to ensure that the monies paid under governmentally-financed projects will remain within and for the benefit of the community and/or the state.

Along these lines, an employer may be required to select local subcontractors and to maintain a minimum level of local employee staffing. These requirements will make it more difficult for out-of-state (or city) employers to bid on government projects.

The advent of the smaller facilities in more diverse locations, the aging of the work force, the right to employment theories and the expanded NLRB protections in the non-union setting will drastically alter the manner in which the 21st century employer will address employee relations.

Because of increased state-imposed restraints on employee terminations, corporations will be required to devote much more time and effort to employment practices and procedures. To reduce employee turnover, greater importance will be placed on interviewing techniques to help identify individuals who will be better suited for the particular work.

Enlightened corporations also will increase efforts in job training to ensure that the employees will be able to adapt to the rapidly changing needs of the corporation and to reduce employee terminations.

Finally, the employer will find it necessary to install a comprehensive system for handling grievances and termination disputes for all employees to successfully meet NLRB and "just cause" requirements, and to avoid exposure to large back-pay awards for "improper" employment decisions.

Although the human resource department may enjoy a higher status within the 21st century corporation, the 21st century human resource manager will also share an increase in responsibility and additional legal burdens due to the changing employment relationships. ☐

Training and retraining workers will be an important challenge for unions in the 21st century.

With the Information Age upon us and the 21st century looming ever closer on the horizon, it is essential that organized labor take a candid look at the future and attempt to anticipate what the changing world of work holds for the century-old labor movement in this country.

Will that future be characterized by growth or gradual decline? Will the rapid change that is affecting every element of society change the labor movement? How will Information Age unions differ from their Industrial Age counterparts? Will worker priorities change with the changing times?

These are important questions, questions that must be addressed if American unions are to retain their relevancy.

In search of answers to these and other important questions about the future of work, our union— the Communications Workers of America (CWA)— recently completed a two-year examination of what living and working in the Information Age will mean to workers and society in general.

Social forecaster John Naisbitt contends future success will require nothing less than all of us reconceptualizing our roles. That is exactly what we attempted to do with our unique Committee on the Future project.

The committee—the first of its kind within the labor movement—was created by CWA's 1981 convention and

GLENN WATTS *is president of the Communications Workers of America and is pointed to by many observers of labor trends as the most progressive of America's contemporary labor leaders.*

gave the mandate to "look at our total environment and at ourselves". The 14-member committee devoted thousands of hours to research to develop a scenario for the future of the union and its members. The idea was to anticipate trends as they evolve and act accordingly to prepare for a changing work place.

The committee's findings and recommendations offer knowledgeable insight into what workers can anticipate in the work place of the 21st century. From the committee's work, it seems clear that the still-evolving Information Age holds both promise and peril for American workers.

There is the definite potential for new and interesting careers for millions of Americans. Tempering that promise is the stark reality that this new information-fueled society also has the potential to create new work place problems.

The next 20 or 30 years could bring serious disruptions and dislocations to the American work force. Basic U.S. industries, such as steel, auto and rubber, will continue to decline, just as the American textile and shoe industries already have done.

Along with this decline in traditional industries, increasing amounts of industrial work will be taken over by robots. The robot factory is essentially a reality today.

...workers in the 21st century will place stronger emphasis on employment security, career development, training and retraining, and support for job relocation.

As a result of these changes and disruptions, workers in the 21st century will place stronger emphasis on employment security, career development, training and retraining, and support for job relocation.

Work patterns in the year 2000 will be quite different from what we know today. New technology will permit many tasks to be done at home and at widely dispersed work locations. The use of electronic work stations and local, regional and international data and communications networks is spreading rapidly today. Before the turn of the century, today's four million work stations will grow to some 30 million.

As the Information Age becomes more firmly entrenched, workers and their jobs will be affected dramatically. New jobs created by technology will require more knowledge and decision-making capabilities on the part of workers; hence, the need for worker training and retraining to satisfy the demands of ever-

Glenn Watts

...a growth-oriented union will probably have some sort of nationwide network of service centers that offer legal, clinical and counseling services for its members...

changing technology.

The 21st century will see a rapid decline in rigidly defined jobs. Career-minded workers will insist on portable skills that they can take from job to job, regardless of the employer.

From the standpoint of organized labor, the message is clear. Unions must be prepared to change with the times— or be prepared to be run over by them.

Traditional unionism will have less appeal to Information Age workers than it has had to workers of the Industrial Age. Single-industry unions seem likely to go the way of the older single-craft unions. The larger, successful unions of the 21st century will be multiple-industry unions.

Successful unions of the future will have to present a fresh image, offer new kinds of services to the members and portray a willingness to enter into new alliances for the collective benefit of members. And the union of the future will need to be more innovative and experimental. In many instances, union growth will be directly related to union flexibility.

In the 21st century, a growth-oriented union will probably have some sort of nationwide network of service centers that offer legal, clinical and counseling services for its members, as well as day-care assistance and other community services.

The priorities of workers are but another facet of the American work place that is changing as we move toward a new century.

When CWA's Committee on the Future presented its final 234-page report to a special union convention in the spring of 1983, nothing within the report took a higher priority than employment security and worker training and retraining.

"The key to employment security is through training and retraining," the committee stated on the opening page of its report. And the emphasis on training and employment security was a recurring theme throughout the document.

In the past, unions have concentrated on protecting specific jobs—from buggywhip makers to cable splicers to Linotype operators. The results were less than gratifying in most cases.

In the future, the emphasis will be on protecting employment through continuing work place education. It has become clear that the key to a worker's employment security is acquired skills and knowledge.

The normal life cycle of many jobs is on an irreversible decline. In the past, it was possible to train for a job and expect the job requirement to remain relatively stable for at least five or 10 years. Today, jobs and the skills and knowledge required to perform them are evolving much more rapidly. A much broader range of abilities is thus needed to keep pace with the ever-present changes.

In the future, the emphasis will be on protecting employment through continuing work place education.

As a direct result of CWA's Committee on the Future, employment security through training and retraining has become one of our union's primary bargaining priorities with all the employers with whom we negotiate.

The most recent contract our union negotiated with AT&T on behalf of 525,000 of our members has, in fact, been called a landmark contract because of its elaborate provisions regarding training and retraining, and its built-in protections for workers whose jobs fall victim to technology. The *Washington Post* editorialized that the new contract is "likely to be cited widely as a precedent." The realities of the Information Age will also demand a greater sense of cooperation between management and labor. One avenue toward greater cooperation is an innovative concept known as Quality of Work Life (QWL).

Cooperation is at the heart of the QWL programs, as opposed to the over-publicized adversary relationship between management and labor. Sensing this need for greater worker involvement in the decision-making process of the work place, CWA joined with management, AT&T in this case, to initiate a QWL program in 1980.

Quality of Work Life as developed by CWA and AT&T is a process by which workers participate in decisions that affect their daily lives at work.

The heart of the process is the work force team composed of five to 10 employees. Team members have the responsibility of defining problems they see at work, proposing solutions and keeping other workers informed of their actions. More than 1,000 of these work force teams have been established throughout the country in the CWA-AT&T Quality of Work Life program.

As a result of this concept, we have jointly resolved work place problems, ranging from such minor but important matters as the proper office temperature to complicated problems involving measuring systems used by management to evaluate employee performance.

Worker participation, in the form of QWL programs and Common Interest Forums, is an idea whose time has come in the United States. It is a concept that will receive considerable attention from both management and labor as the Information Age continues to unfold.

And it represents the kind of innovative approach that will be required of unions in the coming decades to ensure the continued well-being of American workers.

During its first century, the American labor movement has secured collective bargaining rights for millions of American workers and offered those same workers protection from the abuses of employer power.

Those who insist on entering the 21st century with the tools and techniques of the 20th century will almost certainly suffer.

During the next century, workers will look to unions for employment security in the form of training programs to ensure that technology serves people—and not the other way around.

For workers, and indeed for all of society, the preeminent challenge of the 21st century will be the challenge of change.

Those individuals and institutions willing to adapt and change with the times will lead the way in the next century. Those who insist on entering the 21st century with the tools and techniques of the 20th century will almost certainly suffer. There is really but one choice. ☐

Tracking new career categories will become a preoccupation for job seekers and managers.

feingold

S. NORMAN FEINGOLD, EdD, *is president of National Career and Counseling Services in Washington, DC. The most recent of his 45 books is* Emerging Careers: New Occupations for the Year 2000 and Beyond. *He has been on the faculty of American, Boston and George Washington universities. Dr. Feingold also has been a special lecturer at more than 35 colleges and universities in the U.S. and abroad.*

First of all, I want you to know that I am biased. I'm an optimist by conviction and temperament, even though some of the predictions of George Orwell's 1984 already have taken place.

But it was John Galsworthy who many years ago said, "If you don't think about the future, you can't have one." Dr. David Campbell said, "If you do not know where you are going, you'll probably end up somewhere else." As a licensed psychologist in the District of Columbia, I earn my living dealing in futures and career change and know, first hand, the important interplay between the two. Work so often determines where one lives, what one earns, who one marries—if one marries at all—and one's overall lifestyle. It takes up most of a person's time and significantly affects most other important aspects of our lives.

Change is a constant for all facets of living and growing; occupations and careers are no exception. The accelerated speed of change is the new dimension, and it demands faster responses. This acceleration and its inherent challenges can be expected to continue well into the 21st century.

Careers have changed from time immemorial. First, food gathering was done by women, while males did the hunting. Then came a period when most people were engaged in subsistence farming and growing a variety of plants, fibers and animals to meet their needs for food, clothing and shelter.

In the Middle Ages, the new emerging careers were those of craftsmen and artisans. These workers made a living in the villages by serving the needs of the upper classes. The serfs continued to grow food for themselves and overlords and provide military service.

During the Renaissance, a class of craft and artisan guilds developed. Business, trade and manufacturing expanded. People worked in jobs that had not existed in the preceding agricultural age.

Next, the Industrial Revolution expanded the number and types of jobs and careers. And let's not forget that the kind of job disruption going on now occurred when the Industrial Revolution began. With booster shots from developing science and technology, this expansion has been going on ever since.

We are now in what is being called the post-industrial period. Today, only one percent of Singer's business, for example, is in sewing machines; 99 percent is in electronics.

Farmer, laborer, clerk, professional are occupational titles that encapsulate the work history of the United States. Knowledge and how it transforms the tasks of farmer, laborer, clerk and professional is the critical new ingredient of the information or post-industrial age.

Professional workers today are, as they have been in the past, almost always information workers (lawyers, teachers, engineers, accountants, librarians, reporters, etc.). It is the microprocessor that speeds the manipulation, storage and use of numbers, words, ideas and information. Carried another step, information that is properly manipulated, stored and used is lessening the need for human beings as the operators of machines, whether those machines be farm equipment, auto assembly lines, mining excavators, typewriters or cash registers.

Eighty percent of workers employed by the year 2000 probably will be employed in the information industry.

Eighty percent of workers employed by the year 2000 probably will be employed in the information industry. Many, if not most, of those in farming and manufacturing will be using machines made possible by the information industry.

104

S. Norman Feingold

Up to 20 percent of those let go in automobile, steel, rubber and related industries probably will never get their jobs back.

Up to 20 percent of those let go in automobile, steel, rubber and related industries probably will never get their jobs back. They will need to acquire new work, attitude and life- style skills if they are ever to be employed again.

New occupations and careers emerge all the time, while some occupations and careers become obsolete. In comparing the past *Dictionary of Occupational Titles* with the most recent edition, one can readily see many changes. New job titles have been added, and many hundreds of others have been deleted. Some seem to die, but then reappear in new costumes.

For example, one career of short duration in the 19th century was that of the Pony Express rider. Vestiges reappear in today's secret courier and routine messenger services. The elevator operator, the bowling pin setter, the Linotype operator, the milkman, and hundreds of other jobs and careers have passed into oblivion. Instead of reading the gas meter at your home, it has been shown in trial runs that the meters can be tied into a computer on a more cost-effective basis. The meter reader will soon be extinct.

So the ability to recognize new careers is becoming increasingly valuable, both for those who wish to ride these new careers into the next century and for those whose success depends upon the effective recruitment, training and retention of people who can move effectively along these new career paths.

To be able to recognize an emerging career, it is necessary first to know how to define one. Here are the five points I use in my research to measure a particular category of work for its value as an emerging career:

• It has become increasingly visible and distinguishable as a separate career area in recent years.

• It has developed on the job from pre-existing career areas. Examples: legal assistant, community development worker or teacher's aide.

• It has become possible because of advances in technology or physical changes in our environment. Examples: home computers, solar energy research, satellite television, air and water pollution fighting equipment.

• It shows growth in numbers of people employed and attending emerging education and training programs.

- It requires at least two months of special training or preparation before entering.

All traditional jobs are not going to die, of course. The U.S. Bureau of Labor Statistics has projected that between 1978 and 1990 there will be more than 600,000 jobs for janitors and sextons, compared to 200,000 new jobs for computer system analysts; 800,000 jobs for fast food workers and kitchen helpers, compared to 88,000 jobs for computer operators.

A sample of emerging job titles and careers appears in Figure 1, listed in eight major classes and alphabetically within each category. A number of these emerging jobs and careers are already here, but the numbers will increase significantly in the 21st century.

The new jobs/careers will attract both those who want work and those who must work. But one group that may not be able to re-enter the 21st century work force are those people who have 20 to 30 years of experience in declining occupations and who do not have the educational background for retraining, or whose lifestyle is so established that a new career and lifestyle is unthinkable.

The other group that may find adjustment to the new careers and occupations difficult are those who have been educated and trained beyond the skill levels of the jobs/careers that will require the greatest number of workers.

Women will continue to gain full- and part-time work and will soon surpass men in total numbers of those employed. Women are returning to the labor market three to four years after childbirth. They will seek these new careers and will be willing to go the extra mile to get the necessary education and training. Genetic counseling, for example, appears to have attracted more women than men. Moreover, women as a group are changing the fabric of the world of work. More and more women are going into what were traditional male jobs, but the contrary is not as evident. Men do not seem to move as readily into traditionally female work roles.

The skills and training needed for 21st century careers run the gamut from unskilled to professional. There will be heavy demands for job training to prepare employees for positions that did not previously exist. Entry levels for new careers will, in many instances, be vaguely defined. More and more jobs will involve the use of computers and other sophisticated products and machines. The skill requirements for some jobs generally will be higher than they are today, while for others the skills required will be considerably reduced. Companies in the United States spend $137 billion each year to train people for new careers, so training effectiveness will increasingly provide demonstrable impact on bottom-line performance of the organization.

Technology eliminates jobs but it also creates jobs. The big question is whether it will create more jobs or fewer jobs than it eliminates. One significant problem is that the jobs created are frequently in industries other than those where jobs have been eliminated. One estimate suggests robots could replace up to three million operative jobs during the next 20 years. On the other hand, the use of robots creates jobs in industries involved in development, production, design and manufacturing.

Essentially, we have two distinct job training needs. One is to assist the displaced worker to obtain new skills and the other is the education, job and career training of the existing school-age population.

New careers are emerging so rapidly and, in some cases, changing so continuously that it is not possible to compile for each new field standardized information on its advantages and disadvantages, education or training needed, working conditions, number of workers, typical earnings, etc. Many colleges, particularly community colleges, now offer creative courses leading to new careers. Other institutions, including the private sector, are educating and training personnel for new technical work. The shift from menial to mental work is a critical one. An economy based largely on professional work requires a more highly trained work force.

During World War II, management and the federal government developed crash training courses that were eminently successful. From job analysis and employee skill analysis, jobs were restructured and on-the-job training was developed. If we so decide, we can again muster

FIGURE 1
A sample of emerging careers for the 21st century
Professional

Cable TV auditor
Career counselor
Career change counselor
Certified alcohol counselor
Certified financial planner
Child advocate
Communications specialist
Computer designer
Computer scientist
Computer security specialist
Computer systems analyst
Data base designer
Data base engineer
Divorce mediator
Documentation specialist
Ecologist
EDP auditor
Energy auditor
Engineering geologist
Environmental engineer
Ethicist
Family mediator
Forecaster
Forensic scientist
Fusion engineer
Gene splicing worker
Geneticist
Genetic counselor
Geriatric nurse
Health physicist
Hibernation specialist
Human services expert
Image consultant
Information broker

Information research scientist
Lead system analyst
Licensed therapeutic recreation
  specialist
Marine geologist
Mineral economist
Molecular biologist
Neutrino astronomer
Ombudsman
Oncology nutritionist
Phobia therapist
Planetary engineer
Planetary scientist
Professional ethnicist
Public affairs psychologist
Robot engineer
Robotic scientist
Security engineer
Selenologist
Sex therapist
Software writer
Solar architect
Solar designer
Solar energy consultant
Space colonist
Space botanist
Sports psychologist
Strategic planner
Thanatologist
Theoretical chemist
Underwater archeologist
Volcanologist
Wind prospector

Paraprofessional

Exercise technician
Family and planning midwives
Home health aide
Hotline counselor
Lawyer's aide
Library aide

Licensed psychiatric technician
Medical aide
Sex counselor
Social work aide
Teacher's aide
Veterinary aide

Managerial and supervisory

Complaints manager
Data base administrator
Data base manager
Director of human resources
Director of software developments
EDP audit systems manager
Employee relocation
  services director
Executive VIP for international
  product planning

International sales and
  marketing manager
International systems director
New product manager
Site selector specialist
Space launch director
Systems analysis manager
Technical services manager
Telecommunications marketing
  director

Halfway house manager
Information coordinator
Information manager

Transplant coordinator
Underwater hotel, pavilion
   or observatory director

Sales

Cable TV salesperson
Computer salesperson
Digital radiography sales
   representative
Distributor of new business
   equipment
Phonovision salesperson

Robot salesperson
Salesperson for talking
   encyclopedias
Sales trainer
Software salesperson
Telecommunication salesperson
Telephone salesperson

Small business

Aquaculture
Artist (graphic)
Book club sales
Catering and fast food
Child daycare service
Computer games developer
Consultant
Electric car service station
Financial consultant
Financial planner
Fish farmer
Freelance writer
Home correspondence courses
Information salesperson
Inventor

Manufacturer of talking signs
Music store
New health foods
Orthotist
Picture framer
Plant and pet service
Publishing
Self-employment
Shrimp and trout fish farming
Specialized food services
Telephone answering service
Training services
Truffle nursery
Tutor
Videodating services

Skilled

Asteroid miner
Bioconversion technologist
Biomedical technician
Bionic medical technician
Computer assisted design
   (CAD) technician
Computer assisted manufacturing
   (CAM) specialist
Computer axial tomographer
   (CAT) technologist
Computer programmer
Computer service technician
Cryogenic technician
Cyborg technician
Diagnostic medical sonographer
Dialysis technician
Exotic welder
Fiber optic technician
Hazardous waste technician
Hibernation technician

Holographic inspection specialist
House husband and house wife
Industrial robot technician
Laser technician
Lunar miner
Materials utilization technician
Mechanic for hydrogen powered
   automobiles
Medicine aid technician
Microbiological mining technician
Nuclear fuel technician
Nuclear reactor technician
Positron emission tomograph
   (PET) technician
Rehabilitation housing technician
Space mechanic
Solar engineering technician
Telecommunciations technician
Underwater culture technician

Semi-skilled

Battery technician
Bio-gas technician
Computer graphics assistant
Courier
Paramedics

Unskilled

Home companion
House pet and plant sitter
TV monitor (guard)

the goal orientation of World War II and retrain the skilled and unskilled workers who have been displaced by new and high technology.

Schools and industry must get closer to one another in better-sponsored programs during the school year and during the summer. There is no excuse for training for jobs that are declining or have evaporated. The National Association for Industry Education Cooperation and the National Alliance of Business have been, and continue to be, conduits for bringing industry and schools together. The new Job Training Partnership Act also appears to be a step in the direction of greater industry/government/school cooperation in training for jobs that will exist.

Training also must begin to include teaching acceptable work behaviors, the importance of time and attendance; how to look for and keep a job, and how to advance to one's potential.

The work force has more formal education than ever before. The median amount of schooling of the entire labor force has moved past a year of college. Workers in the United States want more from their jobs than money; they want their work to be meaningful and worthwhile. They want to be able to afford a "decent lifestyle." Loyalty to owner, boss or supervisor or concern is a temporary thing. Many high-tech workers, with the help of executive search firms, move up and down the country. Some industries have developed work styles that are in great contrast to the traditional work styles.

> *Personnel professionals will need to understand in depth the tremendous psychological and emotional changes that have occurred within the last 10 years and that will continue to occur.*

Personnel professionals will need to understand in depth the tremendous psychological and emotional changes that have occurred throughout the United States within the last 10 years and that will continue to occur. Unless these professionals participate in continuing human resource training, they can become as obsolete as the Model T Ford.

As the cutting edge in the human resource management field, personnel professionals will need to:
• Constantly update their knowledge of changing qualifications and skills needed for emerging careers.
• Recruit across the spectrum so that the handicapped, minorities, youth, women and displaced workers are knowledgeable about new job and career opportunities.

- Plan site visits to see and meet workers who are successful and working in new emerging careers.
- Act as mentors, advisors, network catalysts, etc., for applicants who are interested in and qualified for new emerging jobs and careers.
- Attend conferences, workshops and seminars to keep up with the latest developments in the field.
- Be active in professional associations.
- Be up to date on the Equal Employment Opportunity Commission and legal implications of the work they are doing.
- Network with colleagues and others in different specialized areas of human resource management.
- Establish links to staff in companies for which they work. Communicate with professionals, managers, salelspersons, paraprofessionals, skilled, semi-skilled and unskilled workers in these companies; show interest and concern about the needs and successes of these colleagues; help them succeed in their jobs; gain information about skill, personality and training needs of their company.

Only by maintaining the highest professional standards will human resource management professionals be able to deal effectively with the new careers—and the people who pursue them—in the 21st century.

Only by maintaining the highest professional standards will human resource management professionals be able to deal effectively with the new careers — and the people who will pursue them — in the 21st century. □

Part-time work will increase, bringing change to social mores and standards of compensation.

*b*arrett

NANCY S. BARRETT *is a professor of economics at American University in Washington, D.C. She is the author of several books, and was a major contributor to* The Subtle Revolution, *report on the growth of the female labor force. She was Acting Assistant Secretary and formerly Deputy Assistant Secretary of Labor for Policy, Evaluation and Research in the Carter Administration, and has directed studies on the status of women for the Urban Institute.*

Within the past generation, a revolution has occurred in attitudes regarding work. Among its many manifestations has been a change in the work patterns and aspirations of women, especially married women with children, a change that has transformed the household economy and increased the participation of women in paid employment.

In 1960, roughly 70 percent of married women between the ages of 16 and 54 were full-time homemakers. By 1980, fewer than 40 percent were in that category. Over the same period, the proportion of married women with pre-school children who were full-time homemakers dropped from 82 percent to 50 percent.[1]

This decline of full-time homemaking as the predominant occupation for married women has been accompanied by a rapid increase in the number of part-time job seekers. Roughly one-third of the former homemakers who have entered paid employment have taken part-time, rather than full-time, jobs. Since the early 1960s, the part-time work force has grown nearly three times as rapidly as the full-time work force.

It is important to note that this rapid growth in the demand for part-time work has been mainly the result of the movement of former homemakers into paid employment, rather than a growing propensity for previously full-time workers to reduce their working hours.[2] Many married women with children see part-time work as a way to benefit from the financial and social advantages of paid employment while continuing home responsibilities. In addition to these married women, many of the growing number of women who head families also seek part-time work as a way to manage their home responsibilities and satisfy their financial needs.

The worklife expectations of the elderly also have changed. Early retirement programs and increased longevity and health have brought the older members of our work force strongly into the part-time market. Although statistically less significant than younger married women in the part-time work force, retirees will constitute a growing number of part-time workers in the future.

The same attitudinal changes that have whetted the appetites of married women for paid employment are also causing them to reject the low pay and menial, dead-end work that part-time jobs have typically offered in the past. They want pay equity, opportunities for upward mobility, fringe benefits, job security and opportunities for personal fulfillment and status achievement. For women who head families, a well paying part-time job may mean the difference between work and welfare.

For women who head families, well paying part-time work may mean the difference between work and welfare.

The legislative climate mandating non-discrimination against women will accommodate these demands. Since the vast majority of part-time workers are female, discrimination in part-time employment can clearly be interpreted as a civil rights issue, a violation of Title VII of the Civil Rights Act of 1964 that prohibits employment discrimination on the basis of sex.

Moreover, as young men and women adjust their family responsibilities to accommodate more egalitarian sex roles, men will begin to seek part-time opportunities outside the traditional clerical and sales jobs usually held by women. Although some men with working wives would undoubtedly like to spend more time at home, these men now find it difficult to reduce their working hours without a severe loss in income, status and opportunities for upward mobility.

All these trends are suggestive of important changes in

Nancy S. Barrett

The growing number and influence of part-time workers will challenge the sanctity of the fixed, 40-hour week...

the structure of worklife in the 21st century. The growing number and influence of part-time workers will challenge the sanctity of the fixed, 40-hour week, and the needs and aspirations of part-time workers will produce a major upgrading of the quality of part-time job opportunities.

Between 1965 and 1980, the number of part-time workers nearly doubled, increasing from 7.6 million to 14.3 million. (These figures refer to workers on voluntary part-time schedules. Those forced to work part-time because full-time work was unavailable are counted as part of the full-time work force). The proporation of part-time workers who were women rose from 65 percent in 1965 to 69 percent in 1980, as the labor force participation of married women increased.

The most rapid increase in part-time employment has been among women aged 18 to 44. Since 1965, roughtly 3.4 million women in this age group have been added to the part-time work force.

In 1980, 78 percent of all part-time workers were in wholesale and retail trade, finance and services. Roughly 70 percent of all female part-timers were in sales, clerical and non-domestic service occupations, while for males the occupational distribution is more diverse. Nonetheless, median part-time pay rates for men are about the same as the median for women, reflecting the fact that most male part-timers are younger or older than average. Only about 30 percent of male part-timers fall into the prime-age category (22 to 55 years) compared with 60 percent of female part-timers.[3]

Hourly earnings for female part-timers are roughly 75 percent of those for full-time female workers. Male part-timers earn about half that of their full-time counterparts, on an hourly basis. In 1982, the median hourly wage for part-time workers was about $4.50, only slightly above the legal minimum wage. Median annual earnings for part-time workers who worked 50 to 52 weeks in 1982 were $4,848 for men and $4,959 for women. Comparable figures for full-time workers were $21,077 for men and $13,014 for women.[4]

Coupled with these low part-time pay rates is the virtual absence of fringe benefits, apart from federally-mandated social security and unemployment compensation. The dead-end nature of most part-time jobs provides little opportunity for training and upward mobility. Without training and career tracking, these employees have little job security. Yet studies show that part-time workers compare favorably with full-time workers with respect to hourly productivity. A 1976 study of federal employees by the General Accounting Office found part-timers to have much lower rates of absenteeism and lower quit rates than full-time workers.[5] Today's part-time workforce—largely female, concentrated in low-paying dead-end jobs—is an anachronism at odds with the emphasis on more egalitarian treatment of women workers. The assumption that these women are working for recreation or "pin money," or that they are intermittent workers without career ambitions is hardly tenable in today's world.

Stereotypes and anachronistic attitudes can be self-fulfilling if workers are not given recognition and responsibility commensurate with their contribution and potential.

Paul Glick and Art Norton, two Census Bureau demographers, have estimated that roughly 40 percent of all marriages contracted today will terminate in divorce.[6] Child support payments are rarely enough to tide these families over, and the availability of a decent part-time job will make the difference between financial security and proverty for many families. Of course, even for two-career couples, the wife's income from a part-time job is often a crucial part of the family budget. Moreover, faced with high and rising probability of divorce, married women are wise to maintain a continuous link to the job market in the event they, too, should experience a marital disruption.

But divorce and financial necessity are not the only factors involved in shaping the new work ethic. Men and women are rejecting traditional gender-based stereotypes. Many women want to break out of traditional occupations not only because they are low-paying, but also because they lack channels for upward mobility, personal achievement and status attainment. Moreover, part-time jobs in traditional female occupations are not very attractive to male retirees or to fathers who would like to share child-rearing work with their wives.

As long as socially acceptable part-time jobs are more prevalent for women than for men, traditional inequalities in the time men and women devote to child care and household work will be perpetuated. Unless fathers can reduce their hours of paid employment as readily as mothers, the causal nexus that prevents a more equal sharing of both financial and emotional responsibilities in marriage will be reinforced.

Expanding and upgrading part-time employment opportunities as a strategy for improving the economic status of women and allowing men to share more of the responsibilities of family life has always been controversial.

Opponents of this approach fear that facilitating part-time employment will only serve to reinforce traditional stereotypes and contribute to further occupational segregation of women. They see little evidence that fathers would move into these jobs in significant numbers.

There surely is considerable merit to this view, particularly as little progress has been made to date in upgrading the quality of the vast majority of part-time jobs. Paradoxically, as millions of married women have left full-time homemaking and entered part-time employment on a wave of egalitarian sentiment, occupational segregation in the labor market has remained remarkably pervasive. [7]

...the needs of part-time workers...will become more pressing in the 21st century.

Nonetheless, there will continue to be a growing demand for part-time work, and the needs of part-time workers—both financial and for broader purposes of personal fulfillment—will become more pressing in the 21st century. While it is true that a part-time work force that is predominantly female may contribute to traditional stereotypes, there are compelling social and economic reasons for improving the earning prospects of part-time workers.

Despite the growing number of part-time jobseekers and their increasing insistence on higher pay, non-traditional jobs and opportunities for advancement, part-time jobs remain low-paying and low-status. What are some of the factors contributing to this weak dynamic for change?

Employers resist change both because they underestimate the potential productivity of part-timers and because there are genuine economic disincentives for employing part-time workers. To the extent that employers themselves hold traditional stereotypes, they may view the part-time jobseeker as less committed and more likely to be called away to take care of home responsibilities than would a full-time worker. This view is somewhat curious in light of the fact that most part-time jobs are in occupations held predominantly by females. Why should a part-time worker necessarily be more burdened with household responsibilities than a full-time worker? An employer concerned that an employee might be overcommitted should prefer that they work fewer, not longer, hours.

Coming together with the continued growth of the part-time work force will be added pressure to upgrade the status of part-time work.

But there are other concerns. In some work settings, a part-time employee can be a real inconvenience, depending on the relation of the job to the total work flow. This raises a broader question of alternative work schedules, which clearly are not amenable to all work settings. Job-sharing, in which two persons share one full-time job, is a possible solution to scheduling problems.

The payoff to training will usually take longer for part-time employee, because they work fewer hours in which newly-acquired skills are applied. Combined with the belief that part-timers, being less committed, might quit, this factor may prevent employers from providing the same training opportunities to part-time employees as they give full-time employees.

There are administrative costs as well. Employer contributions to social security are higher for two part-time workers earning $20,000 each than for one earning $40,000. (However, as long as part-time jobs are low-paid, the social security maximum would usually not be a factor.) There is a fixed paperwork cost associated with employing a worker, regardless of the number of hours worked. Employer costs for health benefits, life insurance, etc., may also be higher for two part-time workers than for one full-time worker. Moreover, in some work settings, notably the federal government, managers are allocated personnel on the basis of a stipulated number of employees, without regard to cost. In such a system, full-time workers are usually preferred.

But employer resistance is not the only factor barring change. More subtle influences also are at work. Given strong legal support for equal employment opportunity, the part-time job market becomes a last bastion for enforcing occupational segregation and keeping wages low for women and the elderly. In extreme cases, the part-time employee is a cheap worker, who is denied fringe benefits and pay increases. Lacking options, part-timers are at the mercy of the employer, fearing that if they quit they will be branded as unstable.

It is important to recognize that many part-time workers are terribly insecure both financially and because they lack the self-esteem that goes with a high-status, full-time job. As a consequence, they become prey to employer paternalism and are potential victims of exploitation. Thus, barriers to change may be at least partially self-imposed as workers themselves resist external efforts to improve their situation.

Recognizing the sources of these barriers to change is an important first step in upgrading employment opportunities for part-time workers. Stereotypes and anachronistic attitudes can be self-fulfilling if workers are not given recognition and responsibility commensurate with their contribution and potential.

Clearly, economic disincentives such as added costs of fringe benefits must be eliminated. Part-time workers must be afforded the same legal protections as full-time workers, but without added cost to employers.

Eventually, affirmative action will extend to the part-time sphere, mandating access to improved opportunities for part-time workers.

Given the strong institutional resistance to change, eliminating penalties on employers who hire part-time workers is not enough. Affirmative action programs must include the provision of part-time jobs for both men and women in higher-paying skills and professional categories.

What do these trends suggest for the work place of the 21st century? First, there is no question that the part-time work force will grow in importance, both in numbers and in status. In 1965, roughly 12 percent of the work force was part-time. In 1982, part-timers (those on voluntary part-time schedules) constituted 15 percent of the work force. By the year 2000, part-time employment could be as high as 20 percent of the total.

Judging from current trends, labor force participation of women with families will continue to rise, and many of these women will seek part-time work. Expansion of the service sector, where part-time job opportunities are most likely to emerge, will facilitate this growth. Retirees and younger males who are fathers will increasingly seek part-time work, as increasing longevity lengthens the post-retirement lifespan and more egalitarian social standards compel fathers to devote more time to non-market work.

Coming together with the continued growth of the part-time work force will be added pressure to upgrade the status of part-time work. Economic needs associated with the higher incidence of divorce and female-headed families, and societal reforms to provide improved employment opportunities for women will increasingly focus public attention on low wages and poor working conditions in part-time employment. Eventually, affirmative action will extend to the part-time sphere, mandating access to improved opportunities for part-time workers.

Once part-timers break out of their traditional occupational ghettos, moving into management and other positions of control, they will increasingly influence the structure and conditions of worklife.

...opportunities for personal achievement will not be governed by the number of hours spent in the office each week, but rather by the contributions and abilities of each individual.

As the rigidity of the 40-hour week erodes and men find socially-acceptable ways to reduce their working hours, the potential for growth in the part-time work force will increase even further. This will mean more experimentation with alternative work schedules and working hours. It will also engender a reassessment of the value of non-market, household work.

To accommodate these changes, laws governing employee rights and working conditions will be reassessed and overhauled. Implicit penalties for hiring part-time workers will be eliminated (just as the implicit "marriage penalty" is being eliminated from the federal income tax code). And new laws governing work in the non-market sector (for instance, social security coverage and workers' compensation for homemakers) will undoubtedly be promulgated.

Only a generation ago, with a traditional division of labor

between a male breadwinner and a female homemaker, the notion prevailed that only those who were committed to full-time days and weeks at the office could be productive and reliable, worthy of high pay and status recognition. In the 21st century work place, pay responsibility and opportunities for personal achievement will not be governed by the number of hours spent in the office each week, but rather by the contributions and abilities of each individual. □

...pay responsibility and opportunities for personal achievement will not be governed by the number of hours spent in the office each week...

References

1. Except where indicated otherwise, all data are from U.S. Department of Labor, Bureau of Labor Statistics, *Employment and Earnings* (various monthly issues) and U.S. Department of Labor, Employment and Training Administration, *Employment and Training Report of the President* various annual issues).

2. Nancy S. Barrett, "Women in the job market", in Smith, Ralph E., (ed.), *The Subtle Revolution;* Washington, D.C.: The Urban Institute, 1979, p. 81.

3. Nancy S. Barrett, *op. cit.,* p. 84.

4. U.S. Department of Commerce, Bureau of the Census, *Money Income and Poverty Status of Families and Persons in the United States: 1982, Current Population Reports, Consumer Income,* Series, P-60, No. 140, July 1983, p. 17.

5. U.S. General Accounting Office, *Part-time employment in Federal Agencies;* Washington, D.C.: U.S. Government Printing Office, 1976.

6. Paul C. Glick and Arthur J. Norton, *Marrying, Divorcing, and Living Together in the U.S. Today, Population Bulletin;* Washington, D.C.: Population Reference Bureau, 1977, p. 18.

7. Barrett, *op. cit.,* pp. 46-54. See also Blau, Francine D., *Equal Pay in the Office;* Lexington Books, 1977.

International forces will prevail, but will unions be able to change with the new global work place?

dale

"What is going to be the main feature of the U.S. work place in the 21st century?" I asked a couple of non-American colleagues who claim to have given the matter some thought. "Silence," replied one. "No smoking," said the other.

The snap answers were not meant to be particularly profound. But they reflected initial personal impressions of new working conditions to which many people are already being exposed as modern technology and late-20th-century social values move into the work place.

REGINALD DALE is U.S. Editor and Bureau Chief for the Financial Times of London, based in Washington, DC. He is a former president of the European Journalists' Organization, Brussels; former vice president of the International Press Union, Brussels, and former committee member and negotiator for the British National Union of Journalists.

When I first started to work for newspapers in the 1960s, the noise of machinery in the press room was so intense that it was hard to conduct a conversation. In the newsroom, it was difficult even to think against the background of raucously ringing telephones, the clatter of typewriters and the shouts of editors from one desk to another.

If you go into a modern newsroom, there is no clatter of typewriters; editing is being done silently on video terminals and even the telephones are quieter. People have more space around them, the air temperature is better controlled and the whole place is much cleaner.

It is also true that fewer of them are smoking. Working conditions are not established simply by formal contracts of one kind or another between management and individual employees or labor unions. Working conditions are also governed by wider trends in society as a whole, whether they involve personal habits like smoking or more fundamental changes in attitudes towards sexual and racial equality and social fairness.

It is not possible to look ahead to the 21st century work place without making some assumptions about the broader society in which we shall be living. If, as I hope, we are progressively, on the whole, moving toward a more enlightened society, that should be reflected in the long run by greater consideration by managers for their employees' working conditions.

Conversely, it is also interesting to note in passing that the new machinery that now fills offices in the information, service and financial industries seems by its very nature to influence human behavior, too. The people who operate the new machines also seem more subdued, calmer and tidier.

That kind of work place is rapidly becoming familiar, particularly in the United States and Japan, but also in Europe and other industrialized countries. But here is a radically different vision—a description of a new high-tech plant in Japan from Bruce Nussbaum's *The World After Oil:*

> There is very little light in this factory. There is none of the fluorescent glare so typical of plant floors. The entire area, two football fields in size, just glows dimly. Something else is also different here. The air-conditioning is turned way down, and the air is stale, full of metallic smells...There are no people here—none at all. No voices, no sneezing, no coughing, no laughing. Just the sound of machines.

In thinking about the American work place in the years ahead, one has to ask how many Americans will have a work place.

The plant was built in 1981. At least on the night shift, it is populated only by robots and machines making more robots and machines, which will turn out yet more robots. By the 21st century, robots will almost certainly have become so sophisticated that they will be able to perform most manufacturing tasks. For many other tasks, computers will be more efficient than the human brain— we are already on the verge of the age of "artificial intelligence," although there is, as yet, no agreement as to exactly what it means.

Reginald Dale

Many West European countries are beginning to grapple with the prospect that large sections of their work forces may in the future go from cradle to grave without ever having a job.

International competition to dominate these new technologies—for the moment predominantly between the United States and Japan, but later including other emerging countries, particularly in Asia and, probably to a lesser degree, the older societies of Europe—can only hasten the advent of this new age in which traditional work forces will largely be dispensed within the advanced countries. In thinking about the American work place in the years ahead, one has to ask how many Americans will have a work place.

It is now commonplace that the old smokestack manufacturing techniques are largely doomed, as production and jobs move to cheaper areas overseas, old plants become obsolete and investment moves into newer industries. Some countries in Europe—particularly ''post-industrial'' Britain— are beginning to face up to the possibility that many of their traditional industries like ship building, textiles, steel and the making of cars and motor-cycles may never be viable (at least without massive government help) again.

The service sector and the new high-technology industries will help to take up the slack. And in the United Kingdom, for example, some of the older ''pre-industrial'' craft industries such as the manufacture of Harris Tweed, Shetland sweaters, Scotch whisky and old-fashioned foods and cosmetics—have gained a new chance at life. Similar trends can be observed in the U.S.

But there is not going to be a big enough market for these products to provide work for everyone who wants it. Many West European countries are beginning to grapple with the prospect that large sections of their work forces may in the future go from cradle to grave without ever having a job.

The Netherlands, for example, exported many of its jobs—with the aid of multinational companies—thanks to high labor costs and an overvalued currency. For some years now, that country has been thinking about the future. If there are not enough traditional manufacturing jobs to go around, it is suggested, there will just have to be a boom in the numbers of actors, artists, school-teachers, social workers and so on.

The problem, of course, will be to generate the wealth

to sustain such a society. Taken to its extremes, a somewhat idealistic Dutchman once told me, it could pay for itself. The actors who earned their living performing in the evenings, for instance, would help to pay their own wages by buying tickets to watch the matinee show, and so on.

The prospects in the U.S. appear somewhat brighter. Unlike the cramped West European countries, the U.S. has vast natural resources, much greater social and economic flexibility and an undefinable quality that is sometimes described as "a capacity for self-renewal." Unemployment is high in the U.S., but not so high as in Western Europe. And while many of Western Europe's economic and industrial problems are clearly structural, those of the United States may be more cyclical.

Internationally, wage and other costs in initially low-cost competing countries will rise as those countries develop, just as they have in Japan. Traditionally U.S. industries, such as the auto industry, are beginning to show that they *can* adjust to foreign competition, even if it is far from easy. But there will still be a steadily growing group of newly industrializing countries, such as Korea, Taiwan, Brazil and Mexico, moving into traditional areas of mass production with lower costs—and the dilemma of how poorer countries can develop without harming the older industries in the richer countries remains unsolved.

It remains true that if U.S. factories are going to remain competitive, both abroad and in their domestic markets, they will have to introduce new production techniques that require less manpower. Indeed, it is already happening. Factories are closing never to reopen, and redundant auto and steel workers are having to take jobs cooking hamburgers in fast-food restaurants or face the prospect of no work at all.

Looking around the world, there is no evidence that this trend will do anything but accelerate. Protectionism—as exemplified by attempts to limit imports of Japanese-made automobiles—will do no more than to postpone the inevitable changes and make them more painful when they ultimately occur.

If protectionism was to lead to a major international outbreak of beggar-my-neighbor policies of 1930s dimensions, the jobs would disappear even faster as world markets collapsed. It must be remembered that, in the past few years, the United States has rapidly become more dependent upon world trade than ever before.

In the absence of such a disaster, the rapidly increasing mobility of capital, the explosion of global communications and the world-spanning activities of the multinational corporations will combine to switch production to wherever it is most profitable—and in many cases that will not be the United States.

In the developed countries, new industries are emerging alongside the new technological industries, most notably in the service and leisure sectors. But that is—in part, at least—precisely because people are likely to have more time on their hands in the future.

The combination of new technology and fewer manufacturing jobs is bound to have fundamental effects on the working conditions of those still at work. One of the most obvious consequences, and one that has been increasingly evident in Europe since the mid-1970s, is that those with a job will be less inclined to endanger it.

The result is that the astonishingly high unemployment in countries like France and Britain has not led to the major labor and social unrest that once was predicted. Even in the United States, the recent period of double-digit jobless figures was swallowed *relatively* calmly by a society that on the whole seems to realize that it will not bring the jobs back by rocking the political boat.

But the phenomenon has been much more striking in Europe. Those with vulnerable jobs are less inclined to go on strike, or otherwise protest, to improve their own pay and working conditions— still less inclined to agitate on behalf of those without jobs, who in any case tend by the nature of things to be less unionized.

What is happening in Europe is a major shift in the nature of the trade unions. By the 21st century, the European trade unions are likely to be virtually unrecognizable compared with the original Victorian organizations that had to struggle for the most basic labor rights. In both Europe and the United States—though not always in Britain—many unions now realize that by

One of the obvious consequences...is that those with a job will be less inclined to endanger it.

demanding constant wage increases they risk ruining their employer and, in the end, reducing the scarce number of jobs.

The trend is to demand compensation in other ways, either through greater participation in company decision-making, for instance with seats on the board as in West Germany, or through the proliferation of fringe benefits such as health care, amenities at the work place and longer holidays. Job security and improved pension and redundancy payments, rather than ever-increasing wages, are likely to become increasingly frequent demands. In Europe, the notion that a worker can automatically expect an annual real wage increase is increasingly coming into question.

For their part, managements are buying off wage demands by offering other inducements, such as company-financed sports facilities, longer paid maternity (and, increasingly, paternity) leave and paid periods away from the work place ("sabbaticals") for employees to gain further training and experience in areas that may be only indirectly related to their full-time jobs.

At the same time, unions in a number of European countries—particularly in Northern Europe—have for some years now seen their role evolving into one of partnership rather than confrontation with management. Relations between management and the work force, they believe, should be based on a bargain under which management admits the unions into the corporate decision-making in exchange for greater responsibility on the part of the workers.

Unions have, so far, failed to organize as an international counterweight to the power of the multinational corporations...

The bargain has worked in some countries, but by no means all. In Britain, for instance, the unions have been loath to give up their traditional confrontational role. And while efforts are under way to extend such practices throughout the European Community—for example, through the European Commission's so-called Vredeling Directive—they are unlikely to be particularly successful in the foreseeable future.

The European Community has wrought some changes in working conditions, for instance, in the field of equal pay for men and women. But one of the many failures of European economic integration so far has been that of the unions to follow its logic and operate effectively across borders at an international level.

The same is true in the wider world. Unions have, so far, failed to organize as an international counterweight to the power of the multinational corporations; they remain beset by national and political differences. There is little reason to think that they will cooperate much better internationally in what is likely to be a much less favorable climate for trade unions in the 21st century.

By dispensing with mass labor, the new technological and information industries rob the unions of their basic source of strength. In the United States, many of the country's most successful enterprises are non-union, and the migration of commerce from the Northeast to the Sunbelt has shifted productive forces into areas where unions have never held sway. One of the many differences between Europe and the United States is that areas comparable to the Sunbelt simply do not exist in Europe.

It is, in fact, far from clear that U.S. trade unions will try to follow their European counterparts very far along the road toward greater participation—or indeed be offered it by future managements. In the past, those American unions that have shown willingness to accept sacrifices in the interests of their members' employers have usually had short memories as soon as the economy picks up.

In the past, those American unions that have shown willingness to accept sacrifices in the interests of their members' employers have usually had short memories as soon as the economy picks up.

My own, perhaps naive, hope is that as union power wanes and the new technologies take hold, management will increasingly see the need for a contented work force without the need for so much prodding as has been necessary. There appears, after all, to be an increasing recognition, both in the United States and abroad, of the substantial investment constituted by a highly trained modern work force—and of the desirability of not losing it.

This is not altruism; it is a hard-nosed calculation. It can be seen most obviously in the increasing attention that employers are paying to their employees' health. It would be nice, too, to think that paid vacations for American workers—ludicrously short in European eyes—will gradually be extended. That, however, I admit is less likely.

But if my optimism about overall social and business trends is justified, management concern for employees should continue to grow in the next century, partly by choice and partly by necessity. Since the dawn of the Industrial Revolution, the historical trend has had its ups and downs—but it has been steadily upwards, at least in the industrialized countries. The seven-day week became the six-day week and then the five-day week. Day-care centers, company health clinics and cafeterias would have been unthinkable in the last century. There is no reason why the humanization of the work place should suddenly stop.

In the shrinking modern world, the United States is more dependent than at any time in its history on global economic trends.

In some fields, employees may even be totally liberated from the work place by the ability to do their jobs at home with the aid of modern information and communication equipment. This is already happening in Britain, where, particularly in the field of finance and investment, some executives are spending up to three days a week at home— often in congenial country surroundings many miles from company headquarters.

In the shrinking modern world, the United States is more dependent on global economic trends than at any other time in its history. But the difficulty of predicting how those trends will affect the work place is compounded by post-war experience, in which the United States has been overwhelmingly an exporter, rather than an importer of social trends. My colleagues' silent, non-smoking offices are more likely to catch on here before they do anywhere else. I don't think they're ready for them yet in Naples Marseilles. □

Retirement will become obsolete in the improved work scheme of our 21st century economy.

bird

CAROLINE BIRD *is the author of seven books that have established themselves as bellwethers of social change, including* Born Female *and* The Two-Paycheck Marriage. *Her most recent is* The Good Years: Your Life in the Twenty-First Century, *in which she predicts a new kind of prosperity based on pleasure, freedom and self-fulfillment.*

Today, the people who grew up in the Great Depression of the '30s look forward to the day when they can quit working. When New York State offered a pension sweetener averaging $150 a month to employees 55 and older for retiring early, it had to buy out twice as many workers as it needed—including many key people who couldn't be replaced easily by lower-paid juniors—to meet the budget target.

Young workers would like to retire early, too, but they fear they won't have the income to do it. Surveys repeatedly report that majorities think their pensions won't be worth the Social Security taxes taken from their paychecks. For those under 40, the stretch-out already has begun. The 1983 package for rescuing Social Security included raising the retirement age, beginning with those now eligible for benefits in 2009.

The current conventional wisdom advises young people to start banking big hunks of their salaries now, or to go to work for a company that does the saving for them through pension plans intended to bind them for life with golden handcuffs. These, of course, are exactly what the private investment community would like them to do. Projections of future disaster are usually intended to scare people into doing something that is going to do somebody else some good *bird*

In spite of the gloom and doom about the future that is fashionable now, a plausible case can be made for a brighter scenario.

right now. The impending bankruptcy of Social Security is a classic example.

In the spring of 1981, David Stockman, director of the Office of Management and Budget, hoped to cut the budget deficit for the year by getting Congress to cut Social Security benefits. He knew the move would be unpopular, so he decided to blame it on the baby boom of the 1950s and make it sound as though he was rescuing Social Security instead of cutting it. He argued that the growing ratio of beneficiaries to workers would bankrupt the system eventually, so we ought to start saving the system now, and the sooner the better. The lurid forecasts didn't say exactly when the crunch would come, but jumped over the decades during which the baby-boomers causing the trouble would be swelling the harvest of payroll taxes.

"It's not a matter of satisfying actuaries," Stockman admitted to William Greider, the journalist friend who spilled the beans. "It's simply one of satisfying the here and now of budget requirements."

The effort backfired. Congress turned the proposal down and Stockman himself eventually was summoned to the President's woodshed, but the image of a bankrupt Social Security remains a powerful force in political life. It created the urgency for a compromise between right and left on the President's National Commission on Social Security, and it seems to have permanently lowered the expectations of today's young people.

But is it likely? Will today's young people really be worse off when they are in their 60s and 70s than people that age today? They won't if the senior boom expected for that time becomes reality.

The ratio of old to young is only one of the factors in the forecast. In their periodic estimates of future taxes and benefits, the Social Security trustees consider trends in fertility, mortality, immigration, marriage, divorce, labor force participation, unemployment, productivity, inflation, retirement patterns, the incidence and duration of disability, as well as prices and wages. In short, the hapless trustees are required by law to forecast the entire economy—and for 75 years into the future!

Past forecasts usually have been wide of the mark, and the batting average of recent economic forecasts does not

Caroline Bird

Instead of inciting a war between young taxpayers sweating to support a plague of greedy pensioners who refuse to budge from the beach, the nature and role of work is likely to change so that nobody would want to retire from it.

suggest that contemporary projections will turn out to be any better. We can no longer safely assume that the economy of the 21st century will work the way we imagine it works today, or that, as they grow older, young people will become like the older people of today whose values were shaped by an entirely different life experience. In spite of the gloom and doom about the future that is fashionable now, a plausible case can be made for a brighter scenario.

If Toffler, Naisbitt and Bird are right, young management trainees can expect to spend their entire careers on the transition to a post-industrial, information-based economy. The changes they are helping to bring about will redefine work and pay in a way that will make the projections of the Social Security trustees meaningless. By the time these young people turn 62, the problem of meeting their pension claims may not have to be solved. Like so many of the problems that worry us in our daily lives, a shift of scene will wipe it from the screen. Instead of inciting a war between young taxpayers sweating to support a plague of greedy pensioners who refuse to budge from the beach, the nature and role of work is likely to change so that nobody would want to retire from it.

Retirement in the sense of withdrawal from paid employment will no longer be based on age, because people now entering the labor force will have been "retiring" all along the way. Young people who have been stopping out from college and postponing children won't march together through a set of predictable stages at predetermined ages. They won't have the midlife crises that rattled the young people of the 1950s—who had too many babies and moved up rigid career ladders too fast.

Then, too, they'll be healthier in their later years than their parents have been. In their 60s, they will find the sedentary work of the 21st century no more stressful than they found it at 30 or 40, and they'll be in better physical shape than their counterparts of today.

The prophets of Social Security catastrophe dwell at length on the fragile and medically expensive years of extra life that medicine is adding to people in their 80s and 90s. But less is said of the increase in the number of people who have escaped the traumas that have traditionally limited the activities of people in their 60s and 70s. So many people are vigorous in their later years that it is getting harder to guess a person's age. Women 50 now look, act and live like women of 30. As the decades pass, they grow ageless instead of old.

Healthy people in their 60s and 70s are not lazy or lethargic. Even those who are dreaming of retirement tell you that it isn't work they are eager to escape, but the nonsense they have to go through to do it. They talk at length about Mickey Mouse rules, office politics, stupid bosses and the straitjacket of a nine-to-five schedule.

Many—on some surveys a majority—say they would like to go on working after retirement—if they could work a little bit less, if they didn't have to trudge to the office when it wasn't necessary or they didn't want to, or if they could work for a different boss or at a kind of work they have always wanted to try. They would like work outside the bureaucracy, and over which they could have some control. Many dream of escaping the work rules by starting their own business.

Imaginative retirees, secure in their pensions, are able to take a chance on the new work the technology is creating.

Those healthy older people who have been lucky enough to find work with one or more of these features are very apt to be doing it. And since those eligible for Social Security have an incentive to work off the books, there are undoubtedly many more of them than we realize. Some of them talk of their second or third "retirements."

Blue-collar workers buy little tractors and plow out the driveways of their neighbors. Accountants find they can earn their corporate-world salaries more comfortably by advising a few small local enterprises. During their last few years on the job, high-powered executives plot how to take a piece of the business with them when they go—or, more frequently, how to exploit a potential the bureaucracy is ignoring.

Imaginative retirees, secure in their pensions, are able to take a chance on the new work the technology is creating. Because there is no name for what they do, they frequently call it "consulting." An engineer whose company moved him around the country becomes a consultant in the management of relocation. A foundation executive advises nonprofit organizations how to plan for the future. A foreign service officer buys American farmland for foreign investors.

Work and retirement are so blurred for these pioneers of the post-industrial economy that it is sometimes hard for them to say whether they are retired or working. Some of them are always being called back to give younger workers the benefit of their experience.

What, for instance, is the status of a maintenance man who has agreed to check out an old coal-fired furnace that a factory has to keep going while the modern furnace is under repairs? Or a 55-year-old who has taken a furlough from his job to decide whether he and his wife want to live on a farm in Oregon? Or the dentist who is building a set of false teeth for the editor who is helping him shape the book he has always dreamed of writing. Swapping skills keeps many retired people comfortably busy.

Now, the interesting thing about the work that the retired—as well as the rest of us—would like to do is that it is exactly the kind of work that most people will be doing in the post-industrial, information-based economy that is being so widely predicted. The next generation of information technology promises more liberation from the shop, the office, the time clock, the chain of command and the work rules. It will enable more people to work at home or at a succession of short, self-contained projects separated by weeks and months of leisure. When jobs are less constricting, there will be less incentive to retire.

The quality of work life is destined to improve. The surest thing about the future is that technological advances will continue to cut the hours of effort required to put a floor of material comfort under everyone. We will use this dividend—as we have in the past—not only to invent new goods and services and to raise the minimum standard below which no one is going to be allowed to fall, but also to eliminate the jobs that nobody likes to do.

Dull, demeaning jobs will go unfilled because no one will be willing to do them at the wage they're worth in competition with other goods and services. It's happening already. So few people are willing to tote trays that cafeteria service now prevails except in the luxurious

The next generation of information technology promises more liberation from the shop, the office, the time clock, the chain of command and the work rules.

establishments where tray toters can expect to earn a middle class income. There'll be less incentive to retire when work is intrinsically more rewarding.

How will we feel about work when toil is no longer essential to survival? Instead of a jail from which to escape as soon as possible, work will become an integral part of human activity, so woven into the fabric of a person's normal activity—prosumption is Toffler's word—that retiring from work would be like retiring from life itself. Artists feel this way now. So do the people we describe as driven workaholics.

Jobs in the information-based economy of the 21st century will be modeled on the employment structures of the institutions that employ our knowledge workers today: schools, colleges, laboratories, newspapers, book publishers, brokerage houses and law and accounting firms. (Hospitals are information exchanging centers too. But they do it so badly that their work rules are going to have to be changed.)

These are places where people like to work, and if you ask them why, they talk about freedom, control, using talents, opportunity to make a contribution, variety, leeway on hours and rules, working relationships that are collegial instead of hierarchic, and the chance to follow changing interests, perhaps to another institution or even a related industry.

Young people in their first jobs can look forward to a time when the job will not be the primary organizer of their life plans and schedules.

Even when there is an attempt to run them on factory lines—the unfortunate example of the hospital comes to mind—knowledge workers have acquired more control over their work than the rules intend, if only because their work is so specialized that it's harder to check up on them.

Young people on their first jobs can look forward to a time when the job will not be the primary organizer of their life plans and schedules. Although everyone will work on and off, through all of their adult life and into their later decades, they'll spend fewer total hours of their lives in paid employment than they do now. A few will join the small cadre of specialists at the top, but most college graduates won't want to work full time all their lives or climb a career ladder in one company.

Like the wives of the mid-20th century, most people will

look for jobs that are compatible with the other things going on in their lives. They'll quit to go back to school, take care of their health, spend time with their children, or pursue a sport, a hobby, a relationship or one of a widening array of nonvocational interests that in our work absorption we now call "outside activities." The arts are not everyone's cup of tea, but there are going to be more people writing novels, making films and painting pictures—often just for the fun of it.

Those who choose to have children will take parenting more seriously and invest more time in it, but they are not rearing families on a standard time-table. Some couples will have their children right after college, but others will have them first and resume education only when their children are old enough to go to school themselves.

There will be all kinds of arrangements. In some families, both parents will quit their highly structured jobs for a year or two while their children are small. In others, both will choose to work part of the day at undemanding jobs, or take turns working full time.

One way or another, the next generation will spend more of their lives in activities that presently do not command an income.

We talk of endless wants, but we haven't been able to think of new products and services that will generate the buying power needed to keep the new technology working to its awesomely high capacity.

A lovely dream, you may be saying to yourself. It's nice to know that working is going to be more fun, even if we are going to be able, after all, to retire from it. But how are you going to pay for all this leisure? Less work means less revenue from payroll taxes. And if all this depends on a different kind of economy, how are we going to get from here to there in time to be of any use to the adults now working?

These are good questions, but they require answers that are political, rather than economic. Some economists warn that the technology ahead will save so much labor that there won't be enough work to go around. Robots don't buy cars. We talk of endless wants, but we haven't been able to think of new products and services that will generate the buying power needed to keep the new technology working to its awesomely high capacity. In the industrial view that imprisons us all, this is a problem instead of a blessing.

137

And it's not a new problem. Eventually, politicians will coin some shiny new variation of the way we tried to solve the "lack of demand" that seemed, at the time, to be the trouble with the economy in the Great Depression.

If you are a young worker in the 1980s, some funny things could happen on the way to your retirement. Already, we are cheating on the work ethic. But instead of going back to the good old days of sweat and toil, we are going to find new ways to cheat even more. We are going to do it not because our moral fiber is snapping, but because it is the only reasonable response to improved technology. We are going to have to find ways to give people the money to buy what the robots turn out, even if we can't think of things the people can do to earn it. If necessary, we will invent work for them to do.

...since we all have a stake in the nation's human capital, it is in our interest to provide an income to people for learning, as well as teaching; restoring their health as well as tending the health of others, and the critical work of bearing and parenting children.

As Toffler has pointed out, work can be anything we decide to say is work. There are many possibilities, but the one with the broadest political appeal would be a massive program to replenish the nation's stock of human capital. The rationale could be persuasive even to the owners of the robots who will have to devote some of their profits to it.

The argument could go like this: The real wealth of every nation is not its bricks and mortar, but the abililties of its people. Yet most of the investment in human capital is outside the Gross National Product. Individuals are expected to invest their time in improving their capacities as if they were the only ones to benefit. But, since we all have a stake in the nation's human capital, it is in our interest to provide an income to people for learning, as well as teaching; restoring their health as well as tending the health of others, and the critical work of bearing and parenting children.

In an information society, people will be "working" less of their lives because they will be investing more of their time in their future productivity. Full-time higher education of various kinds will occupy about as much of adult life as the rearing of children—more years in college than now, and less in child rearing. Both activities are now regarded as private responsibilities, but in the new economy based on information, they will be recognized as capital investments in the health of the economy, as important as public and private investments in roads, bridges, factories and machines.

Who's going to make this investment? It will be funded by a combination of public and private effort, the way elementary schooling is funded now. Parents and the children whose productivity is improved contribute time and effort, but the taxpayers have a big stake in this investment, and they are the ones who put up the cash.

Because we are pragmatic, we'll probably do what is necessary without philosophizing about "socialism" or "free enterprise." There will be private as well as public programs. We could develop new forms of insurance to help individuals invest in themselves and their families. Employers will shoulder some of the costs, but the taxpayers will pick up the rest, if only to enable the United States to compete with other developed countries that are ahead of us in creating human capital.

Where does this leave older people? In the cat bird seat. Older workers possess the human capital. They monopolize the skills that make the economy work. In an information society, their monopoly will increase.

The work that machines create and leave behind is not the kind of technical skill that can be taught to young engineers in a six-week cram course. On the contrary, it is the human work of making sense out of a snowstorm of computer printouts; weighing nonstatistical factors, matching tasks to people, seeing possibilities, taking risks. In an industrial economy, these skills of judgment that come from experience are required only by the bosses. But in the 21st century, most workers will need them. Those skills take decades of living to acquire, so most workers will find themselves growing more valuable as they grow older.

In the 21st century, you are going to want to go on working—not only because work will be more enjoyable, but also because the skills you will accumulate over the years are skills that will be sought aggressively.

In the 21st century, you are going to want to go on working—not only because work will be more enjoyable, but also because the skills you accumulate, over the years, are skills that will be sought aggressively.

One thing is certain: The world into which you retire in the 21st century is not going to be the same world on which you are planning your retirement now. □

About ASPA

The American Society for Personnel Administration (ASPA) is a non-profit, professional membership association of more than 34,000 human resource professionals and some 4,000 student members in the United States and 42 foreign countries. Now in its 36th year, ASPA is the world's largest association devoted exclusively to human resource management and its members represent companies which employ over 40 million people.

ASPA membership includes a variety of publications and services designed to provide professionals with the information necessary to make wise decisions, formulate and implement effective personnel programs and to encourage the opportunity for peer exchange of ideas. ASPA publishes *Personnel Administrator* magazine, the nation's leading monthly publication in the HRM field, and *Resource,* a monthly award-winning tabloid newspaper covering news and trends in HRM. The Society also publishes books and monographs of interest to executives in the field; sponsors an annual conference, seminars and workshops; and offers members access to its information center and lending library for those members who seek in-depth information in any functional area of HRM.

In addition, ASPA's government affairs staff monitors all government actions which could affect human resource management practices. It coordinates testimony on critical issues and sponsors an annual legislative conference which brings together executives with government and agency officials to discuss the effects of regulatory change which could have an impact on the profession.

ASPA is also a charter member of the World Federation of Personnel Management Associations.

For more information on the American Society for Personnel Administration and its services, write ASPA, 606 North Washington St., Alexandria, VA 22314 or call (703) 548-3440.